BIG BOX USA

BIG BOX USA

THE ENVIRONMENTAL IMPACT OF AMERICA'S BIGGEST RETAIL STORES

Edited by

BART ELMORE, RACHEL S. GROSS, AND SHERRI SHEU

UNIVERSITY OF WYOMING PRESS
Laramie

© 2024 by University Press of Colorado

Published by University of Wyoming Press
An imprint of University Press of Colorado
1580 North Logan Street, Suite 660
PMB 39883
Denver, Colorado 80203-1942

All rights reserved

 The University Press of Colorado is a proud member of Association of University Presses.

The University Press of Colorado is a cooperative publishing enterprise supported, in part, by Adams State University, Colorado State University, Fort Lewis College, Metropolitan State University of Denver, University of Alaska Fairbanks, University of Colorado, University of Northern Colorado, University of Wyoming, Utah State University, and Western Colorado University.

ISBN: 978-1-64642-592-1 (hardcover)
ISBN: 978-1-64642-593-8 (paperback)
ISBN: 978-1-64642-594-5 (ebook)
https://doi.org/10.5876/9781646425945

Library of Congress Cataloging-in-Publication Data is available online.

Cover art: "Evening in the Forest," © llvllagic/iStock; store interior © Ethan Payne.

CONTENTS

List of Figures   vii
Acknowledgments   ix

Introduction: Why Big Box and Environmental History?   3
Bart Elmore, Rachel S. Gross, and Sherri Sheu

SECTION I: WELCOME, WALMART CUSTOMERS: THE ORIGIN STORY OF AMERICA'S BIGGEST RETAIL STORE

1 Walmart World: The Ecological Roots of the Largest Corporation on Earth   17
Bart Elmore

SECTION II: CLEANUP, AISLE 2: MANAGING ENVIRONMENTAL IMPACT

2 "Taking Paradise": A Target Distribution Center and a Battle in the Midwest   53
Johnathan Williams

3 Walmart's Ocean: Certifications, Catch Shares, and the Ripple Effects of Corporate Governance on Marine Environments   77
Aaron Van Neste

4 "Building Some Big-Ass Wetlands": Big Box Retail and the Rise of Mitigation Banking   111
Laura J. Martin

SECTION III: ATTENTION SHOPPERS: CREATING CONSUMER MIND-SETS

5 Boxing in the Outdoors: Cabela's, REI, and the Growth of Specialty Retailers   *137*
Rachel S. Gross

6 Bass Pro Shops: Selling Conservative Conservation   *159*
Sherri Sheu

Conclusion   *187*
Shane Hamilton

Index   207

About the Authors   223

FIGURES

1.1. In 2023, Sam Walton's Ford F-150 pickup truck still sat outside the front entrance to Walmart's home office in Bentonville, Arkansas   20
1.2. Walmart truck on rural road   24
1.3. Williston Citizens for Responsible Growth protesting the siting of a Walmart store in Williston, Vermont   27
1.4. Sam Walton's five-and dime store on the downtown square in Bentonville, Arkansas   32
1.5. World-class mountain biking culture in Bentonville, Arkansas   33
2.1. Panorama of Silver Lake   54
2.2. Map created by a Town of Summit employee comparing size of the distribution center to the largest buildings in the area   61
3.1. Small sample of Walmart seafood products, many but not all of which display the Marine Stewardship Council's blue checkmark   84
4.1. Site plan for the Ambassador Town Center in Lafayette, Louisiana   112
4.2. Satellite images of marginal swampland in Lafayette, Louisiana   113
4.3. Total land drained for agriculture by period as reported by the Bureau of the Census   116
4.4. States that lost more than 50 percent of wetland extent before the 1980s   117
4.5. Total acres in wetland mitigation banks in Louisiana and California by year   124
5.1. Displays of political T-shirts and other pieces of merchandise unrelated to the outdoors in Cabela's   148
5.2. The REI flagship store in Denver leans into the aesthetic of the repurposed historic building in which it is located   151

6.1. The Memphis Pyramid Bass Pro Shops is a major Memphis tourist attraction   *158*

6.2. Albert Einstein: "Look deep, deep into nature, and then you will understand everything better"   *165*

6.3. Black Rifle Coffee Company coffee bean display at Bass Pro Shops   *166*

6.4. Donald Trump presidential rally before the 2016 election inside Bass Pro Shops   *175*

ACKNOWLEDGMENTS

The authors in this volume would like to thank the American Society for Environmental History (ASEH) for providing the opportunity for this book to take shape. The contributors in this volume came together for a panel scheduled to be held in Ottawa as part of the 2020 ASEH meeting. Although that conference never happened because of the Covid-19 pandemic, we nevertheless made connections with the editorial team at the University Press of Colorado, which ultimately resulted in this volume finding a home. In 2022, the authors in this book were fortunate to be able to reconvene at ASEH's Eugene, Oregon, conference where we could plan and strategize. In short, we are fortunate to have the support of ASEH, which helps nurture new scholarship in the field of environmental history.

The College of Arts and Sciences at The Ohio State University proved an important partner in our publication journey, providing critical grant support that was essential as we moved toward the final stages of manuscript preparation.

We would also like to offer special thanks to our editor at the University of Wyoming Press, Robert Ramaswamy, who worked tirelessly with us over the years to get this book to publication. He drew on the support of a talented team of copyeditors and staff that helped make this the best possible book it could be. We are deeply indebted to those who dedicated so much time to this project and are delighted that it could be released as part of the new Intersections in Environmental Justice series at the University of Wyoming Press.

Finally, portions of chapter 1 were originally published in *Country Capitalism: How Corporations from the American South Remade Our Economy and the Planet*. Copyright © 2023 Bart Elmore. Used by permission of the University of North Carolina Press (www.uncpress.org). We would like to thank the University of North Carolina Press for granting permission for reuse.

BIG BOX USA

INTRODUCTION

Why Big Box and Environmental History?

BART ELMORE, RACHEL S. GROSS, AND SHERRI SHEU

To drive across America on an interstate is to relive a certain sameness. Whether you navigate through West Texas on I-10, along the West Coast on I-5, or through the Southeast on I-85, familiar names with bright signage punctuate these national arteries. Walmart, Target, Costco, Staples, Dick's Sporting Goods, and other stores dot the landscape, with promises of linoleum floors and fluorescent lights that will be the same from Des Moines, Iowa, to San Bernardino, California. They are seemingly timeless, untethered to any particulars of geography. Yet, it was not always this way. The rise of the big box store has dramatically reshaped the American landscape in the last half century.

This volume focuses on the rise of big box retail in the United States beginning in the 1960s and the radical ways industry retailers transformed local and global environments. Historians have previously studied big box stores in relationship to the rise of the Sunbelt, the evolution of a service economy, and the transformation of consumer culture.[1] While big box stores are now a feature of international commerce, this volume focuses more narrowly on the United States to make a case for understanding the big box as an environmental force with the power to reshape ecologies and cultures on multiple scales.

So, what is a "big box" store? The term *big box*, which first became popular in the 1990s, highlights many of the questions we address in this volume. The words are relational—"big" contrasts with the postwar stores with smaller footprints, often non-chain stores or small businesses. "Box" indicates a barebones design with few flourishes—no time wasted on velvet curtains or expensive holiday window displays here. "Big box" can be a celebration of a streamlined, efficient shopping experience or a critique of the soulless corporation, depending on perspective. While a business journal might offer a clear definition that specifies facility size or the range and turnover of products, we argue here that "big box" matters not because a facility fits those specific parameters but rather because it signals a new kind of story about American retail. Since the 1970s, the big box has made an emotional claim about corporations' role in American life while erasing the link between corporations and the natural environment. The stores have offered comfort in their monotony and their bounty. From the geography of the facilities to the shopping experience inside, the big box has purported to be a ubiquitous provider of affordable goods. Even an anonymous corporation can prompt contentment and loyalty.

Historians have shown that the roots of the big box retail revolution extend back to the late nineteenth century, when the first big retail chain stores emerged. At that time, entrepreneurs such as New Yorker Frank W. Woolworth and Detroit-based S. S. Kresge introduced some of the first variety and "five-and-dime" stores that brought a wide selection of cheap mass-manufactured goods under one roof.[2] These businesses took advantage of new railroad routes and communication networks that helped usher in a flood of cheap goods produced by some of the first vertically integrated firms in the country. The new goods appealed to consumers, as workers in many parts of the United States were becoming wage earners in factories and therefore were less able to devote time to home production of necessities.[3] By the early 1900s, Quaker and former mariner Rowland H. Macy in New York City and J. C. Penney in Wyoming launched the first department stores that at first primarily served urban residents in cities in the American West and on the East Coast.⁴ Like the five-and-dime stores, Macy's and J. C. Penney's offered American consumers attractive retail experiences, abandoning traditional bargaining practices that had been the norm in the mid-nineteenth century and setting fixed prices on goods sold in stores. They also offered credit accounts to customers and implemented home delivery systems.⁵ Simultaneously, mail-order retail businesses such as Sears and Montgomery Ward became profitable by sending mass-manufactured goods on rail lines that radiated in every direction from cities like Chicago directly to consumers in more remote markets across the country.⁶ By negotiating directly with manufacturers, these firms developed advanced accounting systems and integrated distribution networks as well as money-back guarantee programs; they focused primarily on making large-volume sales of cheap, branded goods rather than relying on smaller-volume sales of high-dollar wares.⁷ By the 1910s, consumers throughout the United States had access to many cheap manufactured goods through a variety of retail outlets.

The grocery business also changed dramatically in the early 1900s, with firms such as the Great Atlantic & Pacific Tea Company integrating management of distribution systems and pioneering ways of streamlining the flow of product inventories.⁸ In 1913, the Piggly Wiggly grocery chain in Memphis, Tennessee, introduced the first self-service grocery chain format, which later drew the attention of Michael Cullen, who worked at the Kroger Grocery and Baking Company in Ohio. Cullen left Kroger in 1930 to create his own grocery store chain in New York that took the self-service idea developed by Piggly Wiggly and added another ingredient to the mix: large-format store layouts. Cullen's creation, the King Kullen grocery store, was really the nation's first supermarket, and it emerged at a time when there was vibrant debate in the United States as to whether such big stores were good for society. In the 1920s and 1930s, "chain store wars" rocked the nation, as local merchants fought the expansion of department stores, mail-order companies, and supermarkets in states across America. Politicians sympathetic to local merchants sponsored anti-chain legislation that was designed to halt the growth of the big firms.⁹

But this resistance was ultimately unsuccessful at blocking the growth of department stores, supermarkets, and other big retail outlets. Especially in the lean years of the Great Depression, many Americans came to rely on the cheap goods these firms could provide. By the 1940s, it was clear that the new, large-format, self-service stores were here to stay.

Thus, when Detroit-born Kmart, Minneapolis-based Target, and Arkansas-founded Walmart first launched their big box retail stores in the 1960s, these firms built on innovations launched by Piggly Wiggly, King Kullen, and others that came before. But what made these firms different was the scale at which they operated. The stores often exceeded 50,000 square feet in size and offered the most barebones self-serve retail environments. Kmart and Target focused mainly on large suburban and urban markets. In contrast, Walmart sited its stores in towns of 5,000 people or less, which many people thought was ludicrous. How could a firm like Walmart expect to make profits with such big stores in such tiny markets? Walmart proved that big box stores could generate tremendous cash flow in even the most rural American markets, which ensured that in the second half of the twentieth century, big box stores redefined America's cityscapes and suburbs and became fixtures of the American countryside as well.[10]

Big box retailers also transformed cyberspace, serving as models for e-commerce companies like Amazon.com that emerged in the internet boom of the 1990s. When Jeff Bezos began building his business, he traveled to Bentonville, Arkansas, and courted the distribution wizards that had made Walmart one of the largest corporations in the world. Bezos also read Sam Walton's biography and built Amazon by drawing on the logistics techniques first perfected by the big box firm from Arkansas. It's convenient to label our modern marketplace the "Amazon" economy, but the truth is that Bezos's billions would not have been possible but for a logistics revolution led by a big box store based in the Ozarks.[11]

As a century of evolution in retail suggests, the history of big box stores encompasses a wide range of characters and questions. The business-environment nexus in particular has been a thriving point of inquiry in recent years, and it is this cross-pollination of subfields we call attention to in this volume. Calls to combine the approaches of business and environmental history more than twenty years ago yielded scores of dissertations, monographs, and edited volumes that engaged with the fruitful overlap between the fields.[12] Retail stores, especially big boxes, have remained largely out of sight from this work, however.[13] Part of this omission is about time: recent retail histories often end their time line at the point when the big box came of age. For instance, an excellent recent tracing of the geography of American retail takes us from Main Street to the mall but stops short of the sprawling parking lots and brightly lit aisles of Walmart or Target.[14] This volume uses the questions and tools of the business-environment nexus honed over the last two decades to interrogate the rise of the world's largest retailers.

The question of how capitalism reshaped ecosystems was foundational to the founding of the field of environmental history in the 1970s, and more recent works have added new layers to that question. What is the relationship between government policy and green development? How have corporations addressed past violence inflicted on bodies and landscapes? How skeptical or hopeful should we be about narratives of corporate environmentalism? Using the tools of environmental history, we will examine a quintessential business history topic: big box stores and their development in the last fifty years. We frame this discussion by invoking "big" and "box" to interrogate what these institutions mean for their relationships to the natural world. How have these mega-stores changed ecologies, including not only physical spaces and things but also a cultural ecology of how people think about the natural world?

When scanning a parking lot at Walmart or passing Target-branded semi-trucks on the highway, it becomes clear that big box stores have a major impact on the landscape. Locally, corporate headquarters dictate the construction of new superstores by paving land into parking lots and buildings. Manufacturers use petroleum millions of years in the making, refined and shaped into bobbles and gizmos in a factory before being shipped across the globe. We will look at both smokestacks and coat racks to assess this bigness at various scales. We ask what the impact of stores has been on the environment, in terms of both production and shipping and the local impact of individual retail stores. We explore how these stores relate to surrounding landscapes. Importantly, we assess how corporations have attempted to address environmental problems from the inside. The pollution trails of corporate giants are vast, but so—potentially—are the solutions they have to offer. To assess the environmental impact of stores, we trace their ecological footprint and their relationship to local environments, from brownfields to wetlands.

The connections between big box retail and the environment continue inside the stores themselves. One recent phenomenon is that some of these stores have moved away from cold, utilitarian aesthetics to become destination shopping experiences and now play a pseudo-educational role regarding the American landscape, serving as vehicles of information. The big boxes have become didactic spaces. Taking chain stores in the outdoor industry as a case study, we examine how outdoor retailers began to present visions of the environments in which Americans play. The in-store environment offered technological wonders, cheap goods, and narratives about the American past and future. Stores achieved this through product arrangement, decoration, building displays, and even museums to teach some of these lessons. The buildings have evolved as well. From the bright lights and plain metal shelving of the early days of Walmart, some specialty retailers now create lavish in-store environments that send messages about the products and ideas they want to promote. Far from plain boxes, these stores created new wrappings, even making the move from highway-adjacent fields of concrete to renovations of historic buildings closer to downtowns. The shape of the box and its contents, just like its size, provide a cultural education that also relates to the environment in particular. The emotional appeal of the big box has expanded from predictable contentment to being stimulating and even thrilling.

Of course, an examination of the physical building, its surroundings, and the retail experience it provides inside can hardly be neatly divided from the questions of scale and impact mentioned above. After all, from the 1970s to the 1990s, these retailers' store size grew from 50,000 to over 90,000 square feet. Many supercenters of the twenty-first century top 150,000 square feet. Quite simply, the boxes got bigger. But careful attention to the evolution of the shopping experience and the building aesthetics and architecture reveals that we need to unpack this box more fully.

Many of these trends of the bigger box are not specifically American. Walmart and Target, born in Arkansas and Minnesota, respectively, are joined by counterparts overseas such as Carrefour, Tesco, and Ikea, although these international examples lie beyond the scope of this volume. With our balance between global and local impacts, we show how the American big box model is both an environmental and a cultural phenomenon.

In an America shaped by leisure, consumption, and mobility, big box stores reached a new kind of market. Like the suburban shopping malls that preceded them, big box stores became powerful during the rise of of the Sunbelt. Within the walls of the big box retailer, individual consumers engaged with global commodities markets and supply chains, even as businesses prescribed their own ideas about resources, leisure, waste, and consumption. When Americans bought groceries, office supplies, and sporting goods, they encountered the same patterns of selling first established in big ways by corporate giants Walmart, Kmart, and Target. Mass distribution is one pattern. Other characteristics include self-service, a patriarchal organization of work, and an implicit celebration of free enterprise.

These stores, characterized by their large size—at least 50,000 square feet in the early iterations, or roughly the size of a football field—and variety of products, mark a turning point in American retail history. In the early twentieth century, Main Street and department stores set the standard for shopping in urban areas. After World War II, suburban shopping malls dominated. While none of these earlier models have disappeared entirely, big box stores such as Walmart and Target set a new standard for how Americans shopped and made shoppers think anew about their relationship with the natural world.

Like the Main Streets and malls before them, these austere institutions filled with everything from toilet paper to televisions highlight—or at times hide—the broader networks in which American shoppers in Everytown, USA, are embedded. These retail outlets touch almost every person in the country and connect individuals to a global economy. Yet only sometimes do customers recognize the impacts of the physical buildings and the products in them on a broader landscape. This volume intends to build conversations between the worlds of business and environmental history and will present the opportunity to begin thinking through how big box stores permeate the ways we understand our relationships to the natural world.

The three sections of this volume highlight how an environmental history approach helps us understand the rise and impact of the big box store on American life.

Section I, "Welcome, Walmart Customers," kicks off with Bart Elmore's chapter, "Walmart World: The Ecological Roots of the Largest Corporation on Earth." Elmore's piece explores the ecological roots of the world's largest corporation, Walmart. Elmore shows how the unique commercial ecology of the Arkansas Ozarks gave rise to Sam Walton's business and explores how the firm's rural roots shaped its global environmental footprint.

Section II, "Cleanup, Aisle 2: Managing Environmental Impact," considers how big box stores have impacted the natural world and shaped environmental regulations. Johnathan Williams begins the section with a study of Target distribution centers in "'Taking Paradise': A Target Distribution Center and a Battle in the Midwest." While grassroots resistance to big box store expansion became a common feature in the 1990s, Williams looks at a rare example of resistance against a distribution center in rural Wisconsin. The case study reveals how larger national forces converged on the small community and how, despite opponents raising sound arguments to classify distribution centers as a major polluting source, the massive buildings essential to modern retail proliferated in the following years while escaping environmental regulations. Aaron Van Neste takes this volume to the oceans in "Walmart's Ocean: Certifications, Catch Shares, and the Ripple Effects of Corporate Governance on Marine Environments." Van Neste examines how Walmart has profoundly shaped ocean environments. Through corporate environmental governance—including mandating sustainability certifications and helping concentrate fishing rights in the hands of large capital firms—Walmart alters which fish are caught, who catches them, and who profits. In doing so, Walmart and its partners have redefined marine sustainability to be compatible with cheap commodity extraction and global supply chains, erasing the harm these changes (and Walmart's larger business model) have done to marine ecosystems and fishing communities. Laura J. Martin continues exploring the themes of regulation and environmental change in her chapter "'Building Some Big-Ass Wetlands': Big Box Retail and the Rise of Mitigation Banking." In the 1980s, federal regulations facilitated the conversion of wetlands to Walmarts through a process known as "compensatory mitigation." Wetland mitigation banking uncoupled sites of environmental damage from sites of environmental remediation, reconfiguring wetlands and retail districts at a national scale while paving the way conceptually and procedurally for carbon offsetting and other ecosystem services markets.

In Section III, "Attention Shoppers: Creating Consumer Mind-Sets," we head into the stores themselves to interrogate how consumers experience big box stores. In "Boxing in the Outdoors: Cabela's, REI, and the Growth of Specialty Retailers," Rachel S. Gross examines the outdoor industry's deep ambivalence toward the big box label. As retail stores selling camping and hiking equipment expanded from local specialty shops to national chains, Gross argues, the underlying debate in the industry was about just *who* the outdoors was for. Sherri Sheu ends section III with a study of how a retailer helped reify political conservatism and race through retail in "Bass Pro Shops: Selling Conservative Conservation." Through its retail stores, catalogs, and museums, Bass Pro Shops created spaces that fostered a particular relationship between nature and consumers.

Historian Shane Hamilton takes us home in the conclusion, helping us to see how these various stories about big box stores speak to one another. In addition, he offers ways to think about new research in the space of big box environmental history.

This volume is not—and should not be—the final word on big box stores in business and environmental history. We intend it as an invitation and an invocation for further discussions and research. This volume serves as a sampling of varied approaches and case studies for the future. In the years ahead, scholars may find much to cover at other locations, such as warehouse stores and non-American retailers such as Carrefour. Internet shopping, whose footprint has rapidly changed shopping patterns among consumers, must also be studied in greater depth.

In many parts of the United States, deserted shopping centers dot the landscape—a parallel, ghostly universe of the costs of big box retail. Empty boxes and faded signs with exposed wiring show the remains of once bustling spaces, now silent but for the occasional scurry of rats and the cawing of birds. These are landscapes capital has mined and stripped of value, as surely as any abandoned quarry. Around the country, workers hobble with backs and spirits broken by years of labor at rock-bottom wages and the emotional toil of liaising between the vaunted global supply chain and the individual consumer. Social safety nets strain at supporting full-time workers paid so little that the costs of basic standards such as food and medicine are met by the government and not the paycheck. As we wrote this volume in the middle of the Covid-19 pandemic, it became clear that the linkages between the big box and the environment are not timeless but fragile and friable.

Our call in this volume is for historians and others to pay attention to these landscapes of our everyday lives and to unearth the myriad ways nature links to the big box. For as surely as the big box has reshaped our relationship to consumer goods, the rise of the big box has remade our relationships with nature itself.

NOTES

1. See, for example, Moreton, *To Serve God and Wal-Mart*; Lichtenstein, *The Retail Revolution*; Strasser, "Woolworth to Wal-Mart"; Strasser, *Satisfaction Guaranteed*; Tedlow, *New and Improved*; Vance and Scott, *Wal-Mart*.
2. For the connections between Woolworth and big box stores that emerged in the 1960s, see, for example, Strasser, "Woolworth to Wal-Mart." For a sweeping history of American retail and mass marketing, see Tedlow, *New and Improved*.
3. Strasser, "Woolworth to Wal-Mart," 33.
4. Strasser, *Satisfaction Guaranteed*, 211.
5. Vance and Scott, *Wal-Mart*, 18; Tedlow, *New and Improved*, 293; Strasser, *Satisfaction Guaranteed*, 204.
6. Strasser, "Woolworth to Wal-Mart," 39–43; Strasser, *Satisfaction Guaranteed*, 212–213.
7. Tedlow, *New and Improved*, 11, 259–274; Strasser, *Satisfaction Guaranteed*, 204, 206.

8. Ortega, *In Sam We Trust*, 38; Vance and Scott, *Wal-Mart*, 19; Strasser, "Woolworth to Wal-Mart," 45; Tedlow, *New and Improved*, 182, 189, 214; Thain and Bradley, *Store Wars*, 7–8.
9. Strasser, "Woolworth to Wal-Mart," 51; Vance and Scott, *Wal-Mart*, 22; Ortega, *In Sam We Trust*, 35, 43, 214; Thain and Bradley, *Store Wars*, 8; Moreton, *To Serve God and Wal-Mart*, 18, 64, 68; Hamilton, *Supermarket USA*, 12–14. Hamilton's book offers an excellent examination of how Cold War politics shaped the rise of supermarkets in the United States.
10. Vance and Scott, *Wal-Mart*, 14; Adams, "Making the New Shop Floor," 214; Strasser, "Woolworth to Wal-Mart," 52.
11. Stone, *The Everything Store*, 60–62, 72–75.
12. Rosen, "The Business-Environment Connection"; Rosen and Sellers, "The Nature of the Firm"; Berghoff and Rome, *Green Capitalism*; Elmore, *Citizen Coke*.
13. Stobart and Howard, *The Routledge Companion to the History of Retailing*; see especially Stephen Halebsky, "Big-Box Stores," 216-226, in that volume.
14. Howard, *From Main Street to Mall*.

BIBLIOGRAPHY

Adams, Thomas Jessen. "Making the New Shop Floor: Wal-Mart, Labor Control, and the History of the Postwar Discount Retail Industry in America." In *Wal-Mart: The Face of Twenty-First-Century Capitalism*, edited by Nelson Lichtenstein, 213–230. New York: New Press, 2006.

Berghoff, Hartmut, and Adam Rome. *Green Capitalism? Business and Environment in the Twentieth Century*. Philadelphia: University of Pennsylvania Press, 2017.

Elmore, Bartow J. *Citizen Coke: The Making of Coca-Cola Capitalism*. New York: W. W. Norton & Company.

Hamilton, Shane. *Supermarket USA: Food and Power in the Cold War Farms Race*. New Haven, CT: Yale University Press, 2018.

Howard, Vicki. *From Main Street to Mall: The Rise and Fall of the American Department Store*. Philadelphia: University of Pennsylvania Press, 2015.

Lichtenstein, Nelson. *The Retail Revolution: How Wal-Mart Created a Brave New World of Business*. New York: Picador, 2010.

Moreton, Bethany. *To Serve God and Wal-Mart: The Making of Christian Free Enterprise*. Cambridge, MA: Harvard University Press, 2009.

Ortega, Bob. *In Sam We Trust: The Untold Story of Sam Walton and How Wal-Mart Is Devouring America*. New York: Times Books, 1998.

Rosen, Christine Meisner. "The Business-Environment Connection." *Environmental History* 10, no. 1 (2005): 77–79.

Rosen, Christine Meisner, and Christopher C. Sellers. "The Nature of the Firm: Towards an Ecocultural History of Business." *Business History Review* 73, no. 4 (Winter 1999): 577–600.

Stobart, Jon, and Vicki Howard, eds. *The Routledge Companion to the History of Retailing*. London: Routledge, 2018.

Stone, Brad. *The Everything Store: Jeff Bezos and the Age of Amazon*. New York: Little, Brown, 2013.

Strasser, Susan. *Satisfaction Guaranteed: The Making of the American Mass Market*. New York: Pantheon Books, 1989.

Strasser, Susan. "Woolworth to Wal-Mart: Mass Merchandising and the Changing Culture of Consumption." In *Wal-Mart: The Face of Twenty-First-Century Capitalism*, edited by Nelson Lichtenstein, 31–56. New York: New Press, 2006.

Tedlow, Richard S. *New and Improved: The Story of Mass Marketing in America*. New York: Basic Books, 1990.

Thain, Greg, and John Bradley. *Store Wars: When Walmart Comes to Town*. New York: Wiley, 2001.

Vance, Sandra S., and Roy V. Scott. *Wal-Mart: A History of Sam Walton's Retail Phenomenon*. New York: Twayne, 1994.

Section I

Welcome, Walmart Customers

THE ORIGIN STORY OF AMERICA'S BIGGEST RETAIL STORE

1

WALMART WORLD

The Ecological Roots of the Largest Corporation on Earth

BART ELMORE

The scene would have fit well in the 1972 river adventure flick *Deliverance*. Sam Walton, founder of Walmart and one of the richest men in the world, directed the canoe through the waters of Sugar Creek just outside Bentonville, Arkansas, Walmart's hometown.[1] Walton, wearing his signature crumpled trucker's cap, was old hat at this. Having grown up in Missouri, he had perfected the canoeing craft as a Boy Scout, becoming, according to one close friend, one of the youngest Eagle Scouts in Missouri history. He loved the outdoors, and so did his wife, Helen, who was also in the boat paddling hard.[2]

This was the setting for the 1981 Walmart shareholders meeting—a strange place for such an affair, but that was all part of Walton's design. He loved the idea of getting the Wall Street analysts from up north out into the Ozark wild that he called home. Much like *Deliverance*, there was a certain southern exoticism to it all. Those from out of town had been handed fliers detailing an "Ozark-Cajun 'Bone-Mending' River Stew" that Alice Walton, Sam's daughter, would apparently provide for their journey. The ingredients? A mix of snakes and chicken parts brewed in a pot, tended by an overalls-bedecked Alice Walton puffing on a corncob pipe.³

By all accounts, it was a raucous affair. Many of the Wall Street types got sloppy drunk, to the point of toppling out of their canoes. This bothered Sam Walton, who henceforward made shareholders meetings a dry affair. ("They were never quite the same after that," said one Walmart investor.) At night, the group camped, and chaos ensued as the city slickers tried to cope with the sounds of the wilderness. "That was a real fiasco," Sam Walton said. "A coyote started howling, and hoot owls hooting, and half of these analysts stayed up all night around the campfire because they couldn't sleep. We decided it wasn't the best idea to try something like this with folks who weren't accustomed to camping on the rocks in sleeping bags."⁴

The press picked up on this idea that the ecosystem Walmart called home was something foreign to the captains of capital in the Northeast. Business reporters loved to play with the contradiction that such a "down-home" company from a seemingly backward "small town tucked away in the northernmost corner of Arkansas" could have a balance sheet that was "pure sophistication." They talked about the float trips and barbecues in Arkansas, which seemed to stand in stark contrast to the cold calculation of computer-age capitalism. As historian Bethany Moreton explained, some people could not understand how "high-tech rednecks mastered cybernetics and corporate culture without losing Christ or country music."⁵

But for Sam Walton, the Ozarks had always seemed the perfect environment in which to do business. In the years after that 1981 shareholders meeting, Walton made the Arkansas woods his boardroom for big-deal meetings. In 1987, for example, Walton journeyed down another Arkansas waterway, this time with Procter and Gamble's vice president of sales, Lou Pritchett. Pritchett had proposed the idea because Walton, like himself, had been a Boy Scout. After forging a bond of friendship with the secret Eagle Scout handshake, the two were off, floating down the South Fork of Spring River, discussing how they could revolutionize retail. Pritchett later recounted the story of this journey and spoke of the rugged bus ride that got them between two portage points on the river: "Thick clouds of red dust poured in on us," Pritchett recalled, but the two were unfazed. When they got back on the water, Walton, with his little yellow notepad, jotted down ideas from their conversation as he held on to the gunwale of Pritchett's canoe.[6]

The river proved a fitting place for a conversation that was all about flow. What they devised on this trip was a better way to get goods from producers to consumers: they promised to develop a high-tech computer system that would allow for open sharing of inventory and point-of-sale information between suppliers and retailers. The system, which became known as Retail Link, would allow companies like Procter and Gamble to instantaneously restock items sold in stores. Walmart and Procter and Gamble were essentially removing dams that separated suppliers from retailers further downstream, allowing a flood of goods to course through global commercial arteries. The decision changed Walmart—and then the world—forever.[7]

But to understand why the wealthiest man in the world came to make such a fateful decision on the water that day requires uncovering the ecological roots of the Walmart empire. Hidden in the Ozark Mountains is a history of the retail revolution told from the ground up. So it is that we venture back to the land to see how Sam Walton built the world's biggest corporation in a little town called Bentonville (figure 1.1).

Sam Walton chose Bentonville as the site for his 4,000-square-foot Ben Franklin five-and-dime store in 1950 in large part because of his family's love of the outdoors. Years later, Walton pointed to his wife, Helen, as a key figure that led them to Bentonville. "I'll go with you any place you want, so long as you don't ask me to live in a big city," Helen allegedly told Sam. It helped that the town was also a great location for Sam's favorite pastime. "I wanted to get closer to good quail hunting," Walton said, "and with Oklahoma, Kansas, Arkansas, and Missouri all coming together right there, it gave me easy access to quail hunting in four states."[8]

Beyond the quail it contained, Bentonville proved an ideal ecosystem from which to build the Walmart empire. Perhaps the most important element was the Ozarks topography, which forced Walton to take to the air when planning store expansion. By 1957, Walton had opened several stores, still under the Butler Brothers franchise, in Arkansas

FIGURE 1.1. In 2023, Sam Walton's Ford F-150 pickup truck still sat outside the front entrance to the home office of Walmart in Bentonville—the company's clear effort to show its founder's ties to rural America. Author photo.

and neighboring Missouri and Tennessee; to get to these stores, he often had to take winding roads through hilly terrain. That got old fast and pushed him to get his pilot's license so he could jump up and over the hills to scout potential sites for new stores.[9]

Bentonville's unique geography had forced Walton to do something few other store owners were doing at the time. "We were probably ten years ahead of most other retailers in scouting locations from the air," he said, adding, "I guarantee you [that] not many principals of retailing companies were flying around sideways studying development patterns. From up in the air we could check out traffic flows, see which ways cities and towns were growing and evaluate the location of the competition—if there was any. Then we would develop our real estate strategy for the market."[10] To get around hills hindering his path, Walton went skyward where he began to see the retail landscape like no one else had before. "Once I took to the air, I caught store fever," he said.[11] Seeing the landscape from the clouds inspired a cancer-like vision of conquest. He wanted more and more, and over the next two decades the company's "ultimate real estate strategy," as one Walmart executive put it, "was to saturate a state" until there was nowhere else to put a Walmart store.[12]

In addition to spurring Walton's aerial siting strategy, the Ozarks' mountains and hills also served another important purpose: they insulated Walton from other retailers.[13] Sam Walton liked to say of his Walmart headquarters, built in Bentonville in 1969, that sitting in his office he could "hide back there in the hills" out of competitors' sight.[14] There was a lot of truth to this. The hilly terrain and rural nature of Bentonville and its surroundings inhibited the expansion of road infrastructure—a word the "aw-shucks," folksy billionaire Sam Walton said he couldn't even pronounce during a 1990 congressional hearing on federal funding for Arkansas internal improvements.[15] Few big players wanted to venture into this world of winding roads.

Walton pointed to geography as the key factor that helped Walmart develop its winning way. "We were forced to be ahead of our time in distribution and in communication," he said, "because our stores were sitting out there in tiny little towns and we had to stay in touch and keep them supplied." Rurality, something many believed hindered capital flow, proved essential in stimulating the development of sophisticated distribution systems that radically accelerated the pace of commercial exchange. The financial capital that supercharged this revolution may have come from outside the American South, but Walton's system was nevertheless an Ozark creation, adapted to the environment in which it was born.[16]

Another way Walton saved money was by tapping into a cheap labor market, made possible by farmer flight from the fields of Middle America. Agribusinesses—supported by large federal subsidies, new machines, synthetic fertilizers, and hybrid seeds—had found a way after World War II to plow and plant huge tracts of land with the help of fewer and fewer farmhands. Growers' relationship with the natural environment was changing. Land that had once supported modest family farms, even in the hilly and isolated Ozarks, was swiftly becoming the domain of consolidated agricultural concerns. People pushed off the land, including many poor sharecroppers, were desperate for jobs; for some, the trucking gigs and sales opportunities Walmart offered became the only way to make a living. As historian Bethany Moreton put it, "The agricultural revolution of the early postwar era was in full swing, depopulating Arkansas farms, and putting tens of thousands of white women and men in search of their first real paychecks."[17] It helped that these people, challenged by the natural elements and the hard sun that baked down on America's farming country, were hardened for difficult work.[18] They were the ideal labor force for a firm that looked to drive its workers to accept tough hours for little pay.

Walmart workers, whether women or men, found few protections from southern governments, which proved more interested in attracting businesses to their states than in helping their citizens struggling to deal with the sea change in American agriculture. In 1944, the Arkansas legislature voted in favor of one of the country's first antiunion "right-to-work" constitutional amendments, setting a precedent for other southern states, which soon followed suit with similar amendments or laws.[19] For his part, Walton hated unions, and he fought hard against those who wanted to organize Walmart workers.[20] There would be no union presence in Walmart stores for years to come. Displaced farmers in the Ozarks and beyond would work for Walmart on Walmart's terms.

Facing little pressure from regulators or labor groups, Walton paid many of his workers poverty wages. In 1965, Walton ignored new legislation that set the US minimum wage at $1.15 an hour, paying some of his employees less than half that amount. Ultimately, the federal government sued Walmart and forced Walton to release back pay to his workers. In the years ahead, however, Walmart managers continued to find ways to underpay employees, including by forcing employees to work overtime without compensation.[21]

Instead of using high wages to engender worker loyalty to his firm, Walton did something else. First, in 1971 he created a profit-sharing program that allowed workers to acquire company stock at discount rates after the firm went public in 1970. Walton believed that encouraging his employees to become Walmart stockholders would help defuse any grumbling about low wages.[22] In addition to this program,

Walton also sought to create a corporate culture that served as a kind of salve for young men being wrenched from the land. He created a gendered workspace in his stores: women served in low-paying sales and service positions, while men took on managerial responsibilities. He sent many male managers to nearby Christian universities, where they were indoctrinated into evangelical traditions of servant-hood as they learned business basics. While Walton made billions, his managers earned modest salaries, but they came to accept the financial shortcomings in return for the intangible benefits associated with being atop a patriarchic hierarchy within a new corporate "family" held out as a proxy of the old family farm.[23]

Walmart's long-haul trucking network—the largest in the world by the end of the twentieth century—proved attractive to displaced farmers who desperately wanted independence and freedom but could not find it in the corporate agribusiness landscape of the postwar era (figure 1.2). As New Deal–era farm policies channeled millions of dollars into the pockets of large landowners, machines replaced rural workers, who were forced to trade their tractors for trucks to put bread on the table. Many of these men became deeply resentful of the government, which they saw as the source of the agrarian problem rather than the solution, and they adopted a hardcore allegiance to free-market, antiunion politics. This was extremely beneficial for Walmart, because it meant truckers avoided the minimal opportunities for collective bargaining that still existed in Arkansas and instead engaged in cutthroat competition for business that drove down Walmart's shipping costs.[24]

Yet if rurality helped give birth to Walton's empire, it also threatened its future. Beyond the American South, in hills and valleys known for their natural beauty, cries of resistance to Walmart's retail revolution could be heard. In the waning years of the twentieth century, the epicenter of the fight was a small town called Williston, nestled in the Green Mountains of Vermont.

The battle intensified in 1991 when a local developer, Taft Corner Associates, proposed siting a Walmart store in Williston, Vermont, population circa 4,800. Located just outside Burlington, the town had long

FIGURE 1.2. Walmart's long-haul trucking fleet was the largest in the world by the end of the twentieth century, allowing the company to transport goods to small towns and rural communities across America. *Courtesy*, https://www.alamy.com.

attracted people fleeing New England cities in search of something more rural; Malcolm Gladwell, writing for the *Washington Post*, dubbed them "ecotopians."[25] This included Jerry Greenfield and Ben Cohen of Ben and Jerry's fame, business partners who shared a worldview perhaps best encapsulated by the catchy names of the firm's ice cream flavors, such as "Cherry Garcia" and "Wake and No Bake." Ben and Jerry, who had started their business in Burlington in the 1970s, were going back to the countryside in search of serenity, as farmers in Middle America continued to leave the rural world in search of city jobs.[26]

Walmart had no doubt wanted to come to Williston because it had all the environmental ingredients the firm liked. An isolated mountain community of just a few thousand people, an Ozarks in the North, this was just the kind of place—devoid of discount competitors—where Walmart could make millions.

Yet if it wanted to do that, the firm was going to have to change the rural natural environment that had attracted it—and Ben and Jerry—to this place. After all, digital communication systems and outer-space satellite technology could not, in and of themselves, move Walmart's goods to market. The firm had to touch the ground—or the pavement, as it were—to get the goods it sold to the stores; in towns like Williston, the blacktop simply wasn't adequate for this retail giant. Rural roads, the on-the-ground arteries of Walmart's commercial network, would have to be widened to allow Walmart's trucks and out-of-town customers access to this market. This was a change many Williston residents would resist.

The Williston Citizens for Responsible Growth (WCRG) led the charge against Walmart. In 1988, Ben and Jerry's CEO and Williston resident Fred "Chico" Lager formed the group with like-minded citizens—including Jerry Greenfield and his wife—to combat a series of commercial development projects that threatened to turn this little Vermont town into "any other place, U.S.A.," as Burlington mayor Peter Cavelle put it.[27] By the time local developer Jeffrey Davis decided to propose building a Walmart on the Taft Associates commercial site, members of the WCRG had already successfully blocked an attempt by a New York firm to build a mall in the town's central corridor—which had just one yellow blinking light at its central intersection. The WCRG was organized, experienced, and ready to fight.[28]

And they had a powerful weapon at their disposal: Act 250, a law passed by the Vermont legislature in 1970 designed to prevent sprawl-like development that could sully the state's natural beauty. Passed in response to concerns about a proposed ski resort, the law required developers to conduct extensive environmental assessments to ensure that a project would not cause undue harm to Vermont's ecosystem. It was a unique piece of legislation, a law Walmart had not encountered in other states. In 1991, the firm had failed to site a single Walmart in Vermont. This was the final frontier of Walmart's American conquest.[29]

At first, it seemed that Walmart's odds looked good in Williston. Jeffrey Davis had already navigated the Act 250 approval process in the 1980s and had an umbrella construction permit that ostensibly gave him the right to build a Walmart in the town. But in the early 1990s, the WCRG sought to make the case to the state's regulators that they had not considered the huge impact a Walmart would have on the community when granting Davis's permit. How could the commission grant Act 250 approval before knowing exactly what Davis planned to build on his site?[30]

The WCRG decided that its best tactic was to focus on roads and traffic, covered under provisions of Act 250. During the original permitting process, the local environmental commission had clearly said the Taft Associates development "will be community or county oriented," and it went on to state, "The Interstate has not been represented as a necessary link." This obviously meant, Chico Lager explained, that a Walmart was not something regulators had envisioned in Williston.[31]

The WCRG thought it had Walmart in a tough spot. A traffic study in 1992 made clear that millions of dollars in roadway improvements would have to be completed before a Walmart could be sited in town, and much of that money was going to have to come from taxpayer dollars. The municipality and the state would probably be tapped for more than $15 million in infrastructure costs. With local and state governments facing tight budgets, there was little chance that roads could be widened fast enough to warrant Walmart's entry.[32]

In 1994, three years after WCRG began its wrangling over Walmart, Vermont's Environmental Board ruled that Jeffrey Davis's project could go forward, but not before an estimated $15 million in road infrastructure was completed.[33]

The WCRG thought it had won.[34] These costs were simply too high. Some people thought there was no way the town could make these adjustments anytime soon. Ironically, Williston's rural roads, the thing that had created the discount retail desert that brought Walmart there in the first place, had temporarily forestalled Walmart's expansion into its final frontier. "Some things just don't fit in Williston," a WCRG protest poster read (figure 1.3).[35]

But the battle continued. In the spring of 1995, Jeffrey Davis appealed the 1994 decision and received a serious gift from the Environmental Board: a radical reduction in total outlays required before the Walmart project could go forward. Instead of the $15 million in infrastructure improvements initially projected, the board only demanded that $3 million worth of work be completed before Walmart could break ground. This helped get the Arkansas firm one step closer to landing its first Vermont store.[36] That summer, the WCRG got more bad

FIGURE 1.3. Williston Citizens for Responsible Growth (WCRG) protest against the siting of a Walmart store in Williston, Vermont, in the 1990s. *Courtesy, Vermont Historical Society, Barre.*

news: Davis said he was going to front much of the money for roadway improvements himself. He was tired of waiting; he would go it alone. Davis did not disclose how much money he was going to spend to get the job done, but proposed construction plans included widening on and off ramps on I-89, expanding roadways that cut through town, and making major intersection improvements.[37]

The WCRG would not give up: in the fall of 1995 it appealed the Environmental Board's decision to the Vermont Supreme Court.[38] But the court ultimately decided in favor of Davis and Walmart. The Environmental Board's decision would be the final word on the matter. "As we understand it," a happy Jeffrey Davis told the press, "this is the end of the road." It was a fitting statement for this developer turned road maker.[39]

After that, things got nasty. Eco-saboteurs, stealing a page from environmental radical Edward Abbey's classic *The Monkey Wrench Gang*, took matters into their own hands, sneaking onto the Walmart construction site after hours and dumping a mix of "rice and cornmeal into fuel tanks and hydraulic systems" of earth-moving equipment. It was an expensive act of defiance, one that set a locally contracted construction firm back a few thousand dollars. For Walmart, this was the advantage of operating at arm's length. Because the company typically leased its stores from local developers, it avoided taking on certain risks and financial liabilities associated with store construction. In this case, monkey wrenching carried out by eco-crusaders eager to hurt an out-of-state firm ended up hitting the pocketbooks of people closer to home.[40]

And it did little to stop Walmart from coming to town. By January 1997, roads had been widened, the Walmart was built, and Williston was transformed.[41]

Not everyone thought this was a bad thing. Even though a local poll showed that roughly 70 percent of Chittenden County residents opposed allowing Walmart into Vermont, the *Burlington Free Press* interviewed many citizens who said they welcomed the low prices Walmart would bring to the community.[42] A mother of five, a grocery clerk, an office cleaner from Burlington, a Walmart applicant from nearby St. George: these were just some of the people who wanted to see the big box giant come to town.[43] These voices reflected the way the Walmart debate was refracted through the prism of class. For many working-class people in Vermont, Walmart's low prices offered relief at a time when American wages were stagnating and the cost of living was rising.[44]

But for those concerned about the environment, Walmart's cheap goods came with a high price tag. Pavement, after all, did not just bring a flood of traffic to town. During the approval process, the WCRG had been concerned about the increased flow of storm water from parking lots into drains and the release of harmful air pollutants from idling autos coming to the new Walmart, and they were right to be concerned. Just a few years after Williston's Walmart opened its doors, the US Environmental Protection Agency (EPA) toured Walmart construction sites around the country and "detected a pattern of failures to comply with the requirements of applicable permits for the discharge of storm water from these construction sites."[45] "Inadequate silt fences," faulty retention ponds, and "unprotected slopes" were just some of the problems cited in Delaware, Utah, Colorado, and six other states.[46] In 2001, Walmart agreed to a $1 million settlement with the EPA, but three years later, the environmental agency found that Walmart was still not in compliance with basic storm water rules.[47] The EPA negotiated another settlement with Walmart for $3.1 million, "the largest civil penalty ever paid for violations of storm water regulations."[48]

In Williston, Muddy Brook—a stream that went right by the new Walmart—became an impaired stream, and environmental engineers specifically pointed to Walmart's parking lot as one of the key culprits contributing to tributary erosion and habitat loss.[49] "Stormwater runoff are [sic] causing a decline in biotic integrity," a 2009 watershed report read, noting that urbanization in the Taft Corners area was exacerbating the problems.[50]

Then there were the issues with air quality. In part because Davis made only minimal changes to roadways, not the investment of over $15 million that experts had suggested in the early 1990s, intersections and turning lanes quickly became clogged, with traffic often stalling all the way up the exit ramp on I-89.[51] It was a nightmare for many commuters, especially around rush hour.[52] Ultimately, the Vermont Agency of Transportation had to intervene, spending millions of dollars on infrastructure expansion in Williston to try to fix the problem. In the end, it took state dollars to deal with the inevitable traffic problems the big box store helped bring to this small town.[53]

In the meantime, the backed-up cars belched out pollutants, precisely as the district environmental commission had predicted, although just how much this changed the local air in Williston is not precisely known—in part because the EPA never put an ambient air quality monitoring system in the town. With limited resources and budget, the EPA installs ambient air quality devices only in bigger cities, and the closest one to Williston was in Burlington, more than six miles away. This was an advantage Walmart gained by siting its stores in tiny hamlets: the towns were often devoid of EPA instruments that might track the fine-grained ecological impact of a particular store.[54]

But air pollution was in many ways out of sight and out of mind. What really bothered those who had fought hard against Walmart was the new look and feel of the town. After Walmart came a flood of other box stores—Home Depot, Best Buy, Toys "R" Us, and more. It was as if Walmart had opened the door for a passel of new development. As many saw it, a natural beauty and an ecological aesthetic that defied precise valuation had been damaged and would never be fully restored.

In the words of environmental historian Jack Temple Kirby, it was a "rural world lost."[55]

Williston was not alone. In the 1980s and 1990s, dozens of small-town residents across the country fought Walmart on the grounds that the firm destroyed a certain rural aesthetic. In these battles—and there were many—one of the key concerns was that Walmart's entry would lead to the decline of local businesses and Main Street establishments. Beginning in 1988, Kenneth Stone, a professor and economist at Iowa State University, provided the statistics supporting this claim: he published studies showing that Walmart hurt many local shops and stores over the long run (typically after five years). Digesting nearly ten years of data that looked at small towns in Iowa, Stone concluded in 1997 that "some small towns lose up to 47 percent of their retail trade after 10 years of Walmart stores" doing business nearby. Though in 2012 Stone produced a study that offered a more nuanced view of Walmart's impact on local businesses and concluded that "Walmart's presence" in small Iowa communities actually "helped stabilize and even expand the local retail sector of most rural Iowa host communities," his original findings emboldened opponents of Walmart stores in the 1990s who turned to Stone's economic studies to argue that the Arkansas discount store was not good for local business.[56]

But while these economic arguments proved popular in Walmart debates, roadways and the environmental change those roadways wrought were often at the center of anti-big box discussions. In New York State in the early 1990s, the Otsego County Conservation Association fought a Walmart distribution center in the small town of Sharon Springs that routed trucks through rural roads. "We feel it is unfair for us to bear the brunt of the negative impacts we foresee," association president Bonnie Canning-Hofmann told Walmart vice president H. Lee Scott Jr. in a 1994 letter, listing among her grievances "increased heavy truck thru-traffic, suburbanized traffic patterns, air pollution noise, [and] disturbance to historic villages and to the rural quality of life we deeply appreciate." Canning-Hofmann wanted Walmart to avoid certain rural roads and proposed a traffic plan that would "route large trucks to the interstate highway system built and intended for their use."[57]

Scott, writing in response to Canning-Hofmann, explained that the shorter access roads to the highway had "inclines, curves, underpasses, and weight restrictions," making it impossible to route trucks that way. The physics of shipping huge amounts of goods in big tractor trailers meant that Walmart could only take certain routes through rural America. Though Scott said he appreciated her "concerns regarding traffic," he added that Walmart was going to send its trucks down Highway 20—a road Canning-Hofmann described as "one of the most beautiful . . . in New York . . . nestled among bucolic unspoiled hills, dramatic and magnificent view[s], enhanced by the presence of working farms." Scott said she shouldn't worry because the "peak traffic level on this route will not be reached for several years . . . This should allow all parties time to adjust to the new truck traffic and reevaluate and adjust routes or modify roads if and as needed." It was going to go Walmart's way, even if that way would eventually have to be paved with state dollars.[58]

Walmart did not always win, however. In Westford, Massachusetts, thousands of residents supported a Stop Wal-Mart Committee campaign in the early 1990s to prevent the Arkansas discounter from coming to town. They used the local environment to their advantage, pointing to pools on the prospective Walmart property that were breeding grounds for frogs to thwart Walmart's proposed development. Here was another way roadways and pavement affected the local environment of Walmart sites. Stores designed to increase the flow of out-of-town traffic in a particular community also impeded the free flow of endangered species migration. But the local developer working with Walmart on the Westford project said he would figure out a way to have a biologist onsite who could help frogs get to their breeding grounds—one assumes by directing traffic like a crossing guard for the amphibious. But this never came to pass because Walmart ultimately bowed to the pressure of 4,000 protestors (nearly a quarter of the town) who simply would not give up their fight.[59]

Steamboat Springs, Colorado; Iowa City, Iowa; Ithaca, New York; Jackson Hole, Wyoming: all these towns, east and west, became sites of anti-Walmart flare-ups in the 1980s and 1990s. In these battles, ecology, not just economics, entered the lexicon of protest, as some residents

FIGURE 1.4. Sam Walton's first five-and dime store on the downtown square in Bentonville, Arkansas, a place Walton chose to call home in part because his wife, Helen, loved the outdoors and because he believed the site would allow him easy access to quail hunting grounds. In 2023, the original store was being remodeled and was located next to a children's bike shop. The Walton Family Foundation has spent a lot of money in recent years to make Bentonville "the mountain biking capital of the world." In more ways than one, the hilly environment has brought economic rewards to some in this small Arkansas town. Author photo.

in small towns fought to preserve a rural aesthetic they believed made their towns special.[60]

Between 1998 and 2005, roughly 563 communities protested Walmart store constructions, which represented more than a third of the 1,599 sites proposed during that period. But in the end, Walmart chose to abandon only about 365 projects. Over that eight-year period, the company completed construction on 1,040 stores, bringing its total number of outlets in the United States to well over 3,000 (figure 1.4). These stores helped make Walmart not only the world's largest retailer but also the largest corporation on the planet.[61]

FIGURE 1.5. The mountain biking culture in Bentonville, Arkansas, is world-class. This is a feature on Coler Mountain Bike Preserve, one of the trail networks the Walton family helped build. Author photo.

That power led to global environmental changes that extended well beyond Williston, Vermont. By the 1990s, Walmart had supply chains that stretched across oceans to Asian markets and beyond. The decisions Walmart made at its home office were transforming commerce around the world and the ecosystems of communities thousands of miles away from Bentonville, Arkansas (figure 1.5).

In 1980 and 1981, Walmart opened its first procurement offices in Hong Kong and Taiwan, respectively. The company was not a trailblazer in turning to Asian suppliers to provide cheap consumer goods, but it quickly became a big player in this market. In 1985, Sam Walton announced, with much fanfare, his "Buy American" campaign, pledging to source much of the materials in his stores from domestic companies rather than overseas suppliers.[62] But in 1992, *Dateline* reporters revealed the hollowness of Walton's patriotic appeal, taking viewers on a virtual tour of Walmart stores and showing tags on "Made in America" racks that revealed merchandise that came from China, Bangladesh, and other countries overseas.[63] The exposé also documented horrendous working conditions in sweatshops that supplied the firm in Southeast Asia. The truth was that Walmart, despite its best efforts to bill itself as American-born, was a hawker of foreign wares that were often produced in factories with brutal labor policies. By 2002, 80 percent of Walmart suppliers were based in China.[64] That year, the company ranked ahead of Russia and the United Kingdom in terms of the trade it did with China.[65]

But Walmart was not just an international company because it sourced goods from overseas; it also built stores beyond US borders. Walmart opened its first retail outlet in China in 1996, a year before anti-Walmart Willistonians lost their fight in Vermont. In the 1990s and the first decade of the 2000s, Walmart, like many American companies, took advantage of neoliberal trade policies promoted by new organizations such as the World Trade Organization to open stores across the globe.[66] The company's first foreign foray was in Mexico in 1991 and then in 1994, after President Bill Clinton signed the North American Free Trade Agreement (NAFTA), Canada. Walton saw where Walmart was headed. "I don't know if Wal-Mart can truly maintain our leadership position by just staying in this country [the United States]," he said in 1992. "I think we're going to have to become a more international company in the not-too-distant future."[67] Walmart created an international division and soon opened its first stores in Brazil (1995) and Argentina (1995) and then in Indonesia (1996) and China (1996). Europe soon followed, as the firm bought out competitors and opened new stores in Germany (1997) and the United Kingdom (1999).[68]

In 2006, more than a decade and a half after the firm began opening stores outside the US, international earnings represented only 19.7 percent of sales.[69] Twelve years later, international business remained below 24 percent of consolidated net sales.[70] These statistics made clear that the rural roads in small-town America were still critical veins in Walmart's corporate body.

Yet these veins—a widened road in Williston, for example—would never have pulsed if not for the steady heartbeat of Walmart's suppliers thousands of miles away. For a working family in Vermont to feel like it was worth it to drive fifty miles to a store in Williston, Walmart had to find ways to drive prices of its goods down as far as it possibly could.

In the industry, it was called the "squeeze," and Walmart was one of the best in the business at doing it. This is how it worked. A company would come to Bentonville, hoping to secure a contract to sell its wares to Walmart; in that meeting, Walmart, not the supplier, would dictate the terms of the transaction. Walmart would explain what the price would be for a given good, and the manufacturer would have to figure out how it was going to meet Walmart's demands. There was no real negotiation. Because Walmart was so big and powerful, the company determined what cost what amount. For many companies, the only way to survive the Walmart squeeze was to find cheap labor markets thousands of miles away, especially in China.[71]

This outsourcing strategy might have made smart economic sense, but from an environmental perspective, it meant that a large percentage of Walmart's goods had to be transported extremely long distances on cargo ships, resulting in tremendous greenhouse gas emissions. In 2003, Walmart was the top US importer of shipping containers from overseas markets. Atlanta-based Home Depot, a store whose big box business strategy was very much modeled on discount retailers like Walmart, came in second.[72] As Walmart admitted, roughly 90 percent of the firm's greenhouse gas emissions came from its supply chain, not its retail stores. When it came to Walmart's ecological footprint, Williston's environmental woes were just the tip of a melting iceberg.[73]

This reality had Walmart executives worried. In 2004, Walmart's CEO, H. Lee Scott, admitted that his company—now the largest corporation in the world—was "exposed" on many fronts. Scott, a Missouri native who first joined the company in 1979, had never been an environmentalist. In fact, as journalist Edward Humes put it, "the environment was the last thing on his mind" when he became CEO in 2000. But a series of events culminated in Scott committing to "greening" his company in 2004 because he believed it was the only way to protect the firm's bottom line.[74]

Troubles had been festering since the 1992 *Dateline* investigation that had showed Walmart's Bangladeshi suppliers exploiting child laborers. David Glass, Scott's predecessor, had totally botched the *Dateline* interviews, at one point responding to footage of children working in supplier factories by saying to the NBC reporter on set, "You and I might perhaps define 'children' differently." Then, in 1996, labor rights activist Charles Kernaghan testified to the US Congress that Walmart's Kathie Lee Gifford clothing line was also produced by child laborers working in horrible conditions in Honduran factories. The company said it was taking steps to eliminate these injustices in its supply chain, but clearly there was a deep culture of labor abuse inside the firm. In 2001, for example, a group of women who worked at Walmart filed suit against the firm, charging that the company had systemically paid female employees less than male workers doing the same jobs. Two years later, federal authorities stormed Walmart stores in twenty states, detaining hundreds of undocumented immigrants who were employed in these outlets. At the same time, a damaging confidential internal Walmart report was leaked to the press. The report revealed that roughly 46 percent of the children of Walmart employees had no health insurance or depended on Medicaid or other public welfare programs to meet their healthcare needs.[75]

As all this news was breaking, communities were continuing to battle the environmental and cultural degradation caused by the siting of Walmart stores in rural communities. To be sure, these environmental issues were not as big a concern to folks like Scott in 2004, but they added to the distress top executives felt. That year, the EPA issued its historic $3.1 million fine against the company for its storm water violations; the company also paid $400,000 in penalties to settle complaints about air pollution caused by Walmart's illegal sale of banned CFC refrigerants. In Mexico, activists expressed outrage when the company announced plans to build one of its stores near the ancient city of Teotihuacán, a sacred United Nations Educational, Scientific, and Cultural Organization (UNESCO) World Heritage site. Further, Walmart became a target of environmental activists concerned about the firm's massive contributions to global warming.[76]

Facing this pressure, in 2005, Scott made a bold promise to make his company more environmentally friendly.[77] Over the next decade, the company made major moves—pushing electricity-saving compact fluorescent light bulbs in its stores, radically shrinking product packaging, and improving the energy efficiency of its trucking fleet. Within a decade, the firm boasted that it sourced 26 percent of its electricity from renewable resources and claimed an "87.4 percent improvement" in "fleet efficiency."[78] The company also dramatically increased purchases of organic cotton for its clothing lines—by the 2010s it had become the single largest purchaser of organic cotton in the world—and worked on a series of projects to reduce the greenhouse gas footprint of its dairy suppliers.[79]

Perhaps the most ambitious project was an effort to develop a "sustainability index" that would allow the company to know the entire environmental footprint, from cradle to grave, of every product it sold. Beginning in 2008, the company worked to create a Sustainability Consortium made up of university experts and industry representatives from firms such as Seventh Generation, Procter and Gamble, and SC Johnson, which was tasked with assessing the full life cycle of all Walmart products. As this book went to press, the project was still in existence and was known as the Sustainability Insight System (THESIS) Index. Walmart said in 2022 that it drew on this index to make supply-side decisions but noted that only 1,800 of its 100,000 suppliers participated in the initiative—a far cry from the bold vision proposed back in 2008, when the goal was to track the environmental footprint of every product the firm sold.[80]

Nevertheless, the company continued to make big promises when it came to meeting environmental targets after launching the index.

In 2017, for example, the firm announced Project Gigaton, setting an aspirational goal to eliminate a gigaton of greenhouse gases from its corporate system by 2030. Soon thereafter, Walmart representatives traveled to the climate talks in Bonn, joining a host of American cities, corporations, and state governments in signing the "We Are Still In" declaration—pledging Walmart's commitment to the Paris Accord even as President Donald Trump moved forward with plans to take the United States out of the agreement. Environmental groups and journalists alike gave the firm kudos for being a trailblazer in corporate greening initiatives.[81]

But independently verifying Walmart's progress toward ecological sustainability proved difficult because the company ultimately controlled the numbers. *Atlantic* reporter Orville Schell tried to dig deep in 2011, asking Walmart officials if he could have more details about factories that had been blacklisted from working with the discounter due to standards violations. "A clear answer was hard to come by," Schell said. When he went further and asked whether Walmart auditors could offer greater detail regarding "high-risk" factories listed as being in the "Far East" on the company's audit sheet, he was simply told that the company did not "provide breakouts below the regional level."[82]

One of the biggest problems with Walmart's emissions reporting in the 2010s was that it did not provide a full accounting of greenhouse gases released by container ships carrying Walmart goods to market. In 2013, author Stacy Mitchell explained the absurdity of this omission, noting that Walmart "now accounts for one of every twenty-five containers shipped to the US and its imports are growing faster than the country's as a whole."[83] To truly measure Walmart's impact on climate change, oceanic transport had to be fully integrated into the calculus.

This was a strange situation. A firm that had revolutionized open sharing of information between suppliers and retailers through satellite systems and advanced inventory management technology like Retail Link confessed that it could not pin down its suppliers to obtain basic environmental data or offer full details about the ecological costs of getting its goods to market. Yes, the company had launched an ambitious sustainability index back in 2008, but a decade and a half later, only a fraction of suppliers were included in that index and key data were still missing. The firm had the capacity to replace the smallest trinkets on a store shelf in a matter of hours, activating a sophisticated digital communication network that stretched around the world, but when it came to environmental auditing, it seemed Walmart was still very much in the dark.

It could afford to remain in the dark because no one else was watching. Just as there were no air monitoring devices in Williston to track emissions from idling cars waiting to turn left into the Walmart parking lot, there were no climate auditors keeping track of carbon emissions from ships transporting Walmart wares over oceanic waters. Once in motion, Walmart goods and the consumers they drew to company stores became difficult for regulators to track. Yet it was precisely the long distances both consumers and goods traveled that made the Walmart way of doing business so earth-changing.

Despite all the fanfare about Walmart being a green business committed to curbing climate change, the truth is, the company has produced less than stellar results. According to its self-reported data, Walmart's scope 1 (associated with Walmart stores and distribution center operations) and scope 2 (indirect emissions associated with energy purchases) greenhouse gas emissions increased by over 8 percent from 2006 to 2015. This does not include scope 3 emissions, which cover Walmart's supply network, about which the firm still offers very limited data.[84] What would the numbers look like if Walmart included the scope 3 emissions?[85]

Sam Walton could have predicted this. What he learned in the early days of discount retailing was that firms would only do his bidding if they felt pressure from a third party to meet specific targets. He knew he had to set the rules of the game, not the other way around. It was the "squeeze" that changed the retail world forever. But it only worked because he demanded that his suppliers open their books and show him how they made the sausage or the shirt so he could understand how far they could be pushed. With that knowledge, he made businesses do the impossible. The motivation for him was economic, not ecological.

But environmental regulators would do well to steal a page from Walton's little yellow notepad. For far too long, environmental policymakers have allowed Walmart to operate in the shadows of the US economy.

The company has been free to set its own agenda for dealing with its growing greenhouse gas emissions and to set its own standards for how it is going to meet certain ecological targets. The effects have been less than stunning, certainly not the kind of innovation that would have wowed someone like Walton. So what would Walmart do if it were pressured by regulatory bodies to do the right thing? What would it do if it had to feel the squeeze?

The environmental effects of Walmart's way of making money extend well beyond the boundaries of this Bentonville firm. In so many ways, Walmart has become the model for other retail giants that have reshaped our global economy and ecology, including Amazon.com. In the 1990s, when Jeff Bezos was looking to build his new internet business, he flew to Arkansas to learn more about how Walmart built its distribution network. He read Sam Walton's biography and later poached many Walmart employees to build his distribution network at Amazon—including Rick Dalzell, who had been Walmart's vice president of information systems, and Jimmy Wright, Walmart's vice president of distribution. Wright would play a central role in recruiting other key players from Bentonville, as would a former Walmart engineer, Kal Raman, who joined Amazon in the 1990s and worked to bring more Walmart employees into Bezos's firm. In the end, Walmart sued Amazon for poaching the Bentonville business's top talent, though the case was ultimately resolved without Bezos having to pay Walmart a penny. The point here is that the "Amazon" economy is in so many ways a derivative of the same logistics formula first figured out in the hilly countryside of the Ozarks.[86]

Combined, these two firms have enormous control over our economy. Walmart and Amazon.com enjoyed the number-one and number-two spots atop the 2022 Fortune 500 listing. What a different world this is from fifty years ago, when Ford, General Motors, and General Electric dominated the Fortune list, with retail giants nowhere in sight.[87]

This reality should give policymakers pause as they consider the next generation of environmental legislation in the decades ahead. The Clean Air Act, Clean Water Act, and other environmental laws of the 1970s and 1980s were passed at a time when retail and logistics firms had nowhere near the power they have today. Those laws focused on the smokestacks and effluent pipelines of industrial and chemical firms, not the conduits of commerce constructed by Amazon, Walmart, and other big box retailers that now serve as the veins of the US economy. As we'll see in section II, history suggests that we need to think more about distribution centers and big box retail supply chains, not just manufacturing facilities and coal-powered plants, if we hope to mitigate the worst ecological consequences of our point-click-and-buy, fly-by-night, have-it-now economy.

NOTES

1. Much of this chapter was originally published in *Country Capitalism: How Corporations from the American South Remade Our Economy and the Planet*. Copyright © 2023 Bart Elmore. Used by permission of the University of North Carolina Press. www.uncpress.org. The author would like to thank University Press of Colorado, University of Wyoming Press, and University of North Carolina Press for allowing me to reuse previously published content in this edited volume.
2. Walton, *Sam Walton*, 102–103; Pritchett, *Stop Paddling and Start Rocking the Boat*, 27; "How the Walmart Shareholders Meeting Went from a Few Guys in a Coffee Shop to a 14,000-Person, Star-Studded Celebration," *Business Insider*, June 2, 2017, www.businessinsider.com/history-walmart-shareholders-meeting-2017-6. On Helen Walton's enthusiasm for the outdoors, see Ortega, *In Sam We Trust*, 24; Walton, *Sam Walton*, 19; Trimble, *Sam Walton*, 45, 50.
3. Ortega, *In Sam We Trust*, 190; Walton, *Sam Walton*, 102–103.
4. Walton, *Sam Walton*, 102–103.
5. "The Hot Ticket in Retailing: Wal-Mart Is Making a Bundle by Bringing Big Discounts to the Sunbelt," *New York Times*, July 1, 1984, 4F; Moreton, *To Serve God and Wal-Mart*, 132. For more on the history of cultural representations of southern working-class whites as anti-modern "hillbillies" throughout the twentieth century, see Harkins, *Hillbilly*.
6. Pritchett, *Stop Paddling and Start Rocking the Boat*, 26–31.
7. Pritchett, *Stop Paddling and Start Rocking the Boat*, 29–32.
8. Walton, *Sam Walton*, 19, 21, 31, 33; Bergdahl, *What I Learned from Sam Walton*, 133.
9. Trimble, *Sam Walton*, 64, 71; Ortega, *In Sam We Trust*, 31; Moreton, *To Serve God and Wal-Mart*, 12; Vance and Scott, *Wal-Mart*, 13.
10. Walton, *Sam Walton*, 112.
11. Walton, *Sam Walton*, 40.
12. Soderquist, *The Wal-Mart Way*, 179; Walton, *Sam Walton*, 110.
13. Graves, "Discounting Northern Capital," 51.
14. Vance and Scott, *Wal-Mart*, 51; Moreton, *To Serve God and Wal-Mart*, 12.
15. House Committee on Public Works and Transportation, "To Examine the Future of the Nation's Infrastructure Needs," 158.

16. Walton, *Sam Walton*, 90.
17. Lichtenstein, "Wal-Mart," 14; Moreton, *To Serve God and Wal-Mart*, 11.
18. Moreton, *To Serve God and Wal-Mart*, 84.
19. Moreton, *To Serve God and Wal-Mart*, 39; Cobb, *The Selling of the South*, 101.
20. Trimble, *Sam Walton*, 229; Ortega, *In Sam We Trust*, 87.
21. Humes, *Force of Nature*, 37–38; Lichtenstein, *Retail Revolution*, 117–118.
22. Humes, *Force of Nature*, 39–40.
23. Moreton, "It Came from Bentonville," 82.
24. On long-haul trucking and Walmart, see Hamilton, *Trucking Country*.
25. "Wal-Mart Encounters a Wall of Resistance in Vermont," *Washington Post*, July 27, 1994, A3; US Census Bureau, City and Town Postcensal Tables: 1990–2000, www.census.gov.
26. "Williston Project," *Burlington Free Press*, January 18, 1992, 8A; "Greenfield Seeks Office in Williston," *Burlington Free Press*, January 19, 1993, B1.
27. For extensive records detailing WCRG's extended fight with Walmart, see Williston Citizens for Responsible Growth Records, 1988–1998; "Small Town Worried by Big Retailer," *Daily Chronicle* (DeKalb, IL), January 30, 1997, 5A; "Greenfield Seeks Office in Williston," *Burlington Free Press*, January 19, 1993, B1; "Wal-Mart: Retailer Likely to Put Up a Tough Fight in NCCo," *News Journal* (Wilmington, DE), March 9, 1997, A11.
28. For an excellent summary of WCRG history, see the Vermont Historical Society's WCRG finding aid, https://vermonthistory.org/documents/findaid/WCRG.pdf; author interview with Fred "Chico" Lager, March 29, 2019.
29. "'Sprawl-Mart' Endangers Vermont," *Christian Science Monitor*, December 6, 1993, https://www.csmonitor.com/1993/1206/06111.html.
30. Vermont Environment District #4, Land Use Permit, April 27, 1988, doc. 787, folder 34, part 4; Vermont Environmental Board, Memorandum of Decision Re: Taft Corners Associates, Inc., Application #4c0696-11-EB, doc. 787, folder 1; Memorandum from Chico Lager to Gerry Tarrant and Bob Morris, December 5, 1993, doc. 787, folder 34, part 2, all in WCRG Records.
31. Memorandum from Chico Lager to Gerry Tarrant and Bob Morris, December 5, 1993, Re: Key Points from the Original TCA Act 250 Permit, doc. 787, folder 34, part 2; Memorandum from Chico Lager to Gerry Tarrant and Bob Morris, December 5, 1993, Re: Bob's Testimony—First Draft, doc. 787, folder 34, part 1, both in WCRG Records.
32. Memorandum from Chico Lager to Gerry Tarrant and Bob Morris, December 5, 1993, Key Points from the Original TCA Act 250 Permit, doc. 787, folder 34, part 2; Memorandum from Chico Lager to Gerry Tarrant and Bob Morris, December 5, 1993, Re: Bob's Testimony—First Draft, doc. 787, folder 34, part 1, both in WCRG Records.
33. "Wal-Mart Gets OK, But . . . ," *Burlington Free Press*, July 30, 1994, 1A; "The Issues Slowly Grind through the Courts," *CRG [Citizens for Responsible Growth] Newsletter* (September 1993), 3, doc. 787, folder 7, part 2, WCRG Records.
34. "Endangered Label Was Wake-Up Call for State," *Burlington Free Press*, February 22, 2004, 1C.
35. "From the Co-presidents," *CRG Newsletter* (September 1993), 2, doc. 787, folder 7, part 2, WCRG Records.

36. "State Backs Retailer," *Burlington Free Press*, June 20, 1995, 1A; "Wal-Mart to Pave Own Way," *Burlington Free Press*, August 22, 1995, 1A, 14A; "Timeline: Wal-Mart in Vermont," *Burlington Free Press*, July 30, 1994, 5A; "Wal-Mart Wins in Court," *Burlington Free Press*, October 20, 1994, 1B.
37. "Wal-Mart to Pave Own Way."
38. "Wal-Mart: Retailer Hits Traffic Jam," *Burlington Free Press*, September 9, 1995, 4B.
39. "Wal-Mart Wins Final Approval," *Burlington Free Press*, October 19, 1995, 1A.
40. "Construction Vehicles Damaged at Wal-Mart," *Burlington Free Press*, October 31, 1995, 3B.
41. "Wal-Mart: Symbol or Just Another Store," *Burlington Free Press*, January 27, 1997, 1B, 2B.
42. "More Object to Retail Sprawl," *Burlington Free Press*, January 14, 1996, 1A.
43. "Wal-Mart: Store's Impact on Jobs Unclear," *Burlington Free Press*, October 21, 1996, 12A; "Wal-Mart: Symbol or Just Another Store."
44. Hyman, *Debtor Nation*, 222.
45. *United States of America v. Wal-Mart Stores, Inc.*, 2004, 6.
46. *United States of America v. Wal-Mart Stores, Inc.*, 2004, 7, 12, 19, 23, 31.
47. *United States of America v. Wal-Mart Stores, Inc.*, 2004, 6.
48. "Wal-Mart II Clean Water Act," Environmental Protection Agency, www.epa.gov/enforcement/wal-mart-ii-clean-water-act-settlement.
49. "Town of Williston: Town-Wide Watershed Improvement Plan, Phase I," 95; Rethink Runoff, http://rethinkrunoff.org/explore-the-lake-champlain-basin/muddy-brook/; State of Vermont, 303(d) List of Impaired Waters (September 2018), 5, https://dec.vermont.gov/sites/dec/files/documents/mp_PriorityWatersList_PartA_303d_2018.pdf.
50. Fitzgerald and Parker, "Muddy Brook Phase[s] I and 2 Stream Geomorphic Assessment Summary."
51. "Talking to Neighbors," *Burlington Free Press*, January 20, 1997, 6A; "Hearing on Retail Ban Divides Town," *Burlington Free Press*, May 9, 1997, 4B.
52. "Hearing on Retail Ban Divides Town."
53. "Consultant Rolls Out Plan to Reduce Backups on I-89 Ramp," *Williston Observer*, June 1, 2005, www.willistonobserver.com/consultant-rolls-out-plan-to-reduce-backups-on-i-89-ramp/; "Vt. Lays Out 34 Highway Projects to Ease Chittenden County Traffic Congestion," NBC 5, November 26, 2013, www.mynbc5.com/.
54. To view the EPA's AirData Air Quality Monitors app, which shows the location of air quality monitors around the country as well as air quality data, see www.epa.gov/outdoor-air-quality-data/interactive-map-air-quality-monitors.
55. "Small Town Worried about Wal-Mart," *Daily Herald* (Tyrone, PA), January 30, 1997, 3. "Rural worlds lost" is southern historian Jack Temple Kirby's phrase. See Kirby, *Rural Worlds Lost*.
56. Stone, "The Effect of Wal-Mart Stores on Businesses"; Stone, "Impact of the Wal-Mart Phenomenon on Rural Communities," 2. For the updated study that highlights how Walmart stores in some markets actually increased "host-town retail sales," see Artz and Stone, "Revisiting WalMart's Impact on Iowa Small-Town Retail." For an

archival collection containing Kenneth Stone's research materials, see the Kenneth Stone Papers, 1978–1999, Parks Library, Iowa State University, Ames; also see Neumark, Zhang, and Ciccarella, "The Effects of Wal-Mart on Local Labor Markets"; Basker, "Job Creation or Destruction"; Barcus, "Wal-Mart-Scapes in Rural and Small-Town America," 69; Karjanen, "The Wal-Mart Effect and the New Face of Capitalism," 150; Fishman, *The Wal-Mart Effect*, 143.

57. Letter from Bonnie Canning-Hofmann, president, Otsego County Conservation Association, to H. Lee Scott, vice president of Wal-Mart, December 14, 1994, series: Other Projects and Issues, 1969–2001, box 2, folder 2, Otsego County Conservation Association Records, M. E. Grenander Department of Special Collections and Archives, University Libraries, University at Albany, State University of New York (hereafter OCCA Records).

58. Letter from Bonnie Canning-Hofmann, president, Otsego County Conservation Association, to H. Lee Scott, vice president of Wal-Mart, December 14, 1994; Letter from H. Lee Scott to Bonnie Canning-Hofmann, January 6, 1995, series: Other Projects and Issues, 1969–2001, box 2, folder 2, OCCA Records.

59. "Wal-Mart Cancels Store Plans after Residents Complain," *Rutland (VT) Daily Herald*, September 17, 1993, B8; "In Two Towns, Main Street Fights Off Wal-Mart," *New York Times*, October 21, 1993, A16; "Wal-Mart Ready for Opponents, Right Down to Saving the Frogs," *Rutland (VT) Daily Herald*, September 4, 1993, 11.

60. "Wal-Mart, Builder Drop Plan for Steamboat Springs Store," *Daily Sentinel* (Grand Junction, CO), December 3, 1987, 3A; "Letters from Boynton Middle School, Wal-Mart Foes and a Journal Critic," *Ithaca (NY) Journal*, May 14, 1994, 14A; "Two Communities Rejected Wal-Mart Developments," *Jackson Hole (WY) Guide*, April 26, 1989, A6; "City Panel Challenges Market Study," *Iowa City Press-Citizen*, March 14, 1989, 1B; Ortega, *In Sam We Trust*, 171–172, 176, 180, 186, 300; Vance and Scott, *Wal-Mart*, 153.

61. Ingram and Yue, "Trouble in Store," 53; Soderquist, *The Wal-Mart Way*, 201; Zook and Graham, "Wal-Mart Nation," 15–16.

62. Moreton, *To Serve God and Wal-Mart*, 251–252; Ortega, *In Sam We Trust*, 205; "Walmart's 'Buy American,'" *New York Times*, April 10, 1985, D1.

63. Ortega, *In Sam We Trust*, 223–224; Bergdahl, *What I Learned from Sam Walton*, 16; Moreton, *To Serve God and Wal-Mart*, 253.

64. Moreton, *To Serve God and Wal-Mart*, 251.

65. Zook and Graham, "Wal-Mart Nation," 15.

66. Zook and Graham, "Wal-Mart Nation," 15–16.

67. Walton, *Sam Walton*, 204.

68. Zook and Graham, "Wal-Mart Nation," 16; Burt and Sparks, "Wal-Mart's World," 33–37.

69. Zook and Graham, "Wal-Mart Nation," 15.

70. 2018 Walmart Annual Report, 23.

71. For more on "the squeeze," see Fishman, *The Wal-Mart Effect*, 79–109.

72. Bonacich with Hardie, "Wal-Mart and the Logistics Revolution," 180.

73. 2018 Walmart Global Responsibility Report, 127; 2015 Walmart Global Responsibility Report, 100; Lichtenstein, "Walmart's Long March to China," 15.

74. Humes, *Force of Nature*, 21, 25–26, 53.
75. Moreton, *To Serve God and Wal-Mart*, 49, 253; Ortega, *In Sam We Trust*, 224–227, 331, 341, 345; *Dateline* interview cited in Humes, *Force of Nature*, 43–51; VanderVelde, "Wal-Mart as a Phenomenon in the Legal World," 126.
76. Humes, *Force of Nature*, 49; "Wal-Mart to Pay $400,000 Penalty and Cease Sales of Ozone-Depleting Refrigerants," US Justice Department press release, January 22, 2004, https://www.justice.gov/archive/opa/pr/2004/January/04_enrd_040.htm; Walker, Walker, and Velázquez, "The Wal-Martification of Teotihuacán," 218; Biles, "Globalization of Food," 349.
77. Humes, *Force of Nature*, 53.
78. 2015 Walmart Global Responsibility Report, 5; "Wal-Mart Puts Some Muscle behind Power-Sipping Bulbs," *New York Times*, January 2, 2007, A1; Humes, *Force of Nature*, 87–89, 141.
79. Humes, *Force of Nature*, 84, 132–134, 159–180.
80. "THESIS Index," Walmart Sustainability Hub, www.walmartsustainabilityhub.com/sustainability-index; "THESIS, the Sustainability Insight System," Sustainability Consortium, https://sustainabilityconsortium.org/thesis/; Humes, *Force of Nature*, 182–201.
81. 2017 Walmart Global Responsibility Report, 7, 52, 54; 2018 Walmart Global Responsibility Report, 3; "Walmart Makes Bold Climate Commitments—and Delivers," We Are All In, www.wearestillin.com/success/walmart-makes-bold-climate-commitments-and-delivers.
82. Orville Schell, "How Walmart Is Changing China," *The Atlantic*, December 2011, www.theatlantic.com/magazine/archive/2011/12/how-walmart-is-changing-china/308709/; 2011 Walmart Global Responsibility Report, 101.
83. Stacy Mitchell, "Walmart's Assault on the Climate: The Truth behind One of the Biggest Climate Polluters and Slickest Greenwashers in America," published by the Institute for Local Self-Reliance (November 2013), 7, https://ilsr.org/wp-content/uploads/2013/10/ILSR-_Report_WalmartClimateChange.pdf; Stacy Mitchell, "The Truth behind Walmart's Green Claims," *HuffPost*, June 1, 2014, www.huffpost.com/entry/almart-climate-change_b_5063035. Stacy Mitchell is the author of *Big-Box Swindle*. In the company's 2018 CDP report, Walmart said it was able to "estimate the emissions from our third party logistics coordinators in some of our markets using EPA emission factors for fuels in 2015." This apparently includes rough calculations for some container ships, but reporting here was vague at best. See Walmart, Climate Change Report for Carbon Disclosure Project, 2018, 37–38, www.cdp.net/en.
84. 2015 Walmart Global Responsibility Report, 55; 2017 Walmart Global Responsibility Report, 55.
85. "ESG Commitments and Progress," Walmart corporate website, https://corporate.walmart.com/esgreport/reporting-data/esg-commitments-progress.
86. Stone, *The Everything Store*, 60–62, 72–75.
87. 2022 Fortune 500 rankings, https://fortune.com/ranking/fortune500/; 1972 Fortune 500 rankings, CNN Money, https://money.cnn.com/magazines/fortune/fortune500_archive/full/1972/.

BIBLIOGRAPHY

NEWSPAPERS, PERIODICALS, AND CORPORATE REPORTS

The Atlantic
Burlington (VT) Free Press
Business Insider
Christian Science Monitor
Daily Chronicle (DeKalb, IL)
Daily Herald (Tyrone, PA)
Daily Sentinel (Grand Junction, CO)
HuffPost
Iowa City Press-Citizen
Ithaca (NY) Journal
Jackson Hole (WY) Guide
New York Times
News Journal (Wilmington, DE)
Rutland (VT) Daily Herald
Walmart's 2018 carbon disclosure project report
Walmart's 2018 corporate annual report
Walmart's 2011, 2015, 2017, and 2018 global responsibility reports
Washington Post
Williston (VT) Observer

PRIMARY AND SECONDARY SOURCES

Artz, Georgeanne M., and Kenneth E. Stone. "Revisiting WalMart's Impact on Iowa Small-Town Retail: 25 Years Later." *Economic Development Quarterly* 26, no. 4 (October 2012): 298–310.

Barcus, Holly R. "Wal-Mart-Scapes in Rural and Small-Town America." In *Wal-Mart World: The World's Biggest Corporation in the Global Economy*, edited by Stanley D. Brunn, 63–75. New York: Routledge, 2006.

Basker, Emek. "Job Creation or Destruction? Labor Market Effect of Wal-Mart Expansion." *Review of Economics and Statistics* 87, no. 1 (February 2005): 174–183.

Bergdahl, Michael. *What I Learned from Sam Walton: How to Compete and Thrive in a Wal-Mart World*. Hoboken, NJ: John Wiley and Sons, 2004.

Biles, James J. "Globalization of Food Retailing and the Consequences of Wal-Martization in Mexico." In *Wal-Mart World: The World's Biggest Corporation in the Global Economy*, edited by Stanley D. Brunn, 343–355. New York: Routledge, 2006.

Bonacich, Edna with Khaleelah Hardie. "Wal-Mart and the Logistics Revolution." In *Wal-Mart: The Face of Twenty-First Century Capitalism*, edited by Nelson Lichtenstein, 163–188. New York; London: New Press, 2006.

Burt, Steve, and Leigh Sparks. "Wal-Mart's World." In *Wal-Mart World: The World's Biggest Corporation in the Global Economy*, edited by Stanley D. Brunn, 27–43. New York: Routledge, 2006.

Cobb, James C. *The Selling of the South: The Southern Crusade for Industrial Development, 1936–1990*. Urbana: University of Illinois Press, 1993.

Elmore, Bartow. *Country Capitalism: How Corporations from the American South Remade Our Economy and the Planet*. Chapel Hill, NC: Ferris and Ferris, 2023.

Fishman, Charles. *The Wal-Mart Effect: How the World's Most Powerful Company Really Works—and How It's Transforming the American Economy*. New York: Penguin, 2006.

Fitzgerald, Evan P., and Samuel P. Parker. "Muddy Brook Phase[s] I & 2 Stream Geomorphic Assessment Summary." Prepared for the Vermont River Management Program with funding from the Vermont Clean and Clear Program, February 2, 2009. www.town.williston.vt.us.

Graves, William. "Discounting Northern Capital: Financing the World's Largest Retailer from the Periphery." In *Wal-Mart World: The World's Biggest Corporation in the Global Economy*, edited by Stanley D. Brunn, 47–54. New York: Routledge, 2006.

Hamilton, Shane. *Trucking Country: The Road to America's Wal-Mart Economy*. Princeton, NJ: Princeton University Press, 2008.

Harkins, Anthony. *Hillbilly: A Cultural History of an American Icon*. New York: Oxford University Press, 2004.

House Committee on Public Works and Transportation. "To Examine the Future of the Nation's Infrastructure Needs." 101st Cong., 2nd sess., March 29, June 13, July 16, August 7–8, 30–31, September 8, 17, December 7, 1990.

Humes, Edward. *Force of Nature: The Unlikely Story of Wal-Mart's Green Revolution*. New York: HarperBusiness, 2011.

Hyman, Louis. *Debtor Nation: The History of America in Red Ink*. Princeton, NJ: Princeton University Press, 2011.

Ingram, Paul, and Lori Qingyuan Yue. "Trouble in Store: Probes, Protests, and Store Openings by Wal-Mart, 1998–2007." *American Journal of Sociology* 116, no. 1 (July 2010): 53–92.

Karjanen, David. "The Wal-Mart Effect and the New Face of Capitalism: Labor Market and Community Impacts of the Megaretailer." In *Wal-Mart: The Face of Twenty-First-Century Capitalism*, edited by Nelson Lichtenstein, 143–162. New York: New Press, 2006.

Kirby, Jack Temple. *Rural Worlds Lost: The American South, 1920–1960*. Baton Rouge: Louisiana State University Press, 1987.

Lichtenstein, Nelson. *The Retail Revolution: How Wal-Mart Created a Brave New World of Business*. New York: Picador, 2010.

Lichtenstein, Nelson. "Wal-Mart: A Template for Twenty-First-Century Capitalism." In *Wal-Mart: The Face of Twenty-First-Century Capitalism*, edited by Nelson Lichtenstein, 3–30. New York: New Press, 2006.

Mitchell, Stacy. *Big-Box Swindle: The True Cost of Mega-Retailers and the Fight for America's Independent Businesses*. Boston: Beacon, 2006.

Moreton, Bethany. "It Came from Bentonville: The Agrarian Origins of Wal-Mart Culture." In *Wal-Mart: The Face of Twenty-First-Century Capitalism*, edited by Nelson Lichtenstein, 57–82. New York: New Press, 2006.

Moreton, Bethany. *To Serve God and Wal-Mart: The Making of Christian Free Enterprise*. Cambridge, MA: Harvard University Press, 2009.

Neumark, David, Junfu Zhang, and Stephen Ciccarella. "The Effects of Wal-Mart on Local Labor Markets." *Journal of Urban Economics* 63, no. 2 (March 2008): 405–430.

Ortega, Bob. *In Sam We Trust: The Untold Story of Sam Walton and How Wal-Mart Is Devouring America*. New York: Times Books, 1998.

Otsego County Conservation Association Records. M. E. Grenander Department of Special Collections and Archives, University Libraries, University at Albany, State University of New York.

Pritchett, Lou. *Stop Paddling and Start Rocking the Boat: Business Lessons from the School of Hard Knocks*. New York: Authors Choice Press, 2007.

Soderquist, Don. *The Wal-Mart Way: The Inside Story of the Success of the World's Largest Company*. Nashville, TN: Nelson Business, 2005.

Stone, Brad. *The Everything Store: Jeff Bezos and the Age of Amazon*. New York: Little, Brown, 2013.

Stone, Kenneth E. "The Effect of Wal-Mart Stores on Businesses in Host Towns and Surrounding Towns in Iowa." November 9, 1988. www2.econ.iastate.edu/faculty/stone/.

Stone, Kenneth E. "Impact of the Wal-Mart Phenomenon on Rural Communities." Published in the proceedings *Increasing Understanding of Public Problems and Policies*. Chicago: Farm Foundation, 1997. www2.econ.iastate.edu/faculty/stone/.

"Town of Williston: Town-Wide Watershed Improvement Plan, Phase I—Allen Brook, Muddy Brook, Sucker Brook, Winooski River: Final Report." Prepared by Stone Environmental, Inc., for the Town of Williston, Department of Planning and Zoning. February 28, 2013. www.town.williston.vt.us.

Trimble, Vance H. *Sam Walton: The Inside Story of America's Richest Man*. New York: Penguin, 1990.

United States of America v. Wal-Mart Stores, Inc. Complaint, May 12, 2004. https://

www.epa.gov/sites/default/files/2013-09/documents/walmart2-cp.pdf.

Vance, Sandra S., and Roy V. Scott. *Wal-Mart: A History of Sam Walton's Retail Phenomenon*. New York: Twayne, 1994.

VanderVelde, Lee S. "Wal-Mart as a Phenomenon in the Legal World: Matters of Scale, Scale Matters." In *Wal-Mart World: The World's Biggest Corporation in the Global Economy*, edited by Stanley D. Brunn, 115–140. New York: Routledge, 2006.

Walker, Margath A., David Walker, and Yanga Villagómez Velázquez. "The Wal-Martification of Teotihuacán: Issues of Resistance and Cultural Heritage." In *Wal-Mart World: The World's Biggest Corporation in the Global Economy*, edited by Stanley D. Brunn, 213–224. New York: Routledge, 2006.

Walton, Sam, with John Huey. *Sam Walton: Made in America—My Story*. New York: Doubleday, 1992.

Williston Citizens for Responsible Growth (WCRG) Records. 1988–1998. Vermont Historical Society, Barre.

Zook, Matthew A., and Mark Graham. "Wal-Mart Nation: Mapping the Reach of a Retail Colossus." In *Wal-Mart World: The World's Biggest Corporation in the Global Economy*, edited by Stanley D. Brunn, 15–25. New York: Routledge, 2006.

Section II

Cleanup, Aisle 2

MANAGING ENVIRONMENTAL IMPACT

2

"TAKING PARADISE"

A Target Distribution Center and a Battle in the Midwest

JOHNATHAN WILLIAMS

Tensions remained high in Oconomowoc, Wisconsin, two months after the announcement that Target's Midwest Regional Distribution Center would be locating there. To residents like Ed Rohloff, "life changed" after catching wind of the over 1-million-square-foot project and imagining its impact on the idyllic, pastoral surrounding (figure 2.1). During a National Public Radio (NPR) interview aired on May 31, 1993, the former dairy farmer turned local politician shared his frustration: "Living in sight of something that operates around the clock with lighting and that—noise—and threatening the wells, and of course the water. I think that this is totally incompatible [with the area] and that's why we do resist it." Wisconsin Department of Development secretary Robert Trunzo, a key player in securing the project for the state, sympathized with local concerns like those expressed by Rohloff. However, as he exclaimed to the same reporter, "Some real winds of change . . . are sweeping over all of Waukesha County." As NPR host Noah Adams framed the two opposing sides, the conflict over the

FIGURE 2.1. Panorama of Silver Lake, located less than a quarter-mile west of the distribution center. Author photo, June 2019.

distribution center was "either a story of taking paradise and putting up a parking lot . . . or greenfield development" and "relocating industry from cities to suburbs."[1]

The NPR story rightly assessed the conflict in Oconomowoc as a debate over land use and values; however, the framing failed to grasp its larger significance. Protests against the rapid expansion of big box chains, like the one in Vermont discussed by Bart Elmore in chapter 1 of this volume, were a common feature of 1990s America. Yet these clashes of grassroots resistance against the expansion of big box retailers overwhelmingly centered on individual stores instead of distribution centers like the one in rural Wisconsin. Although they are seemingly simple buildings, as historian Nelson Lichtenstein pinpoints, distribution centers "stand at the center of the production and consumption network that now girdles the planet."[2] The challenge against a single distribution center, therefore, threatened not only Target's expansion during the early 1990s but the entire retail industry.

The conflict in Oconomowoc further highlighted the newness of distribution centers and questions over the environmental impact of big

box stores like Target. Distribution centers—although having similarities with earlier warehouses—diverged greatly in their scale, operation, and location. Whereas warehouses proliferated in urban centers along railroad and waterway connections, distribution centers arose on the outskirts of urban centers along highways. They emerged in significant numbers during the 1980s and relied on new computer and information technologies. Major federal legislation like the Motor Carrier Act of 1980 and the Intermodal Transportation and Efficiency Act of 1991 helped by incentivizing long-haul trucking as the preeminent form of interstate transportation. As federal policies loosened previous transportation restrictions, retailers such as Target looked to rural places like Oconomowoc where they could turn cow pastures into massive facilities able to accommodate hundreds of semi-trucks daily.[3]

While protesters in Oconomowoc raised sound arguments about the environmental impact of distribution centers, such as a source of pollution on air quality and groundwater, the center prevailed. The project promised economic growth and, with the backing of powerful local and state interests, overrode concerns about environmental costs.

Such outcomes played out in communities across the United States during the late twentieth century as landmark environmental legislation failed to address some of the big environmental problems associated with distribution centers. Legislation like the Clean Air and Water Acts proved tremendously successful in curtailing the most harmful industrial pollutants and creating a cleaner environment. Yet such legislation still allowed for the expansion of polluting economic activities such as distribution centers and the carbon-emitting transportation networks supporting them.[4]

Although late twentieth-century legislation had regulatory limits, it still managed to provide revolutionary reform by creating new legal avenues for citizens to challenge new developments. As lobbying and pressuring politicians to intervene to halt the project in Oconomowoc failed, opponents looked to the courts. But here, too, they faced an uphill battle. Legal actions proved a crucial tool for environmental activists in expanding the original interpretation of environmental legislation and pressuring congressional reform. But amid growing partisanship and gridlock during the 1990s, the influence of conservative, pro-corporate politics halted legislative actions and influenced the judiciary—something Oconomowoc opponents experienced firsthand. Such a transition narrowed avenues of legal activism as a means to expand the interpretation of environmental laws and allowed such centers to proliferate and become a staple of twenty-first-century retail.

At the end of 1992, the interests of Wisconsin and Target officials aligned with Target eyeing expansion into the Chicago market, marking another milestone in the company's near century-long history. Tracing its origins back to the downtown Minneapolis department store named after its founder, George Draper Dayton, in 1902, the company played a vital role in the development of twentieth-century retail. By mid-century, the Dayton Company had become one of the largest retailers in the country and an influential voice of an industry gaining more power as it mastered the mass distribution counterpart to mass production.[5] During the postwar years, the company led retail's suburban entrance, revolutionizing American consumerism with the 1956 opening of Southdale in Edina, Minnesota, the first fully enclosed, environmentally controlled regional shopping center in the world—the blueprint for the iconic late twentieth-century American *mall*. In 1962, under the leadership of Dayton's five grandsons, the company once again led the industry by launching a new kind of discount chain: Target Stores. Unlike other discount stores, Target promised shoppers an upscale version by offering quality goods found at its parent company's department stores at a reduced cost. The chain rapidly became the most profitable division of the Dayton-Hudson Corporation following Dayton's 1969 merger with the Hudson Corporation of Detroit, Michigan, as it built a strong middle-class suburban consumer following.[6]

Target's success was evident by the 1990s as it joined the ranks of Kmart and Walmart to form the retail industry's "Big Three," and Target's entrance into Chicago-land marked the first time all three chains were competing in the same major market. All three discount chains opened their first stores in 1962 Middle America and rapidly found success carving out regional markets. Their rise was certainly not guaranteed, as the industry faced fierce consolidation with chains disappearing left and right during the following decades. However, the Big Three survived by maintaining capital to continually expand beyond regional constraints. Scale meant everything for discount retail by the late twentieth century, and it even transformed the physical consumer space. Target, for example, opened its first Target Greatland store format in 1990. Compared to its standard stores, Target Greatland stores were 50 percent larger and reached over 200,000 square feet with expanded departments, greater convenience, wider aisles, and more checkouts. This format set the standard for what would become known as the "big box" store during the 1990s. Yet with more and larger stores, successful discount chains scaled up their distribution systems as well.[7]

To supply hundreds of stores spread across multiple regions, retailers like Target invested heavily in logistics. Nothing symbolized the new retail environment more than the rise of distribution centers during the final decades of the twentieth century, with Target opening its first center in 1969.[8] The centers resulted from standardization of freight handling and computer advancements, including the barcode; their proliferation allowed for national chain expansion by shaving pennies off already low-margin goods.[9] Demonstrating their importance to the retail industry by the end of the twentieth century, a 1992 trade study conducted with more than 100 American retailers revealed that successful companies had "become more efficient, as more and more retail dollars are being spent for the cost of goods and fewer dollars for the services retailers provide." "The weeding of American retailing" the report illuminated, "can be expected to continue, as competition becomes smarter and tougher." Certain companies "are even uncomfortable with the word 'distribution' and prefer concepts such as logistics, systems and merchandise flow which are more appropriate to managing flow of goods from the vendor to the store shelf," the report explained. Nevertheless, an assured level of "agreement" between companies "supersede[s] inherent differences among retailers. The common ground symbolizes what can be described as a new philosophy influencing retailers' approach to distribution," with "out of stock" a "mortal flaw."[10]

As the importance of distribution centers grew for retailers, it also increased for local and state governments. Transportation and warehousing jobs offered new opportunities for economic growth and diversification from traditional industries like manufacturing and agriculture. Western states were prime locations for these new industries as they possessed abundant, cheap land compared to the East Coast. Wisconsin, under the leadership of Republican governor Tommy Thompson, recognized these circumstances and pushed to make the state particularly welcoming to distribution centers.[11] The state's geographic location, sound infrastructure, and focus on core industries for retailers, such as paper manufacturing, offered additional enticements. For Target officials, these variables made Wisconsin an ideal location for its new regional distribution center. After searching more than twenty different locations across Illinois, Iowa, and Wisconsin, Target chose Oconomowoc—with the Thompson administration incentivizing the decision with generous tax breaks, subsidies, and backroom dealings.[12]

With Target, state, and local officials striking an agreement, the next step was assessing the land and acquiring the numerous required permits. From the beginning, state regulators raised red flags. In a March 18, 1993, email, a Wisconsin Department of Natural Resources (DNR) official warned of numerous issues with the project by transforming "a flat

100-acre parcel which has little or no surface runoff to a site that will be made impervious over a large percentage of its surface area." "Past observations suggest that groundwater recharge is important to maintain local bodies of surface water," the official reported. The sensitivity of the area's groundwater basins meant the development required significant engineering feats while the official also frankly raised the possibility that the magnitude of potential damage might be too great to allow Target to gain the needed permits.[13]

The following day, questions continued, with the DNR Bureau of Air Management releasing its preliminary study on the air quality impact from the project. As the report explained: "Any facility which conveys or attracts motor vehicle traffic is considered an 'indirect source' of air pollution because of the air contaminants emitted by the vehicles. Under its rules governing indirect sources, the DNR is required to review any proposal for the development of a new facility with an associated parking capacity of 1,000 or more vehicles in an urban area such as Waukesha County." "Such a project," the report continued, "must have an air pollution control construction permit before construction is begun and an air pollution control operation permit before it is opened to traffic." The study used nearly thirty receptors throughout the local area and computerized the data into several models, including "worst-case" scenario emission rates at the required one- and eight-hour concentration intervals. While the study confidently concluded that the air quality impact from the distribution center would be well below state and federal maximum air contaminant levels, it assessed only one of numerous air pollutants from motor vehicles: carbon monoxide—something opponents would later point to.[14]

On March 24, 1993, Target and Governor Thompson made the first public announcement of the project at Oconomowoc City Hall. During his speech, Thompson claimed the "distribution center could provide up to 400 well-paying jobs for the Oconomowoc area" and noted that it "would be among the 20 largest [centers] in Wisconsin." He added, "We can expect considerable additional economic impact from this project because it will foster the creation of jobs in area industries" while "commend[ing] the City of Oconomowoc and the Department of Development for their outstanding efforts to bring this project to Wisconsin."

The "fast-growing retailer," the governor continued, "has conducted a multi-state site search before deciding to pursue the Oconomowoc site," as the area contained a "superior labor force and outstanding transportation access." "I am confident that Target and Wisconsin can work out a suitable agreement and enjoy a productive partnership in the years to come," Thompson concluded, an onerous prediction as the celebration of economic development quickly collided with public opposition to and environmental concerns about the project.[15]

As Governor Thompson announced the project publicly at an event in Oconomowoc City Hall, city officials prepared their own special public hearing, notifying the neighboring Town of Summit and requesting information on all property owners within direct proximity of the proposed project. As Thompson made the announcement, a city official sent a fax memo to the Town of Summit requesting immediate information on property owners neighboring the proposed project to advance the permitting process.[16] Although the project would be located within Oconomowoc's borders, residents of the Town of Summit would be most affected by the development, as the land had been recently annexed from the latter. As Summit residents discovered that they had been excluded from negotiations, questions over the distribution center began.

Of all the required permits, the conditional use permit was essential for the development to move forward. While state officials ensured Target that it had full resident support, the April 8 public hearing for the permit proved otherwise. As one set of notes outlined, the Plan Commission meeting was attended by a Target architect and company representative, Dean Wenger, and roughly 200 residents. The Target officials detailed plans for the project, including estimated employment, planned hours of operation and estimated volume of goods, and engineering plans to address the environmental and aesthetic alterations caused by the facility—such as plans for berms, a rainwater-runoff retaining pond, and a bordering chain-link fence with inserted slats to alleviate water, noise, and light pollution. Despite the extensive plans to mitigate anticipated challenges and opposition, such as a proposed "stormwater treatment system," not everyone was willing to instantly approve the permit, with several commissioners explicitly opposed.[17]

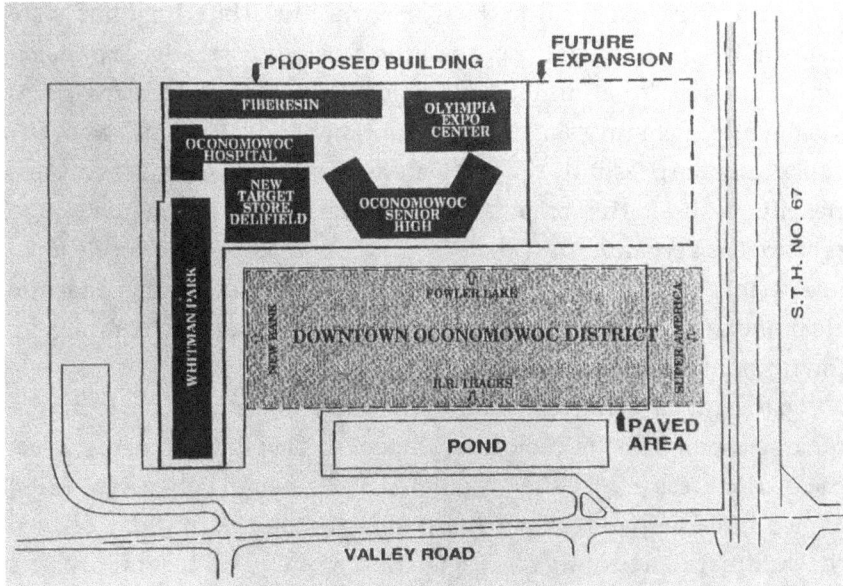

FIGURE 2.2. Map created by Town of Summit employee comparing size of the distribution center to the largest buildings in area. Summit Municipal Records, Target Distribution Center, Summit Village Hall, Summit, WI.

The dissenting commissioners revealed the early divisions sparked by the project, and the expanse of their concerns highlighted the focus of future opposition. One commissioner, for example, "called [the project] an autrosity [sic]," believing the scale of the building was "much too much for [the] property" (figure 2.2). Another raised alarm over the zoning classification of the distribution center, claiming "this is heavy industry," something that "doesn't fit the area." Commissioner Joe Aceto, one of a handful of councilmembers Target had flown to the company's distribution center in Tifton, Georgia, earlier in the month, noted the cleanliness of the facility, both inside and out. Yet even though he noticed little "truck volume"—because the Georgia facility largely received rail shipments—he still expressed great apprehension because the proposed Oconomowoc center would "be twice the size." Aceto also pointed to neighboring homes, insisting that the commission has "an obligation to the nine property owners."[18]

The dissenting voices attempted to negotiate with Target officials, asking if the retailer could "live with a smaller building." The representatives insisted that the scale of the initial building "has got to happen" but did suggest the possibility of a slightly smaller expansion, with potential "to eliminate <u>one door</u>," according to meeting notes. Meanwhile, a commissioner's interruption of a DNR official who was explaining the possibility of well water pollution caused more concern. Despite the dissenting voices and the revelation that the city had yet to prepare the actual permit, the commission approved the conditional use permit. With the vote approved, the project essentially needed to clear one final bureaucratic hurdle before beginning construction: an Environmental Impact Statement (EIS).[19]

The federal government first began requiring detailed environmental assessments of the ecological impact of new developments when the US Congress passed the National Environmental Policy Act (NEPA). Signed into law by President Richard Nixon on the first day of 1970, the landmark environmental legislation required all federal projects to perform an environmental assessment, placing a check on large-impact developments such as interstate highway construction. State and local governments quickly followed the federal government's lead, creating what one historian described as "rebellions against a decades-old tradition of local control of development." Americans began to realize the extent of ecological boundaries, ones that persisted beyond delineated lines on a map. While the boom in land-use legislation implemented new hierarchical jurisdictions to accommodate ecological complexities, it also created new problems and collided with a centuries-old tradition of private property as the epitome of rights.[20]

In Oconomowoc, the rising conflict over the proposed distribution center challenged the effectiveness of land-use legislation. First, placing responsibility for environmental oversight outside of local control allowed for government regulation of expansive ecosystems; yet in doing so, that oversight also became more susceptible to outside influence and interests that had little to no direct relationship with or responsibility to local concerns. The Midwest Regional Distribution Center highlighted the inclinations dictating environmental concerns, as the investments and power of the gubernatorial administration and a distant corporation favored approval. At the same time, the distancing of governing responsibility outside of local control created the potential for less transparency and local involvement. While the City of Oconomowoc maintained noteworthy influence over approval of the project through zoning regulations and permit processing, it did not allow outside municipalities like the Town of Summit to be involved in the process. Such exclusive power held by a single municipality ignored the reality of late twentieth-century metropolitan relations in which city, suburbs, and towns became growingly enmeshed through increased urbanization.

The bureaucratic loopholes in the EIS process were evident regarding the distribution center in the Wisconsin DNR environmental assessment. First, the department assigned responsibility for the assessment to an outside district, one that had no direct relationship to the community or even to the larger surrounding lake ecosystem. Second, the environmental engineer appointed to conduct the assessment, Ashok K. Singh, was inexperienced with such studies, especially at the scale required for the proposed site. The assessment itself contained several contradictions. Notably, the environmental engineer identified the project as "located next to a corporate park and not in a residential area" despite the presence of more than a handful of neighboring homes and an elementary school. Perhaps more striking, the report only assessed carbon monoxide impact on the air quality while concluding that the project could lead to "substantial increase in ground level ozone." Regardless of the likelihood of adverse effects, Singh dismissed a full EIS for the project as plans appeared to abide by government rules and promised economic benefits.[21]

With the dismissal of a full EIS for the distribution center, local opposition to the project erupted. In an April 12, 1993, editorial published in a local paper, for example, Oconomowoc resident Lars Anderson addressed his concerns to local and state officials. "Congratulations on the fine reception Target Stores has given you," Anderson began sarcastically. He chided the celebrated economic benefits from a "nonpolluting industry coming to town." As he saw it, "POLLUTION is the real issue involved." "What is this business all about," Anderson asked rhetorically. "Target makes their selection and in 45 days they have to be under construction. It sounds like we're being driven instead of being the driver." In conclusion, he acknowledged that the area "may be hungry" for new development, "but we don't have to eat Carp [a large, invasive, un-savory freshwater fish] just because it gets hooked on our line. We've landed a big catch but let's throw it back. Let's keep looking for that Rainbow Trout or Walleye."[22]

Thompson's administration attempted to compromise with residents like Anderson, but catch and release was not an option for an economic development opportunity promising hundreds of new jobs. Writing to Governor Thompson on April 14, Department of Development secretary Robert Trunzo shared his frustrations toward the dissenting residents. Trunzo railed against what he saw as unprofessional hostility from opponents during a recent public hearing and prepped the governor for an upcoming meeting with Town of Summit councilmember Ed Rohloff. "This is not his determination to make. Our client [Target] selected this site because it meets every requirement. Nothing prohibits this type of development at the site," Trunzo insisted. "The property is in a TIF [tax incremental financing] district, zoned M-3 for commercial development, and will be developed anyway." Lastly, Trunzo dismissed concerns over air quality and missteps by the DNR as "pure garbage."[23]

Yet while Trunzo ensured Thompson that there was no legitimate threat to the project, an exchange between two DNR officials told a different story. On April 15, following the full approval of the conditional use permit by the Oconomowoc City Council, Ralph Patterson wrote "this looks like a looming problem" to a department colleague. "Our permit is the only permit they need to complete construction," he explained. Patterson noted that a department attorney shared his concerns because "the environmental assessment states that this project will 'cause a significant increase in ground level ozone.'" The decision not to conduct an EIS with no "justification," combined with the admission of major environmental concerns from the substituting assessment, did not bode well for the DNR or the state. Thompson predicted that "if we are brought to court on this . . . we may be forced into completing an EIS which would delay the permit." With "Target want[ing] to dig dirt on May 1," he remarked that the potential of delay "would not make Governor Thompson look very good."[24]

With the state continuing to push forward with the project despite internal concerns, local opponents began organizing under the grassroots STOP TARGET Coalition. While records do not explicitly state the demographic makeup of the environmental group, sources suggest it largely included older white, affluent residents living near the proposed site. They decried misinformation and lack of transparency with the project. The group united under the credence that "the cost of polluted wells, destroyed lakes, or even one case of cancer" from the distribution center "is too high" and believed an "informed" public was the key to a successful challenge. To inform the public, the STOP TARGET Coalition distributed numerous bright yellow newsletters—largely written and illustrated with permanent markers—detailing the byzantine process behind the distribution center's approval and promoting a holistic view toward potential pollution.[25]

In one handout, for example, the group expressed that it agreed with the secretary that development was bound to happen. "That destiny was set in 1989 by the city when they annexed the land and zoned it M3," it acknowledged. However, the two sides' comprehension of M3 zoning diverged greatly, with the STOP TARGET Coalition focusing on how the city code defined acceptable development for the industrial zone as "'an attractive grouping' of light industrial uses 'of limited intensity' with 'aesthetically pleasing open spaces.'" A "truck terminal," it concluded, "is one of many dirty industries specifically prohibited" by the city's definition. Backing its position on the code's semantics, the group highlighted that "shopping centers and other large traffic generating uses are prohibited on this land by the city already." Zoning the land for low-impact development was a precondition for the annexation of Town of Summit land to the City of Oconomowoc, and the city's bending of the definition to differentiate a distribution center from a truck terminal became one of many legal concerns set aside as the project moved forward.[26]

The STOP TARGET Coalition realized the limits of decades of reform on regulating environmental impacts. Managing air pollution, as the DNR's environmental assessment demonstrated, selectively accounted for airborne pollutants, leaving more complicated ecological processes that cannot be directly connected to an individual source—such as the creation of low-lying ozone—unregulated. Nevertheless, although non-point-source airborne pollutants like ozone were not managed for individual projects, regional, state, and federal efforts were under way to mitigate and reduce the worst impacts—especially in southeast Wisconsin, where atmospheric conditions from continental wind currents and the bordering Great Lakes contributed to the region suffering some of the poorest air quality in the country. Nevertheless, the regulatory differentiation made a legal challenge daunting.[27]

Water pollution shared the exemptions for non-point sources. The STOP TARGET Coalition recognized the distinctions between point and non-point source pollution regulations central to the Clean Air and Water Acts and how they would affect pollution from the distribution center. "Won't state and federal laws protect us from harmful effects?" one pamphlet asked rhetorically. "There are state laws preventing water pollution and there are laws enforcing certain air quality standards. Target says they meet these minimum standards. But let's look more closely. For example, on water pollution the state guidelines for evaluating runoff water have not yet been written. THERE ARE NONE!"[28]

The hundreds of trucks entering and leaving the terminal daily and the thousands of square feet of impervious surface they would drive on meant that while each vehicle presented the possibility of leaking trace amounts of harmful chemicals, the vast number of trips to and from the center cumulatively threatened local water systems. Possible contaminants from automobiles range from gasoline and antifreeze and other associated fluids to salt and other additives to remove snow and ice during the winter months. Yet while these pollutants, such as vehicular exhaust, were inevitable, government regulation dividing pollution into two distinct categories—one required to abide by regulation and the other to avoid it altogether—excluded any party from responsibility. An EIS, the coalition concluded, was the only means for legal consideration of the otherwise unregulated pollutants the opposition rallied behind—something, the coalition pointed out, even some state officials were becoming weary about not conducting.[29]

Grassroots efforts to prevent the proposed distribution center in Oconomowoc continued with a campaign focused on writing letters to public officials and newspaper editorial departments in an effort to sway opinion. Many of the pleas for officials and residents to resist the distribution center focused on the environmental impacts of the project and the inappropriateness of the site for a distribution center. Virg Einck, a Summit resident who lived within a quarter-mile of the proposed center, for example, wrote to the Wisconsin Department of Justice pleading for the state judicial branch to intervene in the "railroaded" approval process to protect "the safety and health of residents and [the] environment."[30] Milwaukee resident Linda Jon similarly asked in her letters to various officials that they "consider the health and safety of future generations, not just your short-term monetary profit in developing the land." Jon's concerns, like many others, extended beyond the physical environment. "I don't think you realize how difficult it is to live in the Oconomowoc area on the wages you promise, $8 to $10 an hour. The employees probably won't be able to live there," raising alarm over the cost of living and the area's affluent economic demographics. While surely building public support, such measures failed to derail the project.[31]

With defensive measures dwindling by early June as a result of the finalization of agreements and permitting between the City of Oconomowoc and Target Stores, two options remained for opponents: government intervention or a legal challenge. With the Thompson administration deeply committed to the project and the state justice department not intervening, federal action was in essence opponents' only hope. While the US Environmental Protection Agency (EPA) would later investigate contamination at the site, this occurred after the project's completion.[32] Legal action also required time and money. Time was limited, with the rapid construction deadline Target had set to open the center the following year. A lawsuit could take months or even years for a decision; even then, it did not guarantee a favorable outcome for the plaintiff.

Legal action also cost money. On June 27, 1993, hundreds of Summit residents and organizations, including the STOP TARGET coalition and the Silver Lake Environmental Association (SLEA), gathered at the Oconomowoc Town Hall for an ice cream social fundraiser to support the growing number of lawsuits challenging the project. Attendants enjoyed cold treats while listening to music by a local band, and they celebrated the news of additional lawsuits—including one by the statewide environmental group the Environmental Decade. SLEA president

David Barquist confidently concluded: "We now have very strong evidence [that] these studies were seriously flawed and underestimated the air and water pollution hazards. We suspected all along there was something wrong when environmental studies which normally take many months or years took only a couple weeks in the case of Target's project. Now we can prove it."[33]

Not all Summit residents, however, celebrated the news about lawsuits challenging the distribution center. A letter to Ed Rohloff from an anonymous Summit resident replying to an invitation to the fundraiser, for instance, insisted that "no matter how much you charge you will not collect the amount of taxes you were throwing away on a hopeless and stupid cause." The deprecating letter accused those supporting the lawsuits of being "cronies" and "snooty ARISTOCRATS." "You could fight this case to The Pope in Rome and all it would do would be to make the rest of the Summit people look like ... Jackasses," the author wrote. "When are you going to try to stop all of the BAD air pollution coming from I 94, K-MART and other expanding stores near [Oconomowoc]? It seems that you are NOT consistent," they wrote in a "P.S."[34]

Local resident Fred Kurtz more politely shared his objections to the lawsuits. "The Target Center is not a factory producing material which in turn leaves a toxic or hazardous residue. This building is a warehouse for boxes. A box comes in, a box goes out," Kurtz argued. Their financial situation further influenced their position. "I am in my seventh month of unemployment," they wrote. "I need this opportunity and so do thousands of others in my situation. What Target proposes will be a boon to this area. We should be embracing it[,] not bringing on lawsuits." Unemployed and "gouged" with taxes every year "to support local schools which I never have used nor will I ever use," Kurtz pleaded for spending "tax dollars on something worthwhile," like new street lights, instead of "trying to fight a battle you will most definetly [sic] lose and it would be much cheaper."[35] Such class concerns likely were largely ignored by those opposing the project and were shared by other residents, yet the neighboring towns and villages continued with their lawsuits.

Against the backdrop of legal challenges, experts in the retail industry looked to Oconomowoc as a warning for other retailers. An August

1993 cover story in the major trade magazine *Transportation and Distribution*, for example, explored "how to avoid rough landings" by featuring Target Stores' situation in Wisconsin. "What should have been a straightforward siting project for Dean Wenger turned into a protracted lesson in politics," one that placed him "center stage in a turf war," wrote associate editor and author Tom Andel. "Target considered 55 sites in three states, taking into account proximity to market, transportation costs, and the cost and availability of the labor pool. Wenger, project manager for Target Stores, used in-house computer modeling software to analyze the costs and tax incentives offered by the communities," leading to the Oconomowoc decision. "That's when the turf hit the fan," Andel wrote.[36]

The cover story did not ignore dissenting voices or give Target a free pass. Instead, the trade magazine used the Target case as an example to highlight a changing business environment and a warning to "inspire a new chapter on surmounting political obstacles." Environmental sentiments and laws were some of the most significant hindrances for companies seeking to expand their logistics networks, and the article did not shy away from encouraging its readers to study and understand changing environmental laws. "Get familiar with provisions of the Clean Air Act and the Clean Water Act," Andel heeded, noting that reforms in the laws—such as the designation of non-attainment areas and rainwater-runoff provisions for warehouses—presented challenges for Target. "Community fit" was also important, with Andel suggesting that small-town residents were "much more sensitive these days to the impact of any facility, especially large ones[,] on their infrastructure" and insisting that citizen participation was essential for site selectors.[37]

Target's rush to complete the project, combined with the lack of local input, resulted in months of legal challenges by local opponents. Case after case, local, state, and federal judiciaries struck down the plaintiffs' charges. The court decisions favored the autonomy of private property and local control in issuing, regulating, and enforcing building permits and zoning laws. In invoking the Clean Air and Water Acts, the courts further rejected the charges along lines similar to the federalist structure of the acts, which entrusted enforcement to municipalities and states.[38] These decisions did not mean the opponents' position had no merit; instead, a conservative legal interpretation opposing judicial activism prevailed. Seventh District US Court of Appeals judge Daniel Manion—a controversial Ronald Reagan appointee and son of the conservative talk radio pioneer Clarence Manion—for example, conceded the possibility of an expansive interpretation of the acts, writing: "Before federal courts begin deciding under the Clean Air Act whether or not such things as shopping malls are permissible because of their side effects, we should ensure that Congress has specifically authorized the EPA to regulate at that level. Nor would I suggest that the EPA can figuratively 'wade in' to ground water as part of the waters of the United States without first having specific direction from Congress."[39]

Despite the legal setbacks, lawsuits against the center persisted even after it opened, leading Target officials to finally publicly enter the debate through a purchased full-page advertisement in a June 6, 1994, Waukesha County edition of the *Milwaukee Journal*. "For the 28th time," the public outreach source began, "the people [are] taking legal action to attack the now-completed Target Midwest Regional Distribution Center. During this folly," it continued, "the City of Oconomowoc, the Village of Oconomowoc Lake, and the Town of Summit have had to spend approximately $1 million in legal fees, with taxpayers footing the bill." Instead of "improving parks, adding more teachers, helping the elderly, or simply reducing property taxes," Target officials argued that taxpayer "money being senselessly wasted on this nonissue should be used to finance the real community needs . . . And yet," the advertisement continued, legal challenges have repeatedly failed: "After losing 27 legal challenges, you'd think the Village Board would realize their claims are baseless."[40]

Regardless of what impact Target's advertisement had on influencing the legal challenges, resistance to the project fizzled in the following months. The promise of jobs and the taxpayer burden triumphed in the face of continuing challenges to a project already operating. Oconomowoc would be one of dozens—if not hundreds—of communities to challenge the expansion of big box retail at the turn of the twenty-first century, yet its focus on a distribution center remained unique. Such uniqueness implies that the lessons learned by Target were widely received by others in the retail industry. Transportation and warehousing continued to grow in states like Wisconsin, with the number of jobs in those areas increasing by more than 70 percent between 1990 and 2018—accounting for nearly 4 percent of all jobs in the state—and with jobs relating to trade, transportation, and utilities in general amounting to over one-fifth of the state's workforce by the end of the same period.[41]

Since the conflict in Oconomowoc, hundreds of distribution centers have opened across the United States—even more following the explosion of online retail since the beginning of the twenty-first century. Yet in recent years, a peculiar change has occurred. Whereas distribution centers have traditionally been constructed on the outskirts of urban development, they have increasingly found a new home in urban environments, particularly in poor, non-white neighborhoods. This transition has been fueled by increasing industry concentration and the emergence of urban big box stores—something Target has successfully mastered over its largest brick-and-mortar rival, Walmart—and by cities taking aggressive urban renewal approaches to attract new development. Yet while such projects still promise jobs and growth, communities like the largely Mexican American neighborhood of Little Village in Chicago are attempting to unmask the environmental consequences of such centers. In a community plagued by some of the highest rates of asthma in the Windy City and disproportionately affected by the Covid-19 pandemic, residents have rejected such promises and are demanding a "right to breathe" instead of the choking effects of hundreds of semis passing their streets daily.[42]

NOTES

1. Hosted by Noah Adams, "Wisconsin Conflict," *All Things Considered*, National Public Radio, May 31, 1993, Summit Municipal Records, Target Distribution Center, Summit Village Hall, Village of Summit, WI. Municipal records from the Village of Summit, formerly Town of Summit, are maintained in three large, unlabeled binders in Village Hall. The records were accessed in person on June 9–10, 2019, upon request. Author maintains digital copies of all documents cited. Special thanks to village planner Henry Elling.
2. Lichtenstein, *Retail Revolution*, 40.

3. For warehouses, see Orenstein, *Out of Stock*. For the Motor Carrier Act of 1980 and long-haul trucking, see Hamilton, *Trucking Country*.
4. For late twentieth-century environmental legislation and limits, see Andrews, *Managing the Environment*, 227–228.
5. Howard, *From Main Street to Mall*, 10.
6. For the history of Target, see Rowley, *On Target*; Dayton and Green, *Birth of Target*.
7. Rowley, *On Target*, 69. For examples of Target and scaling operations, see Sandra Salmans, "A Retailer That's Leading the Way," *New York Times*, December 12, 1982, F1, 30.
8. Target opened its first distribution center in Fridley, Minnesota, in 1969. See "Target to Build Big Warehouse Center in Fridley," *Minneapolis Tribune*, July 19, 1968, 20.
9. Lichtenstein, *Retail Revolution*; Levinson; "Founding of Target," https://corporate.target.com/about/purpose-history/History-Timeline?era=2.
10. "Retail Distribution and Logistics: Overview," *Chain Store Age Executive with Shopping Center Age* 68, issue 4 (April 1992): 5A.
11. For an example highlighting the changing economic portfolio of the Midwest during the early 1990s, see NBC Universal Inc., "Economy: Midwest," NBC Evening News, January 15, 1992, Vanderbilt Television News Archive, #583116, https://tvnews.vanderbilt.edu. For distribution centers and Wisconsin during the late twentieth century, see Buss, "Move It Out," 8–10; Wisconsin LMI Data Access, https://www.jobcenterofwisconsin.com/wisconomy/query.
12. For Wisconsin and commitment to secure the distribution center, see Robert N. Trunzo, letter to Governor Tommy G. Thompson, January 28, 1993, Wisconsin Governor (1987–2001: Thompson), Box 5, Folder "Target Distribution Center 1993," Wisconsin Historical Society, Madison; Dale W. Arenz, Testimony Outline from State of Wisconsin, County of Waukesha, July 21, 1993, Summit Municipal Records, Target Distribution Center, Summit Village Hall, Summit, WI [hereafter SMR-TDC].
13. Percy Mather [environmental engineer, Non-point Source and Land Management Section], email to Mike Campbell, P.E. [Ruekert and Mielke, Inc.], "Summary of February 25 Meeting—Berry Farm Development," March 18, 1993, SMR-TDC. For a time line of events, see "Synopsis of TARGET DISTRIBUTION Project," May 11, 1993, SMR-TDC.
14. Wisconsin Department of Natural Resources, Bureau of Air Management, "Analysis and Preliminary Determination on the Approvability of Target Midwest Distribution Center: Oconomowoc, Wisconsin" (93-JFM-024), March 19, 1993, SMR-TDC.
15. Tommy G. Thompson, Governor State of Wisconsin Office, [press release], March 24, 1993, SMR-TDC.
16. Jenni, fax to Town of Summit, Ardyce Senfleben, Notice of Public Hearing, March 24, 1993, SMR-TDC. For estimated residents, see "Synopsis of TARGET DISTRIBUTION Project," May 11, 1993, SMR-TDC.
17. Details of the Plan Commission meeting were recorded in two sets of handwritten notes, with details corroborating each other; Notes from Plan Commission Meeting on Target, City of Oconomowoc, April [8], [19]93, Summit Municipal Records, Target

Distribution Center, Summit Village Hall, Summit, WI. For suburban, corporate structures and pastoral-like landscaping, see Mozingo, *Pastoral Capitalism*.

18. Notes from Plan Commission Meeting on Target, City of Oconomowoc, April 8, 1993, SMR-TDC.
19. Notes from Plan Commission Meeting on Target; original emphasis.
20. Quote in Rome, *Bulldozer in the Countryside*, 229. For NEPA and land-use legislation, see Rome, 221–253. For NEPA and federally mandating EIS, see Andrews, *Managing the Environment*, 286–289.
21. Ashok K. Singh [DNR environmental engineer], "Environmental Analysis and Decision on the Need for an Environmental Impact Statement: Target Midwest Distribution Center," State of Wisconsin Department of Natural Resources, March 31, 1993, SMR-TDC.
22. Lars Anderson [Oconomowoc resident], "Concerns about Pollution" [letter to editor], *Oconomowoc Independent*, April 12, 1993, SMR-TDC.
23. Wisconsin secretary of the Department of Development Robert Trunzo, letter to Wisconsin governor Tommy Thompson, April 14, 1993, Wisconsin Governor (1987–2001: Thompson), Policy staff files, 1987–2001, Box 5, Folder 60SS, Target Distribution Center, 1993, Wisconsin Historical Society, Madison.
24. Ralph Patterson, email to Don Theiler "This Looks Like a Looming Problem," April 15, 1993, SMR-TDC.
25. STOP TARGET Coalition, Questions and Answers [newsletter], [undated], SMR-TDC.
26. STOP TARGET Coalition, Questions and Answers.
27. STOP TARGET Coalition, Questions and Answers.
28. STOP TARGET Coalition, Questions and Answers.
29. STOP TARGET Coalition, Questions and Answers.
30. Virg Einck, letter to Jordon Lowe [State of Wisconsin Department of Justice], April 30, 1993, SMR-TDC.
31. Linda Jon, copy of letter to Ed Rohloff, April 26, 1993, SMR-TDC.
32. Roy F. Weston, Inc.; Dames and Moore; Engineers International, Inc.; Life Systems, Inc.; Hubbell, Roth and Clark, Inc.; Reid, Quebe, Allison, Wilcox and Associates, Inc.; and Mary Sexton Associates, *Integrated PA/SSI Assessment Report: Summit Corner—Northwest Oconomowoc, Wisconsin*, Waukesha County, WI0000472969: "Region V: Remedial Planning Activities at Selected Uncontrolled Disposal Sites" January 1996, SMR-TDC.
33. Silver Lake Environmental Assn., Inc., News Release, June 28, 1993, SMR-TDC.
34. [Anonymous], letter to Mr. Rohloff, [undated], SMR-TDC.
35. Fred Kurtz, letter to Edwin Rohloff, June 23, 1993, SMR-TDC.
36. Andel, "Site Selection," 30–31
37. Andel, "Site Selection," 30–31, 34–35.
38. For example, see *State ex rel. Town of Summit*, 1993.
39. For Manion and controversy, see Chicago Council of Lawyers, "Evaluation of the United States Court of Appeals," 673–857; Glen Elsasser, "Nomination Advances with No Comment," *Chicago Tribune*, May 9, 1986; Nicole Hemmer, "How Conservative Media Learned to Play Politics," *Politico*, August 30, 2016, https://www.politico.com

/magazine/story/2016/08/conservative-media-history-steve-bannon-clarence-manion-214199/; *Village of Oconomowoc Lake v. Dayton-Hudson Corporation*, 1994.

40. "Village of Oconomowoc Lake Should Stop Wasting Money, Start Supporting the Community" [full-page advertisement], *Milwaukee Journal*, June 6, 1994.
41. Employment statistics calculated using Wisconsin LMI Data Access, 2019, https://www.jobcenterofwisconsin.com/wisconomy/query.
42. For Little Village, see "Support Little Village's Right to Breathe," 2022, http://www.lvejo.org/support-little-villages-right-to-breathe/. For an example of the health impact of increasing distribution centers, see Trade, Health, and Environment Impact Project, *Storing Harm*.

BIBLIOGRAPHY

Andel, Tom. "Site Selection: How to Avoid Rough Landings." *Transportation and Distribution* 84, no. 8 (August 1993): 30–35.

Andrews, Richard N. L. *Managing the Environment, Managing Ourselves: A History of American Environmental Policy*. New Haven, CT: Yale University Press, 2006.

Buss, Dale. "Move It Out: Wisconsin Is Attracting Big-League Product Distribution Centers." *Corporate Report Wisconsin* (June 1993): 8–10.

Chicago Council of Lawyers. "Evaluation of the United States Court of Appeals for the Seventh Circuit—Report." *DePaul Law Review* 43, issue 3 (Spring 1994): 673–857.

Dayton, Bruce B., and Ellen B. Green. *The Birth of Target*. Minneapolis: Privately published, 2008.

Hamilton, Shane. *Trucking Country: The Road to America's Wal-Mart Economy*. Princeton, NJ: Princeton University Press, 2008.

Howard, Vicki. *From Main Street to Mall: The Rise and Fall of the American Department Store*. Philadelphia: University of Pennsylvania Press, 2015.

Lichtenstein, Nelson. *The Retail Revolution: How Wal-Mart Created a Brave New World of Business*. New York: Metropolitan Books, 2009.

Mozingo, Louise A. *Pastoral Capitalism: A History of Suburban Corporate Landscapes*. Cambridge, MA: MIT Press, 2011.

Orenstein, Dara. *Out of Stock: The Warehouse in the History of Capitalism*. Chicago: University of Chicago Press, 2019.

Rome, Adam. *The Bulldozer in the Countryside: Suburban Sprawl and the Rise of American Environmentalism*. New York: Cambridge University Press, 2001.

Rowley, Laura. *On Target: How the World's Hottest Retailer Hit a Bullseye*. Hoboken, NJ: Wiley, 2003.

State ex rel. Town of Summit, Village of Oconomowoc Lake Silver Lake Environmental Association, Anne Treloar Carl and Delores Kirkpatrick, Robert La Venture, and

Thomas A. and Karri L. Fritz-Klaus v. City of Oconomowoc, City of Oconomowoc Plan Commission, and Target Stores. 514 N.W. 2d 725, 179 Wis. 2d 853 (1993).

Trade, Health, and Environment Impact Project. *Storing Harm: The Health and Community Impacts of Goods Movement Warehousing and Logistics.* January 2012. https:// envhealthcenters.usc.edu/wp-content/uploads/2016/11/Storing-Harm.pdf.

Village of Oconomowoc Lake v. Dayton-Hudson Corporation. 24 F. 3d 962 (7th Cir. 1994).

3

WALMART'S OCEAN

Certifications, Catch Shares, and the Ripple Effects of Corporate Governance on Marine Environments

AARON VAN NESTE

Walmart is a global actor with a distinct worldview and opinions—and a Walmart-size policymaking capacity. In the twenty-first century, corporate and philanthropic choices, as much as if not more than state policies, govern and shape the more than human ocean ecosystem. Despite humble beginnings, Walmart's economic scale has surpassed that of many countries, granting it influence over supply chains and giving weight to the company's policy initiatives and philanthropic funding campaigns.[1] This chapter takes a critical look Walmart's partnership with the Marine Stewardship Council (MSC) and the Walton Family Foundation's advocacy for catch shares. It argues that both initiatives are at best a double-edged sword. While they may offer substantive environmental improvements, they also advance a definition of sustainability that benefits transnational retailers by driving continual growth, simplifying the supply chain, solidifying the power of the large-scale fishing industry, and limiting the imaginative scope of marine conservation and sustainable fishing initiatives. The necessities of global hyper-markets ultimately make these initiatives pursue and achieve important but less than optimal environmental outcomes.

Much research has shown how large transnational retailers exercise influence through capital accumulation, supply-chain manipulation, and the discursive power of defining concepts like sustainability.[2] Sustainability programs and other "corporate social responsibility programs" are vehicles for this influence, which increasingly has taken the form of *governance*. Walmart's sustainability programs, like others that empower third-party certifications, can be seen as exemplars of a trend toward private corporate environmental governance in an era of weakening state power and neoliberal globalization.[3] This chapter looks at how Walmart and the Walton Family Foundation portray themselves and argues that while they may never have been entirely independent of the state (no retailer that receives state subsidies and follows state regulations could be), their positioning has shifted from market-driven sustainability to government partnerships and direct policy interventions.[4]

In implementing seafood sustainability policies, Walmart and the Walton Family Foundation have also defined what a sustainable ocean means, discursively and in practice. The 1987 UN Brundtland Commission defined sustainability as "meeting the needs of the present without compromising the ability of future generations to meet their own needs."[5] Teresa Ish, the Walton Family Foundation's Environmental Program senior program officer and Oceans Initiative lead, applies this definition to fisheries, defining sustainable fisheries as "fish populations that are in balance, where we can continue to take fish out of the ocean at a rate that allows them to replenish themselves."[6] On its face, this seems reasonable. However, fish populations are inherently dynamic because environmental conditions can cause massive fluctuations in the survival of baby fish; a good year may see thirty times more fish survive to adulthood than a bad year.[7] Fishing exacerbates these fluctuations, which may lead to shifts in the composition of entire ecosystems.[8] Combined with difficulties in counting fish underwater, this means that determining whether fish are being taken out faster than they can replenish themselves is more complicated than it seems, complicated enough that experts regularly disagree about the size, trajectory, and health of a population—in other words, whether a fishery is sustainable. Another problem is that this definition is about a rate, not a number; a fishery can be sustainable under this definition even if the fishery biomass is at 10 percent of what it was before fishing began and even if there are other serious ecosystem or bio-geochemical impacts of that reduced biomass. In other words, sustainable fisheries are not necessarily synonymous with an ecologically healthy ocean or ecologically healthy planetary systems.[9]

Through exercising corporate governance, Walmart has essentially declared that certain seafood policies are sustainable (e.g., those used by fishing companies certified sustainable by the MSC). Walmart's suppliers—fishing companies—also adopt those working definitions, giving them global legibility and legitimacy. Walmart's definition of sustainable fisheries—distinct from ecologically healthy oceans—thus becomes the ideal toward which both public- and private-sector environmental action strives. Indeed, one can observe a trend even among environmental organizations toward using the metrics of sustainability instead of conservation ecology when evaluating marine fish populations and ecosystems. Furthermore, even by their own metrics, Walmart's policies have demonstrated mixed results at making fisheries sustainable. We might well ask, what is really being sustained—marine ecosystems, fishing communities, or supply chains clinically designed to produce low prices all the time?

HOW BIG IS WALMART'S FISHPRINT?

What began as Walton's 5 and 10 in 1950 has become almost incomprehensibly vast.[10] Until the mid-1980s, Walmart remained a regional chain particular to the rural South and Southwest; its headquarters remain in Bentonville, Arkansas, an Ozark town of fewer than 50,000 people (where it was illegal to buy a six-pack of beer until 2012). From this self-consciously humble and homespun locus, Walmart executives assembled an empire. In 1990, shortly after Walmart decided to expand into the fresh grocery market, it had 9 supercenters. By 2000, it had 888 supercenters and was the number-one grocery retailer in the nation.[11] In 2020, Walmart reported $559 billion in revenue, slightly more than the GDP of Sweden; if it were a sovereign nation, Walmart would be China's sixth largest export market.[12] Walmart is the largest private company in the world, with 2.2 million employees on payroll, and it has more than 11,500 stores worldwide (3,571 supercenters in the US alone).[13] Each week, 265 million people shop at Walmart.[14] While seafood-specific numbers are hard to find, Walmart constitutes 26 percent of the grocery market share in the US (as much as 90% in some locations), and it is reasonable to believe its share of the seafood market is similar.[15] Between 1990 and 2006, US seafood imports nearly doubled, from 1,308,444 metric tons to 2,449,468 metric tons. Given the vast expansion of Walmart's grocery share in that time and how many of its seafood products are imported, a good portion of that growth is likely due to Walmart.[16]

When one considers Walmart's size and environmental impact, one might first think about the size and impact of a typical Walmart store. The average supercenter is 178,000 square feet, with the largest clocking in at a staggering 260,000 square feet (not including the parking lot). As of 2021, every Walmart in the US occupied 703 million square feet of retail sales floor, an area larger than Manhattan.[17]

But this metric doesn't begin to indicate the environmental impact of Walmart's supply chain. The area needed to grow, mine, and harvest the raw materials; the facilities to extract and assemble them, the secondary spaces that house and transport the laborers doing that work are all *ghost acres*—essential but hidden pieces of the vast machine that is Walmart.[18] They are generally not owned by Walmart itself but by its suppliers; 90 percent of Walmart's environmental footprint is estimated to come from outside its immediate corporate operations.[19] To grasp the impacts of Walmart's supply chain on the marine ecosystem, one must consider both the direct and indirect impacts of extraction—including the method of capture, how, when, where, which sub-populations and year-classes were disproportionately affected, what other marine life was caught as by-catch and its fate, *and all the ecosystem relations involving that fish*. These ecosystem relations inevitably include relations with people, including fishers, who aren't part of Walmart's supply chain but are deeply affected by its governance.

Our inability to measure the scale and complexity of marine fish harvesting and its ecosystem-level impacts is just one aspect of a larger perception of the ocean as a "no-place."[20] This perception is advantageous for a keystone actor like Walmart. It allows the sometimes disturbing conditions that make low prices possible to remain hidden, like importing products from suppliers in poorer countries with poverty-level wages and slavery-like labor conditions. Walmart is not, technically speaking, vertically integrated; it does not own its suppliers and is not liable for their ethical failings or their financial margins. Nonetheless, it reaps the benefits of vertical integration—given its power as a near monopsony, many of its suppliers functionally have little choice but to sell to Walmart, according to journalist Charles Fishman. Walmart sets a price and its suppliers accept it, and when the company tells its suppliers to drop that price by 5 percent the following year, they must accept that too. Says Fishman, "The fear of Wal-Mart isn't just the fear of losing a big account . . . [The] more business you do with Wal-Mart, the deeper you end up inside the Wal-Mart ecosystem, and the less you are actually running your own business."[21]

What does Walmart want? The omnipresent slogan is unequivocal: "Low prices. Always." What this means in the Anthropocene is an interesting question. The goal of achieving "low prices" consumed Walmart executives throughout the twentieth century. In the twenty-first century, amid growing global uncertainty about climate chains, ecosystem stability, and supply-chain disruption, the word *always* takes on new significance. What does it mean to *always* have low prices on consumer goods? For Walmart, it implies a supply chain that is reliable, costs that remain externalized, employees with low wages and few benefits, and suppliers that are always willing to respond to the retailer's carrots and sticks.

Fishman claims that more than profit or power, "Wal-Mart is greedy for control. Walmart has created the most elaborate, sophisticated ecosystem in the history of business . . . a real place in the global economy where the very metabolism of business is set by Wal-Mart."[22] Walmart is a literal ecosystem that exists around the globe and throughout the sea, composed of human and non-human life forms that may never interact with Walmart directly. It is an orchestra played by suppliers of suppliers running salmon pens in Patagonia, pollock factory ships in Ohtosk, tuna canneries in Indonesia, and shrimp farms in Thailand—all conducted from Bentonville, 500 miles from the nearest coastline.

MAKING SUSTAINABLE SEAFOOD: WALMART AND THE MARINE STEWARDSHIP COUNCIL

THE RISE OF SUSTAINABILITY CERTIFICATIONS

The primary means through which Walmart impacts seafood sustainability is market power: Walmart only buys and sells seafood products that fulfill its sustainable certification criteria. By giving legitimacy to certain certifications, particularly those of the MSC, Walmart has encouraged hundreds of seafood companies to undertake the certification process. It is less clear how well certifications actually acknowledge, let alone create, sustainable fisheries or healthy oceans.

In 2006, Walmart was facing a nadir of public opinion after a series of scandals relating to employee wages, sexism, and horrific supplier conditions—including child labor. Walmart's seafood department, a decade and a half old, faced a different problem—insecurity in its supply chain. Walmart's business model requires suppliers to be consistent, reliable, transparent, and agreeable to changes, particularly price reductions. Its complex seafood supply chain (a single fillet might change hands half a dozen times on its way from the sea to the shelf) met none of these criteria, and Walmart was concerned about receiving inferior products—or possibly none at all. "I am already having a hard time getting supply," Peter Redmond, Walmart's vice president for seafood and deli reported. "If we add 250 stores a year, imagine how hard it will be in five years."[23] Redmond wasn't alone in his concerns; that same year, a controversial and widely reported scientific paper warned that *all* commercially fished stocks could collapse by 2048.[24]

Into this breach stepped Rob Walton, son of Walmart founder Sam Walton. The Waltons continue to own a controlling share of Walmart and remain by far the most influential investors, and Rob was growing concerned about both the company's image and the planet's environmental trajectory. Walton arranged for his close friend and diving buddy Peter Seligmann, chair of the environmental non-government organization (NGO) Conservation International, to meet with Walmart's CEO, H. Lee Scott. Seligmann helped convince Scott that a commitment to sustainability would provide much-needed good publicity (especially for younger demographics particularly hostile to Walmart) while helping secure the continued stability of potentially volatile supply chains, including seafood.

In August 2006, Walmart announced a multifaceted campaign to go green. What this meant in terms of seafood was introducing the MSC label on Walmart seafood products. They started with ten products from Beaver Street Seafood and AquaCuisine but had bigger ambitions. "We have set a goal to procure all wild-caught seafood for North America from fisheries certified by the MSC within the next three to five years," Redmond announced.[25]

Inspired by the catastrophic collapse of the Grand Banks cod stocks in 1992, the multinational consumer goods conglomerate Unilever (at the time of the collapse the biggest buyer of Grand Banks cod) and the environmental NGO World Wildlife Fund founded the Marine Stewardship Council in 1997. The MSC is an independent NGO that allows fisheries to apply to receive the "certified sustainable" label (a blue checkmark in the shape of a fish) (figure 3.1). A fishery seeking certification (through either a single company or a consortium of companies) hires a third party to assess the degree to which the fishery fulfills each of twenty-three MSC sustainability principles. Most important, "A fishery through its practices cannot lead to overfishing, and, if a fish stock is considered overfished, it must take action to bring it back to healthy levels" *and* "must take into account the ecosystem to which the fish belongs... and not degrade the habitat or engage in practices which lead to declining biological diversity of other functional fish stocks." The fishery must be managed and obey all relevant laws.[26] A fishery that passes the certification body's assessment is opened to public comment and objections (from environmental NGOs, concerned citizens, or other fisheries), redrafted, and then certified or rejected. Certified fisheries undergo reassessment every five years.[27]

FIGURE 3.1. A small sample of Walmart seafood products, many but not all of which display the Marine Stewardship Council's blue checkmark. *Top*: Frozen. *Bottom*: Dried and canned. Author photos, taken at the San Diego Walmart, 2021.

The MSC's early self-promotion and media reporting centered on the roles of consumers, environmental groups, and industry and sometimes explicitly rejected the role of governments. A 1996 paper by MSC founder Michael Sutton featured a prominent epigraph from the secretary-general of the UN Environment Program stating simply "the market is replacing our democratic institutions as the key determinant in our society."[28] To Sutton, this was not a problem but an opportunity; the state had failed to manage fisheries sustainably, so it was time to let market forces work their magic. "Government, laws, and treaties aside," Sutton wrote, "the market will begin to determine the means of fish production."[29]

But what did Sutton mean by "the market"? Consumers were not the principal force driving fisheries to adopt MSC-certifiable practices. Corporate pressure—corporate *governance*—was the driving force. Scholars consider the sustainable seafood movement "different from previous social movements," focused on establishing legitimacy and authority not through government or consumers but among supply-chain actors, motivating them to "participate in non-state market driven governance regimes."[30] Within the non-government trinity of consumers, environmental NGOs, and industry, consumers were given substantial lip service: for example, another article coauthored by Sutton was titled "The Marine Stewardship Council: Sustainable Fisheries through Consumer Choice."[31] But reading beyond the headline, it is clear that from the very beginning, Sutton envisioned the MSC achieving marine sustainability through corporate, not individual, decisions. Sutton described the MSC's long-term vision as one in which from their certification, fish had not just market saturation but universal acceptance: "As progressive seafood companies and food retailers make commitments to buy their fish products only from well-managed fisheries certified to MSC standards, the future of the fishing industry and the marine environment will become more secure than is the case today."[32] This is not an open marketplace where consumers have the ability to choose sustainable or non-sustainable fish; it is a marketplace in which all fish are sustainable, where retailers only sell MSC-certified fish.

Teresa Ish started her career with the seafood certification organization FishWise. She describes this retailer's and the industry-targeted approach to limiting consumer choice to sustainable options as "choice editing": "We wanted to get to a point with sustainability, where ... the customers wouldn't even have the choice to choose an unsustainable product."[33]

Choice editing is nothing new. The concept encompasses restricting or removing anything seen as undesirable from the market through regulations and restrictions, from bans on plastic bags and leaded gasoline to food and drug standards and chemical safety regulations.[34] What *is* newer is that choice editing is now consciously performed by NGOs and corporations with little to no government oversight. From an environmental perspective, private-sector–driven choice editing can lead to a preferable outcome, but the method by which that outcome is achieved is less democratic than either the governmental choice-editing regime it replaced or the consumer choice regime the MSC initially claimed to embody. Walmart understood this vision, which Peter Redmond made explicit at a 2010 World Aquaculture Society conference: "How many people actually believe that retailers have customers banging down the doors saying, 'I want to know what you're doing about this, that and the other' ... I probably met with 25 retailers in the last 12 months ... they all said, 'Absolutely not. It's our initiative. We're doing it to make sure what we're doing is right.'"[35]

The focus on retailers rather than consumers turned MSC certifications from a value-added product to a necessity for seafood suppliers. The advantage to being a mega-corporation was that Walmart's supply chain now had to partner with the MSC as well.[36] Rupert Howes, then chief executive of the MSC, focused on suppliers in his statement for Walmart's press release: "Wal-Mart supply fisheries have begun to engage in the early stages of the MSC assessment process. We hope that this commitment will encourage other fisheries to join the MSC assessment process and provide a powerful new route for consumers to support sustainable fishing."[37] Walmart wasn't the first retailer to adopt MSC certifications (perhaps unsurprisingly, Whole Foods Market had made that commitment earlier), but it was the biggest; where Walmart went, other industry players followed. Within a decade, many other major retailers including Aldi, Carrefour, Ikea, and Tesco, as well as restaurant chains like McDonalds and Darden (owner of Red Lobster and the Olive Garden), had partnerships with the MSC.[38]

Starting in 2007, the Walton Family Foundation began donating millions of dollars to the MSC. In 2010, it was the MSC's largest single donor, contributing $4.5 million.[39] While technically independent, the foundation is run directly by the children and grandchildren of Sam Walton, who helped convince Walmart's CEO to embark on the conservation program in the first place. That year, in the same newsletter announcing the partnership with Walmart, the MSC announced a "new strategic plan [that] sets out how we will scale up our activities and accelerate the delivery of our mission. It was developed following an intensive planning process generously funded by the David and Lucile Packard Foundation and the Walton Family Foundation."[40]

Scaling and accelerating accurately describe what happened to the MSC after partnering with Walmart and the Waltons. Its budget increased dramatically, and the number of certified fisheries increased sevenfold from 2006 to 2013.[41] But scaling rarely comes without turbulence, and a Walmart-size MSC quickly found itself navigating rougher seas.

DOES CERTIFICATION MAKE FISHERIES MORE SUSTAINABLE?

When Walmart chose to partner with the MSC in 2006, "Ex post studies of seafood awareness campaigns['] impacts on the seafood market [were] virtually nonexistent."[42] Many of the research studies before and after the partnership were focused on the consumer (e.g., whether consumers could navigate the certification market or which consumer markets would buy sustainable fish if it cost more).[43] Walmart wasn't particularly concerned about consumer behavior, provided it could be certain that its suppliers were eating the cost of sustainable fishing methods (so it could continue to provide consumers with guaranteed "low prices always"). But by the early 2010s, MSC's newfound ubiquity brought increasing scrutiny. An increasing number of scientists and conservation groups—from Greenpeace to the Pew Environmental Group to MSC's founding organization, the World Wildlife Fund—found fault with MSC practices.

A number of scientific papers raised concerns about MSC's governance structure, which featured several practices that scientists feared would incentivize overly permissive certification. First, a market of independent consultants who served as certifiers favored firms that would help fisheries achieve certification; the consultancy acquired a reputation for failing fisheries that would have trouble acquiring future customers, even after they paid between $15,000 and $150,000 for the assessment services.[44] Second, the objection process—ostensibly the most democratic aspect of the certification—did not encompass biological critiques, only errors in the bureaucratic process. The adjudicators appointed to handle objections were lawyers, not scientists. The MSC wrote, "It is not the purpose of the Objections Procedure to review the subject fishery against the MSC Principles and Criteria for Sustainable Fisheries, but to determine whether the certification body made an error." Objections were also prohibitively expensive, costing objectors up to £15,000 until August 2010 and up to £5,000 after August 2010.[45] The effects of this perceived culture of permissiveness were noticeable: nineteen objections were filed between 1999 and 2013, and only one fishery was failed. This meant that 12 percent of the MSC-certified fisheries, representing 35 percent of total certified tonnage, had received a formal objection.[46]

The impartiality of MSC's governance was also called into question by its significant financial interest in certifying fisheries. A leaked WWF report showed that the MSC charged seafood companies 0.05 percent of the wholesale value of certified seafood sales to use its label, which amounted to US $14 million, or 73 percent of the organization's income in 2015. The MSC thus had direct financial incentive to certify more fisheries and allow larger catches. The WWF characterized the MSC as having "aggressively pursued global scale growth," adding that it "has begun to reap very large sums from the fishing industry."[47] The result is that some suppliers now view the council as another market actor, one whose rules are inescapable but have little direct correlation with actual sustainability.[48]

But there was an even deeper critique. MSC's definition of sustainable fishing was loose enough to justify the certification of fisheries that were overfished or in which overfishing was ongoing. Perhaps surprisingly, the word *overfished* does not have a universally agreed-upon definition. The MSC used a relatively lax definition of overfishing, allowing stocks as low as half the population size that is supposed to generate maximum sustainable yield—which some scientists call overfished—to be called "depleted" but not "overfished." This seemingly semantic debate meant that under the more stringent definition, 31 percent of MSC-certified stocks were overfished; even under the MSC's definition, 16 percent were "overfished" and an additional 11 percent were "depleted."[49]

MSC-certified fisheries can also do enormous environmental damage. Even though an MSC principle clearly states that fisheries should not damage ecosystems, the only fishing techniques that are explicitly banned are dynamite and poison fishing and shark finning.[50] Other fishing methods attributed to high rates of bycatch and ecosystem damage, including bottom trawling and long-lining, are not considered inherently unsustainable but still run against MSC principles. Dynamite and poison fishing are most commonly used in small-scale fisheries in the global South, whereas bottom trawling and long-lining are used in larger, better-capitalized fisheries from wealthier countries. (This is just one of the ways MSC certification benefits wealthier fisheries. Smaller fisheries, often from heavily fishing-dependent communities, are also less able to afford the certification fees and never get certified in the first place, losing market leverage even if they use more environmentally friendly techniques and are more sustainable than fisheries that are certified. Interestingly, small-scale fishing vessels are disproportionately featured on MSC's promotional material.)[51]

Perhaps the bigger question is whether the MSC actually improved the stocks of the fisheries themselves. It is one thing for a retailer to sell 100 percent certified products and another for that certification to substantially and positively impact the ecosystem. On a theoretical level, proponents of the MSC argue that it serves as an incentive to avoid overfishing (lest the label be lost), while detractors suggest that it can greenwash unsustainable and environmentally damaging fisheries and keep demand high among unsuspecting consumers. For instance, the MSC touts collaborations with the Ross Sea Chilean seabass fishery to implement practices that make its long-lines dramatically less likely to catch albatross and other seabirds. After the improvements were made, the fishery received its certification.[52] But that unquestionably positive change must be considered along with the fact that the Chilean seabass are long-lived and slow to reproduce, and the ecological role of Chilean seabass has not been well-established in the Ross Sea. Some scientists believe large Chilean seabass populations are critical for sustaining marine mammal populations.[53] Certifying the fishery without knowing its life history and environmental impacts implies a level of confidence in the fishery's environmental harmlessness that these scientists argue is not supported by data.

FROM "CERTIFIED SUSTAINABLE" TO "ON THE WAY TO ON THE WAY"

Around this time, Walmart also made a significant change to its sustainability goals: it amended its initial goal of only stocking sustainably labeled fish to include fisheries "on their way" to earning a sustainability label. As of 2021, Walmart's official seafood policy claimed that by 2025, all seafood would be sourced from fisheries that are "third party certified" by the MSC (or some other certifier recognized by the Global Sustainable Seafood Initiative) or "actively working toward certification."[54] The MSC itself also began to issue certifications for fisheries aspiring toward but not yet achieving sustainability. For example, in 2018 and 2020, two Atlantic bluefin tuna fisheries operated by Japan and France, respectively, acquired MSC certification even though that stock had fallen by over 25 percent between 2017 and 2020—from 18 percent of 1950 levels to 13 percent—and was at the time listed as endangered by the International Union for the Conservation of Nature.[55] The World Wildlife Fund, no longer affiliated with the MSC, raised the alarm;[56] certification for the Japanese fishery was granted with "the condition that by 2025 the fishery will need to prove that the stock reached sustainability level," which the WWF argued put the cart before the horse.[57] Wasn't the MSC supposed to certify fisheries that were already sustainable, not reward aspirations alone? Now Walmart's "100% sustainable" seafood department could stock from fisheries "on their way" to receiving a certification that said they were on their way to sustainability.[58]

Walmart's partnership with the MSC has had a clear effect on the fishing industry, which now must navigate an expensive new market of certification consultancies that favor large industrial fisheries over small, community-based ones.[59] It has made the concept of sustainable fish—the concept of sustainability itself—into a commodity, sellable through a blue checkmark. The effect of the partnership on fish in the ocean is contingent on the decisions of particular consultants; in some cases, it may have saved thousands of seabirds, while in others it may have greenwashed unsustainable fishing practices and hurt other conservation efforts.

CATCH SHARES

CREATING A MARKET FOR FISHING RIGHTS

Partnering with the MSC was not Walmart's only foray into corporate governance of marine fish capture or its only effort to restructure the fishing industry using neoliberal market-based strategies. The Walton Family Foundation has also become a major donor behind campaigns to privatize and create a market for the right to fish, through a system called catch shares. *Catch shares* is a term for various forms of dedicated rights-based access privileges, including individual tradable quotas (ITQs), community quotas, community development quotas (implemented in Alaska, where Indigenous and other fishing communities receive a share of the profits from fishing), and territorial use rights (which assign reefs or shellfish grounds to individuals or communities). What they all have in common is a total allowable catch for the entire fishery (which was already standard policy in theory, if not practice) that is divided into quotas assigned to fishers, corporations, nonprofits, or communities. In tradable quota systems, quota holders can buy and sell their shares of the catch, much like stock or real estate. The design of a quota system can be variable: quotas can be permanent or temporary and renewable every two or three years.

The intellectual history of catch shares has roots in free-market ideology that places a high value on private property. They were first conceived by fisheries economists as a means of allowing fishers to acquire greater profits by reducing the number of fishing vessels without resorting to government regulation (in economic terms, to collect rent from fishing that otherwise would not exist due to overcapacity). Catch shares were viewed as a solution to the tragedy of the commons, in which (in theory) an unlimited number of fishers would compete for a limited number of fish, incentivizing unsustainable fishing. For example, when regulators stepped in to address overfishing without addressing overcapacity, they created perverse "race to fish" systems like the Alaskan halibut's infamous three-day open season, which encouraged unsafe fishing conditions. Catch shares were effective at ending the race to fish, but advocates believed their utility extended further. Some supporters believed ownership would promote stewardship (e.g., fishers would maximize long-term profits by not overfishing in the short term), increase fish biomass, eliminate the need for government regulation, and even reduce the federal deficit.[60] From a retailer perspective, catch shares were also seen as a tool to manage and control supply. There is no futures market for wild fish, and annual total allowable catch (TAC) and harvest are variable, so vertical coordination from either contracting or acquiring subsidiaries is critical for ensuring continued supply. The consolidation of seafood supply chains enabled by catch shares allows for this increased vertical coordination.[61]

Throughout the 1990s and early 2000s, the most prominent supporters of catch shares included large fishing companies that stood to benefit and free-market environmental think tanks such as the Property and Environment Research Council, the Competitive Enterprise Institute, the Reason Foundation, the Alex C. Walker Foundation, the Bradley Foundation (through its subsidiary, the Sand County Foundation), the Charles C. Koch Foundation, and the Wilkinson Foundation.[62] There was one apparent exception: the Environmental Defense Fund (EDF), a large environmental nonprofit with historical credibility in the environmental community and also a history of corporate partnerships.

The EDF partnered with the Reason Foundation and the Property and Environment Research Council in 2004 to form a new pro-catch share organization, IFQs4Fisheries, which successfully lobbied for a congressional moratorium on catch shares to expire and helped convince regional fisheries management councils to implement catch share programs in marine fisheries across the US.[63] The EDF had stated its preference for stricter standards to mitigate social impacts on fishing communities; as both proponents and skeptics identified early on, consolidation and absentee leasing could be mitigated by capping the percentage of the total quota one individual could own, requiring a quota to stay in a community, requiring quota holders to fish onboard themselves, or having a quota be distributed to communities rather than individuals.[64] However, the EDF's partners did not always share these preferences, and many programs progressed without them. While implementation often involved some form of voting on the part of fishers, in cases like that of the New England Groundfish Fishery, catch shares were presented as the only alternative to an untenable status quo—leaving discussion incomplete and lacking democratic consensus.[65] At this point in time, there was scant evidence that catch shares led to healthier fish stocks and considerable evidence that they led to major socioeconomic disruptions in fishing communities. ITQs allowed a quota to accumulate in the hands of a few companies that leased it to others, forcing some fishers to leave the industry (a goal of ITQs, since the presence of fewer vessels increases efficiency) and dividing those who stayed into either self-described "sea-lords" or "sharecroppers."[66]

ENTER THE WALTONS

In the first decade of the twenty-first century, around the time Walmart adopted its sustainability goals, the Walton Family Foundation began a three-pronged approach to increasing the adoption of catch shares. It started by donating millions of dollars to the EDF, Seligmann's Conservation International, and other large environmental NGOs for the purpose of promoting and implementing catch shares. Some of this funding went to catch share design programs, like EDF's Catch Share Design Manual,[67] and advocacy reports, like the 2008 Oceans of Abundance Project (convened by the EDF and the Marine Conservation Biology Institute and consisting of major political figures, scientists, and environmental advocates). The latter urged that all federal fishery management plans be considered for catch shares by 2012 and that half of all plans feature catch share management by 2016. The working group also urged the US Congress to pass legislation requiring that catch shares be considered in all federal fishery management plans by 2012.[68] Other funding went to implementation; between 2016 and 2020, the Walton Family Foundation dedicated $36.6 million to fisheries sustainability programs in Mexico, Peru, Chile, and Indonesia—much of which is dedicated to building catch share programs (or in the Walton press release's phrasing, "empowering fishermen and local communities through rights-based management approaches").[69] These countries are key components of Walmart's seafood supply chain. The foundation acknowledges this fact obliquely in a press release: "The [Walton Family Foundation] strategy leverages the buying power of major seafood importers and engages the supply chain in building support for sustainable fisheries practices."[70]

The Waltons also recently expanded into personal investments in fisheries where their foundation is implementing management changes such as catch share programs. Zoma Capital, the private investment company of Ben and Lucy Ann Walton, invested $10 million in Pescador Holdings, a sustainable seafood investment holding company. Pescador's first investment was Geomar, a vertically integrated "shore-to-shelf" seafood company in Chile, where the foundation supports projects that implement catch share rights. Catch shares will allow Pescador's suppliers—and perhaps even the company itself—to have a secure and permanent share of these fisheries. So far, this alignment of interests has received almost no media attention; instead, the Waltons have enjoyed glowing press for both their investment and philanthropic interests.[71]

A final portion of the $36.6 million went to funding researchers who demonstrate that catch shares improve environmental outcomes and can prevent overfishing.[72] These improved environmental outcomes were often attributed to increased stewardship on the part of fishers due to catch shares, but this idea was contested by independent studies that showed no clear environmental benefits from catch shares and serious methodological flaws in the studies that indicated otherwise.[73] Other studies found that catch shares might improve compliance with TAC but not yield the ecological benefits of increased biomass.[74]

Like other retailers, Walmart has benefited from catch shares by having a shorter, more easily controlled seafood supply chain, one either manipulable and ownable by the Waltons (when direct ownership is desirable) or disposable (when it isn't). Walmart suppliers tend to have low-gross margins and exhibit a "dependency model of market power," in which they are deeply reliant on Walmart.[75] Walmart intentionally cultivates this situation, and executives have suggested that overseas suppliers are too diversified. Andy Ruben, Walmart's first chief of sustainability, suggested shortly after the company launched its first wave of sustainability programs that in the seafood market, "right now we account for two percent of a lot of people's business, especially overseas. We know that needs to be a lot larger—maybe 50 or 60 percent."[76] Being a monopsony (a single buyer that substantially controls the market) enables Walmart to apply more control over its supply chain. In the tangled world of international seafood markets, that might mean the difference between knowing the chain of custody and who the original suppliers are—necessary for both sustainability and exerting pressure—and being left in the dark.

Peter Redmond talked about the advantages of a shorter supply chain:

> One of the problems we had was how much of our fish was coming to us third-, fourth-, or even fifth-hand. Sometimes our supplier turned out to be nothing more than a packer that was going out to a market saying, "I need 50,000 pounds of salmon no matter where it comes from." Through the chain of custody, we started to see when fish was being handled four or five times, and we knew it couldn't be good for the fish [since the texture and flavor of fish degrade over time, especially through freezing and refreezing]. And it's certainly not good for traceability. It brought us a lot more awareness about our supplier base, so now things come to us a lot more directly.[77]

In a post-hoc analysis, Stanford Business School professor Erica L. Plambeck found that "by simplifying its supply chain, Wal-Mart reduced the frequency of seafood stock-outs, improved the quality of the fish it was receiving, reduced paperwork and transaction costs, and reduced the costs and environmental impacts of transportation."[78] But by not vertically integrating directly, Walmart also avoided (at least to a degree) the negative headlines and liabilities associated with its suppliers.

THE LIMITS OF CORPORATE GOVERNANCE

At the beginning of its ventures into environmental policy, in the 1990s and early 2000s, Walmart, the Walton Family Foundation, and their NGO and think tank partners believed the free market was the best means by which to enact sustainability. By the 2020s, after decades of implementing socially disruptive market-driven policies that reshaped the way people around the world fished and who profited from that fishing, that confidence in the market was substantially moderated. Walmart, the MSC, and the EDF may be discovering what other observers believed from the start—markets have not demonstrated themselves to be single-handedly capable of enforcing sustainable fishing. Governments are still required because only governments can enact legal changes in property rights and enforce the compliance that certifications generally require.[79] Actors who for decades advocated successfully for market-based environmentalism now had to turn to traditional governing bodies so they could meet their sustainability commitments. Teresa Ish called this "a further choice editing approach where . . . there aren't any unsustainable fisheries, and you can only do that when your engagement is at the level of management. It is kind of ironic that it all comes back to that management side, but that's where we are now."[80]

What this means in practice is that the Waltons, long advocates for free-market environmentalism and limited regulation, have recently been in the position of "asking" the governments of countries in which Walmart has suppliers to bolster their fishery management and regulatory efforts (with the implicit threat that any country that says no risks losing one of its fishing industry's biggest buyers).[81] This can take the form of open letters, like the one signed by Walmart, Carrefour, Nestlé, Publix, and Tesco in May 2020 calling on governments to allow electronic monitoring of tuna vessels during the Covid pandemic so the retailers could still meet their sustainability commitments without exposing human monitors to disease risk. Consultants for the Walton

Family Foundation agree that governments are still necessary for effecting fisheries policies; one consultancy for the foundation's strategy on fishery improvement plans (FIPs) found that "to succeed, FIPs *must compel governments to adopt changes* needed to reform the fishery."[82]

In some ways we have come full circle, back to traditional environmental strategies like government regulations that use lawsuits to enforce them, except this time both the regulations and the lawsuits are coming from profit-motivated entities. This changes their nature. For instance, Walmart was a major party in a lawsuit against price fixing in the canned tuna industry, which happened to find (among other things) that tuna companies had illegally collaborated to resist environmental improvement measures.[83] However, it is unclear whether Walmart would have joined the suit if it wasn't also losing money because of the tuna companies' price fixing. This is how governance works in a neoliberal world: environmental actions still require government mechanisms, but the environmental action that does occur is substantially determined by profit-motivated companies.

CONCLUSION

Sustainability certifications and catch shares are tools of corporate governance that increase Walmart's control over its supply chain (encompassing a massive market share) and the marine environment (human and more than human). Both measures also allow the company, rather than any government or intergovernmental organization, to be the one monitoring and enforcing fisheries management through supplier agreements.

Walmart's corporate governance strategies allow the company to define sustainability. Walmart and the Walton Family Foundation have defined marine sustainability in such a way that their programs can achieve it without fundamentally changing their business model. This reformulated sustainability doesn't solve the problems associated with producing low-cost disposable goods and shipping them across the world or relying on the continued "predictable" harvest of wild animals with naturally fluctuating population dynamics. This is a definition of sustainability compatible with late-stage capitalism; it is unlikely to be compatible with complex ecosystems, unpredictable population fluctuations, and a changing climate.[84]

This contradiction at the heart of a sustainable Walmart gets elided by the company's rhetoric. By declaring that MSC certification means a fishery is sustainable or that catch shares improve ecological outcomes, Walmart is defining both these actions themselves and whatever ecological results they have as positive environmental outcomes, as sustainable. This is an important aspect of corporate greenwashing that hasn't received much attention: when it comes from a company the size of Walmart, it has a similar effect as a government changing the goalposts by redefining definitions of healthy or sustainable. There is some indication that this mismatch between reality and rhetoric could become even more problematic: in 2020, Walmart president Doug McMillan announced that the company aims to become "a regenerative company—one that works to restore, renew and replenish in addition to preserving our planet."[85] Walmart's stated goal of restoring and preserving the planet is seemingly a recognition that sustainable fisheries are not equivalent to healthy marine ecosystems. But how can a company whose business model depends on moving cheap goods and extracted resources be, on net, ecologically regenerative? Barring a substantial shift in that business model, which may entail higher prices on consumer goods, it seems more likely that regenerative—like sustainable—will become a word whose meaning is determined by Walmart.

The history in this chapter reveals that contrary to Walmart's supposed support of a free market, the Waltons have successfully shifted the fishing industry to an unequal hybrid governance model. Here, sustainability policies are chosen by corporations and private philanthropy but codified and enforced by governments—giving the Waltons the control they ultimately desire.

This control is Walmart's ultimate impact on the sea. Who fishes and who doesn't, what fish consumers have access to, how fishing operates and is managed, and the definition of sustainability itself are all now questions decided in part by the Waltons. The sea may be divided into territorial waters, but it is united by dictates emerging from Bentonville.

NOTES

1. Fishman, *The Wal-Mart Effect*; Copeland and Labuski, *The World of Wal-Mart*; Bianco, *The Bully of Bentonville*; Gereffi and Christian, "The Impacts of Wal-Mart"; Levy, "Walmart's Lead in Groceries Could Get Even Bigger"; Lichtenstein, *Wal-Mart*; Moreton, *To Serve God and Wal-Mart*; Mottner and Smith, "Wal-Mart"; Muñoz, Kenny, and Stecher, *Walmart in the Global South*; Ortega, *In Sam We Trust*.
2. Falkner and Kalfagianni, *Corporate Power in Global Agrifood Governance*; Konefal, Mascarenhas, and Hatanaka, "Governance in the Global Agro-Food System"; McMichael and Friedmann, "Situating the 'Retailing Revolution.'"
3. Hatanaka, Bain, and Busch, "Third-Party Certification in the Global Agrifood System"; Constance and Bonanno, "Regulating the Global Fisheries."
4. For more on hybrid governance and its limits, see Dauvergne and Lister, "Big Brand Sustainability"; Dauvergne and Lister, *Eco-Business*.
5. United Nations, "Sustainability."
6. Interview with Teresa Ish by Aaron Van Neste, Zoom, June 17, 2021.
7. Hjort, "Fluctuations in the Great Fisheries of Northern Europe."
8. Hsieh et al., "Fishing Elevates Variability in the Abundance of Exploited Species"; Anderson et al., "Why Fishing Magnifies Fluctuations in Fish Abundance"; Baumgardtner, Soutar, and Ferreirabartrina, "Reconstruction of the History of the Pacific Sardine and Northern Anchovy Populations."
9. Assuming that large-scale fishing continues, sustainable fishing would be a prerequisite for a healthy ocean, a necessary but not sufficient condition. It is also possible that large-scale fishing isn't compatible with a healthy marine ecosystem or indeed a healthy global planetary system. A recent paper found that fish biomass plays a critical role in global bio-geochemical cycles; as fishing has reduced global fish biomass by over half, nutrient cycling including the carbon sequestration necessary to slow climate change has also fallen by half. The total "biogeochemical impact of fisheries has been comparable to that of anthropogenic climate change." A fishery that reduces fish biomass by half is by the definition of overfishing not overfished but well within normal range, indicating that sustainable fishing is not the same as a sustainable planet. Bianchi et al., "Estimating Global Biomass and Biogeochemical Cycling of Marine Fish."
10. Vance and Scott, *Wal-Mart*, 10–11.
11. Fishman, *The Wal-Mart Effect*, 4–5.
12. Kohan, "Walmart Revenue Hits $559 Billion,"; "Country Profile—Sweden."; Moreton, *To Serve God and Wal-Mart*, ch. 1.
13. "U.S. Largest Employers List—Statistic Brain"; Szecsei, "39 Walmart Statistics."
14. Szecsei, "39 Walmart Statistics"; "FACT SHEET: Walmart's Made in America Pledge."
15. Levy, "Walmart's Lead in Groceries Could Get Even Bigger"; "Who Are the Top 10 Grocers in the United States."
16. "U.S. Imports of Edible Fishery Products from 1940 to 2020."
17. "Walmart Retail Sales Area by Division 2021."

18. The term *ghost acres* was recently re-popularized in Pomeranz, *The Great Divergence*; it was first used in Borgstrom, *The Hungry Planet*.
19. Nichols-Vinueza, "Evaluating NGO-Corporate Partnership Effectiveness"; Hyatt and Johnson, "Expanding Boundaries."
20. For more on the trans-historical construction of the ocean as a "placeless void," see Steinberg, *The Social Construction of the Ocean*.
21. Fishman, *The Wal-Mart Effect*, 235. Walmart changed its legal name from Wal-Mart Stores, Inc., to Walmart Inc. in 2018 but has used the unhyphenated "Walmart" in its logo since 2008. Hence, some quotations and earlier references refer to Wal-Mart rather than Walmart.
22. Fishman, *The Wal-Mart Effect*, 235.
23. Quoted in Plambeck and Denend, "The Greening of Wal-Mart," 55.
24. Plambeck and Denend, "The Greening of Wal-Mart"; Worm et al., "Impacts of Biodiversity Loss on Ocean Ecosystem Services."
25. Marine Stewardship Council, "Wal-Mart Stores, Inc. Introduces New Label to Distinguish Sustainable Seafood—MSC."
26. Bonilla, "Eco-Labeling for Change," 54.
27. Bonilla, "Eco-Labeling for Change."
28. Sutton, "The Marine Stewardship Council," 10.
29. Sutton, "The Marine Stewardship Council," 12.
30. Gutiérrez and Morgan, "The Influence of the Sustainable Seafood Movement," 1.
31. Cooper and Sutton, "The Marine Stewardship Council," 62.
32. Cooper and Sutton, "The Marine Stewardship Council."
33. Interview with Teresa Ish by Aaron Van Neste, Zoom, June 17, 2021.
34. Maniates, "Editing Out Unsustainable Behaviour."
35. Hedlund, "Redmond: Certification Is Retailer-Driven."
36. Moore, "Dredging up a Fight."
37. Marine Stewardship Council, "Wal-Mart Stores, Inc. Introduces New Label to Distinguish Sustainable Seafood—MSC."
38. Marine Stewardship Council, "Buy MSC Labelled Sustainable Seafood."
39. Walton Family Foundation, "Grants Database"; Walton Family Foundation, "Walton Family Foundation Invests $71.8 Million in Environmental Initiatives in 2010."
40. Marine Stewardship Council, *Annual Report 2005/6*.
41. McCambridge, "Sustainable Org. or Sustainable Seafood."
42. Jacquet and Pauly, "The Rise of Seafood Awareness Campaigns." This article considered certifications to be consumer-focused "seafood awareness campaigns," which quickly proved to be a nearly irrelevant mechanism; more accurately, certifications have become "supply-chain control campaigns."
43. Gutierrez and Thornton, "Can Consumers Understand Sustainability through Seafood Eco-Labels"; Jacquet and Pauly, "The Rise of Seafood Awareness Campaigns."
44. Jacquet et al., "Seafood Stewardship in Crisis."
45. Jacquet et al., "Seafood Stewardship in Crisis."
46. Christian et al., "A Review of Formal Objections to Marine Stewardship Council Fisheries Certifications." More recently, the Australian Orange Roughy Fishery

was approved by a consultant and an objection from environmental groups was upheld—but only on the legal technicality that Australia categorized the fish as threatened. The adjudicator otherwise considered the fishery "well managed and currently sustainably fished in terms of the prevailing science," based entirely on the consultant's report and contrary to the opinion of other scientists. See Carter, "Objections to the Proposed Certification of the Australia Orange Roughy"; Kilvert, "Orange Roughy Fishery Report Recommends 'Sustainable Seafood' Status."

47. White, "Leaked WWF Report Levels Harsh Criticism of MSC."
48. Davis, "Challenges to Effective Third-Party Certification in Environmental Policy."
49. Froese and Proelss, "Is a Stock Overfished if It Is Depleted by Overfishing"; Froese and Proelss, "Evaluation and Legal Assessment of Certified Seafood"; Christian et al., "A Review of Formal Objections to Marine Stewardship Council Fisheries Certifications."
50. "MSC Handbook: Guidelines for Developing MSC Pre-Assessment and Full Assessment Projects."
51. Frédéric Le Manach et al., "Small Is Beautiful, but Large Is Certified."
52. Marine Stewardship Council, "Chilean Sea Bass."
53. Abrams, "How Precautionary Is the Policy Governing the Ross Sea Antarctic Toothfish (Dissostichus Mawsoni) Fishery"; Stokstad, "Behind the Eco-Label."
54. Walmart, "Walmart Policies and Guidelines: Seafood Policy."
55. Baurick, "Population of Prized Tuna Species Decline [sic] as Protections Ease in the Gulf of Mexico."
56. Campogianni, "New Flawed MSC Certification of Bluefin Tuna Risks Reaching the Mediterranean Market."
57. Campogianni, "MSC Certification of Bluefin Tuna Fishery before Stocks Have Recovered Sets Dangerous Precedent." There was also precedent for MSC adjudicators to reject a stock considered threatened or endangered, but the bluefin certification decision was not challenged—by this point, the WWW had lost faith in the objections process.
58. Walmart's concept of sustainability as something that can be approached and eventually attained permanently seems more suited to some of its other green projects, like converting its vehicle fleet to electric, than to fisheries. A fishery can be sustainable one year and overfished the next; it takes consistent monitoring to guarantee consistent sustainability. Walmart does not currently sell bluefin tuna but does sell New Zealand orange roughy and several stocks of Chilean seabass, long-lived deep sea fish that are caught using bottom trawls or long-lines. Orange roughy have experienced dramatic population declines and are far from fully recovered, and both Chilean seabass ecology and the environmental effects of the Chilean seabass fishery on marine mammals are highly uncertain. Both fisheries have controversial MSC certifications. See Stokstad, "Behind the Eco-Label."
59. Le Manach et al., "Small Is Beautiful, but Large Is Certified."
60. Arnason, "Minimum Information Management in Fisheries"; Fujita, "Letters to the Editor: Fishing Quotas"; Fujita et al., "Rationality or Chaos"; Grimm, "Can Catch Shares Reduce the US Federal Deficit."

61. Dawson, "Vertical Integration in Commercial Fisheries," 36.
62. Macinko, "A New England Dilemma," 81.
63. IFQs include individual tradable quotas as well as non-tradable individual quotas.
64. The North Pacific Fishery Management Council's Halibut and Sablefish ITQ program is a good example of successful limitations on vertical and horizontal integration in an ITQ fishery. Dawson, "Vertical Integration in Commercial Fisheries," 71.
65. Macinko, "A New England Dilemma."
66. Carothers and Chambers, "Fisheries Privatization and the Remaking of Fishery Systems"; Copes, "A Critical Review of the Individual Quota"; McCay, "ITQs and Community"; McCay, "Social and Ecological Implications of ITQs"; McCay and Acheson, *The Question of the Commons*; Pálsson and Helgason, "Figuring Fish and Measuring Men"; Pinkerton and Edwards, "The Elephant in the Room."
67. Bonzon, McIlwain, Strauss, and Van Leuvan, "A Guide for Managers and Fishermen," 188.
68. "Oceans of Abundance."
69. Kiernan, "Walton Family Investing $36M in Sustainable Seafood"; "Walton Family Foundation Outlines Seafood Markets Strategy."
70. "Walton Family Foundation Outlines Seafood Markets Strategy."
71. Kiernan, "First-Ever Sustainable Seafood Investment Holding Company Launched."
72. Grimm et al., "Assessing Catch Shares' Effects Evidence."
73. Acheson, Apollonio, and Wilson, "Individual Transferable Quotas and Conservation"; Chu, "Thirty Years Later"; Branch, "How Do Individual Transferable Quotas Affect Marine Ecosystems."
74. Melnychuk et al., "Can Catch Share Fisheries Better Track Management Targets."
75. Mottner and Smith, "Wal-Mart."
76. Plambeck, "The Greening of Wal-Mart's Supply Chain."
77. Plambeck, "The Greening of Walmart's Supply Chain."
78. Plambeck, "The Greening of Wal-Mart's Supply Chain."
79. Levine et al., "2020 Global Landscape Review of Fishery Improvement Projects."
80. Interview with Teresa Ish by Aaron Van Neste.
81. These are generally countries where fishery management infrastructure is smaller and less well developed. Levine et al., "2020 Global Landscape Review of Fishery Improvement Projects."
82. Levine et al., "2020 Global Landscape Review of Fishery Improvement Projects," 85, emphasis added.
83. Peter Whoriskey, "Three Popular Tuna Brands Conspired to Fix Prices, Court Records Allege," *Washington Post*, May 16, 2017, https://www.washingtonpost.com/business/economy/three-popular-tuna-brands-conspired-to-fix-prices-court-records-allege/2017/05/16/bcfdde66-3a7d-11e7-a058-ddbb23c75d82_story.html.
84. Britten, Dowd, Kanary, and Worm, "Extended Fisheries Recovery Timelines in a Changing Environment."
85. Walmart, "Toward Regeneration, Together."

BIBLIOGRAPHY

Abrams, Peter A. "How Precautionary Is the Policy Governing the Ross Sea Antarctic Toothfish (*Dissostichus Mawsoni*) Fishery?" *Antarctic Science* 26, no. 1 (February 2014): 3–14.

Acheson, James, Spencer Apollonio, and James Wilson. "Individual Transferable Quotas and Conservation: A Critical Assessment." *Ecology and Society* 20, no. 4 (2015).

Anderson, Christian N. K., Chih-hao Hsieh, Stuart A. Sandin, Roger Hewitt, Anne Hollowed, John Beddington, Robert M. May, and George Sugihara. "Why Fishing Magnifies Fluctuations in Fish Abundance." *Nature* 452, no. 7189 (April 2008): 835–839.

Arnason, Ragnar. "Minimum Information Management in Fisheries." *Canadian Journal of Economics / Revue Canadienne d'Economique* 23, no. 3 (1990): 630–653.

Baumgardtner, Timothy R., Andy Soutar, and Vicente Ferreira-bartrina. "Reconstruction of the History of the Pacific Sardine and Northern Anchovy Populations over the Past Two Millennia from Sediments of the Santa Barbara Basin, California." *California Cooperative Oceanic Fisheries Investigations Report* 33 (1992): 24–40.

Baurick, Tristan. "Population of Prized Tuna Species Decline [sic] as Protections Ease in the Gulf of Mexico." September 13, 2020. https://www.nola.com/news/environment/article_9612fa64-f449-11ea-adcf-efaf33d0785c.html.

Bianchi, Daniele, David A. Carozza, Eric D. Galbraith, Jérôme Guiet, and Timothy DeVries. "Estimating Global Biomass and Biogeochemical Cycling of Marine Fish with and without Fishing," *Science Advances* 7, no. 41 (2021).

Bianco, Anthony. *The Bully of Bentonville: How the High Cost of Wal-Mart's Everyday Low Prices Is Hurting America*. New York: Currency, 2006.

Bonilla, Aileen. "Eco-Labeling for Change: The Marine Stewardship Council and the Creation of Sustainable Fisheries." PhD thesis, Tufts University, 2008. 54.

Bonzon, Kate, Karly McIlwain, C. Kent Strauss, and Tonya Van Leuvan. "A Guide for Managers and Fishermen" 1 (n.d.): 188. https://fisherysolutionscenter.edf.org/sites/catchshares.edf.org/files/CSDM_Vol1_A_Guide_for_Managers_and_Fishermen.pdf.

Borgstrom, George. *The Hungry Planet: The Modern World at the Edge of Famine*. New York: Macmillan, 1965.

Branch, Trevor A. "How Do Individual Transferable Quotas Affect Marine Ecosystems?" *Fish and Fisheries* 10, no. 1 (2009): 39–57.

Britten, Gregory L., Michael Dowd, Lisa Kanary, and Boris Worm. "Extended Fisheries Recovery Timelines in a Changing Environment." *Nature Communications* 8, no. 1 (May 19, 2017): 15235.

"Buy MSC Labelled Sustainable Seafood | Marine Stewardship Council." 2021. https://www.msc.org/what-you-can-do/buy-sustainable-seafood.

Campogianni, Stefania. "MSC Certification of Bluefin Tuna Fishery before Stocks Have Recovered Sets Dangerous Precedent." World Wildlife Fund. July 31, 2020. https://wwf.panda.org/wwf_news/?364790/MSC-certification-of-bluefin-tuna-fishery-before-stocks-have-recovered-sets-dangerous-precedent.

Campogianni, Stefania. "New Flawed MSC Certification of Bluefin Tuna Risks Reaching the Mediterranean Market, Warns WWF." World Wildlife Fund. October 28, 2020. https://wwf.panda.org/wwf_news/?1011266/New-flawed-MSC-certification-of-bluefin-tuna-risks-reaching-the-Mediterranean-market-warns-WWF.

Carothers, Courtney, and Catherine Chambers, "Fisheries Privatization and the Remaking of Fishery Systems." *Environment and Society* 3, no. 1 (2012): 39–59.

Carter, Melanie. "Objections to the Proposed Certification of the Australia Orange Roughy—Eastern Zone Fishery." Independent Adjudicator, Marine Stewardship Council. February 23, 2021.

Christian, Claire, David Ainley, Megan Bailey, Paul Dayton, John Hocevar, Michael LeVine, Jordan Nikoloyuk, Claire Nouvian, Enriqueta Velarde, Rodolfo Werner, and Jennifer Jacquet. "A Review of Formal Objections to Marine Stewardship Council Fisheries Certifications." *Biological Conservation* 161 (May 2013): 10–17.

Chu, Cindy. "Thirty Years Later: The Global Growth of ITQs and Their Influence on Stock Status in Marine Fisheries." *Fish and Fisheries* 10, no. 2 (2009): 217–230.

Constance, Douglas H., and Alessandro Bonanno. "Regulating the Global Fisheries: The World Wildlife Fund, Unilever, and the Marine Stewardship Council." *Agriculture and Human Values* 17, no. 2 (June 1, 2000): 125–139.

Cooper, Laura, and Michael Sutton. "The Marine Stewardship Council: Sustainable Fisheries through Consumer Choice." *Endangered Species Update (School of Natural Resources and Environment, the University of Michigan)* 15, no. 4 (1998): 59–66.

Copeland, Nick, and Christine Labuski. *The World of Wal-Mart: Discounting the American Dream*. London: Routledge, Taylor, and Francis Group, 2013.

Copes, Parzival. "A Critical Review of the Individual Quota as a Device in Fisheries Management on JSTOR." *Land Economics* 62, no. 3 (August 1986): 278–291.

"Country Profile—Sweden." UN Stats. 2021. https://unstats.un.org/unsd/snaama/countryprofile.

Dauvergne, Peter, and Jane Lister. "Big Brand Sustainability: Governance Prospects and Environmental Limits." *Global Environmental Change* 22, no. 1 (February 1, 2012): 36–45.

Dauvergne, Peter, and Jane Lister. *Eco-Business: A Big-Brand Takeover of Sustainability*. Reprint edition. Cambridge, MA: MIT Press, 2015.

Davis, Tyler Blake. "Challenges to Effective Third-Party Certification in Environmental Policy." PhD dissertation, University of Washington, Seattle, 2018.

Dawson, Robert. "Vertical Integration in Commercial Fisheries." PhD dissertation, Virginia Tech, Blacksburg, 2003.

"FACT SHEET: Walmart's Made in America Pledge." *Alliance for American Manufacturing* (blog). June 27, 2016. https://www.americanmanufacturing.org/press-release/fact-sheet-walmarts-made-in-america-pledge.

Falkner, Robert, and Agni Kalfagianni. *Corporate Power in Global Agrifood Governance*. Cambridge, MA: MIT Press, 2009.

Fishman, Charles. *The Wal-Mart Effect: How the World's Most Powerful Company Really Works and How It's Transforming the American Economy*. New York: Penguin Press, 2006.

Froese, Rainer, and Alexander Proelss, "Evaluation and Legal Assessment of Certified Seafood." *Marine Policy* 36 (2012): 1284–1289.

Froese, Rainer, and Alexander Proelss. "Is a Stock Overfished if It Is Depleted by Overfishing? A Response to the Rebuttal of Agnew et al. to Froese and Proelss 'Evaluation and Legal Assessment of Certified Seafood.'" *Marine Policy* 38 (March 2013): 548–550.

Fujita, Rodney M. "Letters to the Editor: Fishing Quotas." *SFGATE*, October 6, 2000. https://www.sfgate.com/opinion/letterstoeditor/article/letters-to-the-editor-2735248.php.

Fujita, Rod, Kate Bonzon, James Wilen, Andrew Solow, Ragnar Arnason, James Cannon, and Steve Polasky. "Rationality or Chaos? Global Fisheries at a Crossroads." In *Defying Ocean's End: An Agenda for Action*, edited by Linda K. Glover and Sylvia Earle, 139–149. Washington, DC: Island Press, 2004.

Gereffi, Gary, and Michelle Christian. "The Impacts of Wal-Mart: The Rise and Consequences of the World's Dominant Retailer." *Annual Review of Sociology* 35, no. 1 (2009): 573–591.

Grimm, Dietmar. "Can Catch Shares Reduce the US Federal Deficit?" *Journal of Sustainable Development* 3 (2010): 118–131.

Grimm, Dietmar, Ivan Barkhorn, David Festa, Kate Bonzon, Judd Boomhower, Valerie Hovland, and Jason Blau. "Assessing Catch Shares' Effects Evidence from Federal United States and Associated British Columbian Fisheries." *Marine Policy* 36, no. 3 (May 1, 2012): 644–657.

Gutiérrez, Alexis, and Siân K. Morgan. "The Influence of the Sustainable Seafood Movement in the US and UK Capture Fisheries Supply Chain and Fisheries Governance." *Frontiers in Marine Science* 2 (2015): 1–15.

Gutiérrez, Alexis, and Thomas Thornton. "Can Consumers Understand Sustainability through Seafood Eco-Labels? A U.S. and UK Case Study." *Sustainability* 6, no. 11 (November 18, 2014): 8195–8217.

Hatanaka, Maki Carmen Bain, and Lawrence Busch. "Third-Party Certification in the Global Agrifood System." *Food Policy, Private Agri-Food Standards: Implications for Food Policy and Agri-Food Systems* 30, no. 3 (June 1, 2005): 354–369.

Hedlund, Steven. "Redmond: Certification Is Retailer-Driven." *Seafood Source* (March 2, 2010). https://www.seafoodsource.com/news/aquaculture/redmond-certification-is-retailer-driven.

Hjort, Johan. "Fluctuations in the Great Fisheries of Northern Europe Viewed in the Light of Biological Research." *Journal Du Conseil—Permanent International Council for the Exploration of the Sea* 20 (1914): 1–228.

Hsieh, Chih-hao, Christian S. Reiss, John R. Hunter, John R. Beddington, Robert M. May, and George Sugihara. "Fishing Elevates Variability in the Abundance of Exploited Species." *Nature* 443, no. 7113 (October 2006): 859–862.

Hyatt, David G., and Jonathan L. Johnson. "Expanding Boundaries: Nongovernmental Organizations as Supply Chain Members." *Elementa: Science of the Anthropocene* 4 (March 2, 2016): 000093.

Ish, Teresa. Interview with the author. June 17, 2021.

Jacquet, Jennifer L., Daniel Pauly, David Ainley, Sidney Holt, Paul Dayton, and Jeremy Jackson. "Seafood Stewardship in Crisis." *Nature* 467, no. 7311 (September 2010): 28–29.

Jacquet, Jennifer L., and Daniel Pauly. "The Rise of Seafood Awareness Campaigns in an Era of Collapsing Fisheries." *Marine Policy* 31, no. 3 (May 2007): 308–313.

Kiernan, Lynda. "First-Ever Sustainable Seafood Investment Holding Company Launched." *Global AgInvesting* (blog). February 15, 2017. https://www.globalaginvesting.com/zoma-capital-encourage-capital-launch-first-ever-sustainable-seafood-investment-holding-company/.

Kiernan, Lynda. "Walton Family Investing $36M in Sustainable Seafood." *Global AgInvesting* (blog). June 14, 2017. https://www.globalaginvesting.com/walton-family-investing-36m-sustainable-seafood/.

Kilvert, Nick. "Orange Roughy Fishery Report Recommends 'Sustainable Seafood' Status—but Is Slammed by Conservation Groups." ABC News. July 4, 2020. https://www.abc.net.au/news/science/2020-07-05/orange-roughy-ngos-blast-sustainability-msc/12395812.

Kohan, Shelley E. "Walmart Revenue Hits $559 Billion for Fiscal Year 2020."

Forbes (February 18, 2021). https://www.forbes.com/sites/shelleykohan/2021/02/18/walmart-revenue-hits-559-billion-for-fiscal-year-2020/.

Konefal, Jason, Michael Mascarenhas, and Maki Hatanaka. "Governance in the Global Agro-Food System: Backlighting the Role of Transnational Supermarket Chains." *Agriculture and Human Values* 22, no. 3 (September 1, 2005): 291–302.

Le Manach, Frédéric, Jennifer L. Jacquet, Megan Bailey, Charlène Jouanneau, and Claire Nouvian. "Small Is Beautiful, but Large Is Certified: A Comparison between Fisheries the Marine Stewardship Council (MSC) Features in Its Promotional Materials and MSC-Certified Fisheries." *PloS One* 15, no. 5 (2020). https://doi.org/10.1371/journal.pone.0231073.

Levine, Max, John B. Thomas, Sydney Sanders, Michael F. Berger, Antonius Gagern, and Mark Michelin. "2020 Global Landscape Review of Fishery Improvement Projects." CEA Consulting report. March 2020, 123. https://oursharedseas.com/wp-content/uploads/2020/03/2020-Global-Landscape-Review-of-FIPs.pdf.

Levy, Adam. "Walmart's Lead in Groceries Could Get Even Bigger." *Motley Fool* (October 11, 2018). https://www.fool.com/investing/2018/10/11/walmarts-lead-in-groceries-could-get-even-bigger.aspx.

Lichtenstein, Nelson, ed. *Wal-Mart: The Face of Twenty-First-Century Capitalism*. New York: New Press, 2006.

Macinko, Seth, and William Whitmore. "A New England Dilemma: Thinking Sectors Through." Final report to Massachusetts Division of Marine Fisheries. June 2009. https://www.savingseafood.org/news/management-regulation/report-a-new-england-dilemma-thinking-sectors-through/.

Maniates, Michael. "Editing Out Unsustainable Behaviour." In *State of the World 2010: Transforming Cultures, from Consumerism to Sustainability*, edited by Erik Assadourian, 119–126. New York: W. W. Norton, 2010.

Marine Stewardship Council. "Chilean Sea Bass: How Patagonian Toothfish Was Saved." January 2018. http://patagonian-toothfish-story.msc.org/.

Marine Stewardship Council. *Annual Report 2005/6*. 2006. https://web.archive.org/web/20070204155802/https://www.msc.org/assets/docs/MSC_annual_report_05_06.pdf.

Marine Stewardship Council. "Wal-Mart Stores, Inc. Introduces New Label to Distinguish Sustainable Seafood—MSC." August 31, 2006. https://web.archive.org/web/20120706091134/https://www.msc.org/newsroom/news/wal-mart-stores-inc.-introduces-new-label-to/?searchterm=walmart.

McCambridge, Ruth. "Sustainable Org. or Sustainable Seafood: A Business Plan Question?" *Nonprofit Quarterly*, February 13, 2013. https://nonprofitquarterly.org/sustainable-org-or-sustainable-seafood-a-business-plan-question/.

McCay, Bonnie J. "ITQs and Community: An Essay on Environmental Governance." *Agricultural and Resource Economics Review* 33, no. 2 (October 2004): 162–170.

McCay, Bonnie J. "Social and Ecological Implications of ITQs: An Overview." *Ocean and Coastal Management, Property Rights and Fisheries Management* 28, no. 1 (January 1, 1995): 3–22.

McCay, Bonnie J., and James M. Acheson. *The Question of the Commons: The Culture and Ecology of Communal Resources*. Tucson: University of Arizona Press, 1987.

McMichael, Phillip, and Harriet Friedmann. "Situating the 'Retailing Revolution.'" In *Supermarkets and Agri-Food Supply Chains: Transformations in the Production and Consumption of Foods*, edited by David Burch and Geoffrey Lawrence, 291–319. Cheltenham, UK: Edward Elgar, 2007.

Melnychuk, Michael C., Timothy E. Essington, Trevor A. Branch, Selina S. Heppell, Olaf P. Jensen, Jason S. Link, Steven J. D. Martell, Ana M. Parma, John G. Pope, and Anthony D. M. Smith. "Can Catch Share Fisheries Better Track Management Targets?" *Fish and Fisheries* 13, no. 3 (2012): 267–290.

Moreton, Bethany. *To Serve God and Wal-Mart: The Making of Christian Free Enterprise*. Cambridge, MA: Harvard University Press, 2010.

Moore, Kirk. "Dredging up a Fight." *National Fisherman* 92, no. 1 (May 2011): 26–28.

Mottner, Sandra, and S. Smith. "Wal-Mart: Supplier Performance and Market Power." *Journal of Business Research* 62, no. 5 (2009): 535–541.

"MSC Handbook: Guidelines for Developing MSC Pre-Assessment and Full Assessment Projects." WWF-US Oceans Program. January 2015. https://seafoodsustainability.org/wp-content/uploads/2015/10/MSC-Handbook-1-12-15.pdf.

Muñoz, Carolina Bank, Bridget Kenny, and Antonio Stecher. *Walmart in the Global South: Workplace Culture, Labor Politics, and Supply Chains*. Austin: University of Texas Press, 2018.

Nichols-Vinueza, Alex. "Evaluating NGO-Corporate Partnership Effectiveness: A Case Study of the Environmental Defense Fund." Masters project, Duke University, Durham, NC, 2020. https://hdl.handle.net/10161/20501.

"Oceans of Abundance, Environmental Defense Fund: Frequently Asked Questions." November 27, 2008. https://web.archive.org/web/20081127004004/https://www.edf.org/documents/8831_OceansAbundance_FAQs.pdf.

Ortega, Bob. *In Sam We Trust: The Untold Story of Sam Walton and How Wal-Mart Is Devouring America*. 1st ed. New York: Times Business, 1998.

Pálsson, Gísli, and Agnar Helgason. "Figuring Fish and Measuring Men: The Individual Transferable Quota System in the Icelandic Cod Fishery." *Ocean and Coastal Management, Property Rights and Fisheries Management* 28, no. 1 (January 1, 1995): 117–146.

Pinkerton, Evelyn, and Danielle N. Edwards. "The Elephant in the Room: The Hidden Costs of Leasing Individual Transferable Fishing Quotas." *Marine Policy* 33, no. 4 (2009): 707–713.

Plambeck, Erica L. "The Greening of Wal-Mart's Supply Chain." *Supply Chain Management Review* 11, no. 5 (July 2007): 18–25.

Plambeck, Erica L., and Lyn Denend. "The Greening of Wal-Mart." *Stanford Social Innovation Review* 6, no. 2 (Spring 2008): 53–59.

Pomeranz, Kenneth. *The Great Divergence: China, Europe, and the Making of the Modern World Economy*. Revised edition. Princeton, NJ: Princeton University Press, 2001.

Steinberg, Philip E. *The Social Construction of the Ocean*. Cambridge, UK: Cambridge University Press, 2001.

Stokstad, Erik. "Behind the Eco-Label, a Debate over Antarctic Toothfish." *Science* 329, no. 5999 (September 24, 2010): 1596–1597.

Sutton, Michael. "The Marine Stewardship Council: New Hope for Marine Fisheries." *Naga, the ICLARM Quarterly* 19, no. 3 (1996): 10–12.

Szecsei, Szabolcs. "39 Walmart Statistics to Showcase the Retailer Giant's Power." April 3, 2021. https://capitalcounselor.com/walmart-statistics/.

United Nations. "Sustainability." 2021. https://www.un.org/en/academic-impact/sustainability.

"U.S. Imports of Edible Fishery Products from 1940 to 2020." *Statista*. June 2021. http://www.statista.com/statistics/197994/us-imports-of-edible-fishery-products-since-1940/.

"U.S. Largest Employers List—Statistic Brain." 2021. https://web.archive.org/web/20160210023938/http://www.statisticbrain.com/u-s-largest-employers.

Vance, Sandra Stringer, and Roy V. Scott. *Wal-Mart: A History of Sam Walton's Retail Phenomenon*. Twayne's Evolution of Modern Business Series. New York: Twayne, 1994.

Walmart. "Walmart Policies and Guidelines: Seafood Policy, Corporate—US." November 7, 2017. https://corporate.walmart.com/policies.

Walmart. "Toward Regeneration, Together, Corporate—US." 2021. https://corporate.walmart.com/newsroom/2021/10/06/toward-regeneration-together.

Walmart. "Walmart Retail Sales Area by Division 2021." *Statista*. 2021. http://www.statista.com/statistics/241194/sales-area-of-walmart-group-stores-since-2008/.

Walton Family Foundation. "Grants Database." 2007. https://www.waltonfamilyfoundation.org/grants-database?q=marine%20stewardship%20council&s=1&f1=00000169-a64e-d132-adeb-b77e35700000.

Walton Family Foundation. "Walton Family Foundation Invests $71.8 Million in Environmental Initiatives in 2010." August 16, 2011. https://www.prnewswire.com/news-releases/walton-family-foundation-invests-718-million-in-environmental-initiatives-in-2010-127835788.html.

Walton Family Foundation. "Walton Family Foundation Outlines Seafood Markets Strategy." 2021. https://www.waltonfamilyfoundation.org/about-us/newsroom/walton-family-foundation-outlines-seafood-markets-strategy.

White, Cliff. "Leaked WWF Report Levels Harsh Criticism of MSC." 2019. https://www.seafoodsource.com/news/environment-sustainability/leaked-wwf-report-levels-harsh-criticism-of-msc.

"Who Are the Top 10 Grocers in the United States?" *FoodIndustry.Com* (blog). November 21, 2019. https://www.foodindustry.com/articles/top-10-grocers-in-the-united-states-2019/.

Worm, Boris, Edward B. Barbier, Nicola Beaumont, Emmett J. Duffy, Carl Folke, Benjamin S. Halpern, Jeremy B. C. Jackson, Heike K. Lotze, Fiorenza Micheli, Stephen R. Palumbi, Enric Sala, Kimberley A. Selkoe, John J. Stachowicz, and Reg Watson. "Impacts of Biodiversity Loss on Ocean Ecosystem Services." *Science* 314, no. 5800 (November 3, 2006): 787–790.

4

"BUILDING SOME BIG-ASS WETLANDS"

Big Box Retail and the Rise of Mitigation Banking

LAURA J. MARTIN

Big box stores are often built on top of wetlands. An old joke about wetlands indicators goes: How can you tell if a site is a wetland? Look for water-adapted plants, hydric soils, and whether there's a Walmart.[1] There are a few reasons why developers routinely choose wetlands as building sites for big box stores and other low-density or strip development. Wetland sites are often less expensive than uplands; relatedly, many Americans already consider wetlands to be wastelands, places to be drained, ditched, and developed. For more than three centuries, wetlands have been relegated to the peripheries, the same liminal spaces zoned for malls and shopping centers. Since the 1980s, federal wetlands regulation meant to reverse wetland loss has only paved the way for the paving-over of wetlands.

Federal regulations facilitate the conversion of wetlands to Walmarts through a process known as "compensatory mitigation." To understand the process, let's visit the intersection of Ambassador Caffery Parkway and Kaliste Saloom Road in Lafayette, Louisiana. Leaving our car in

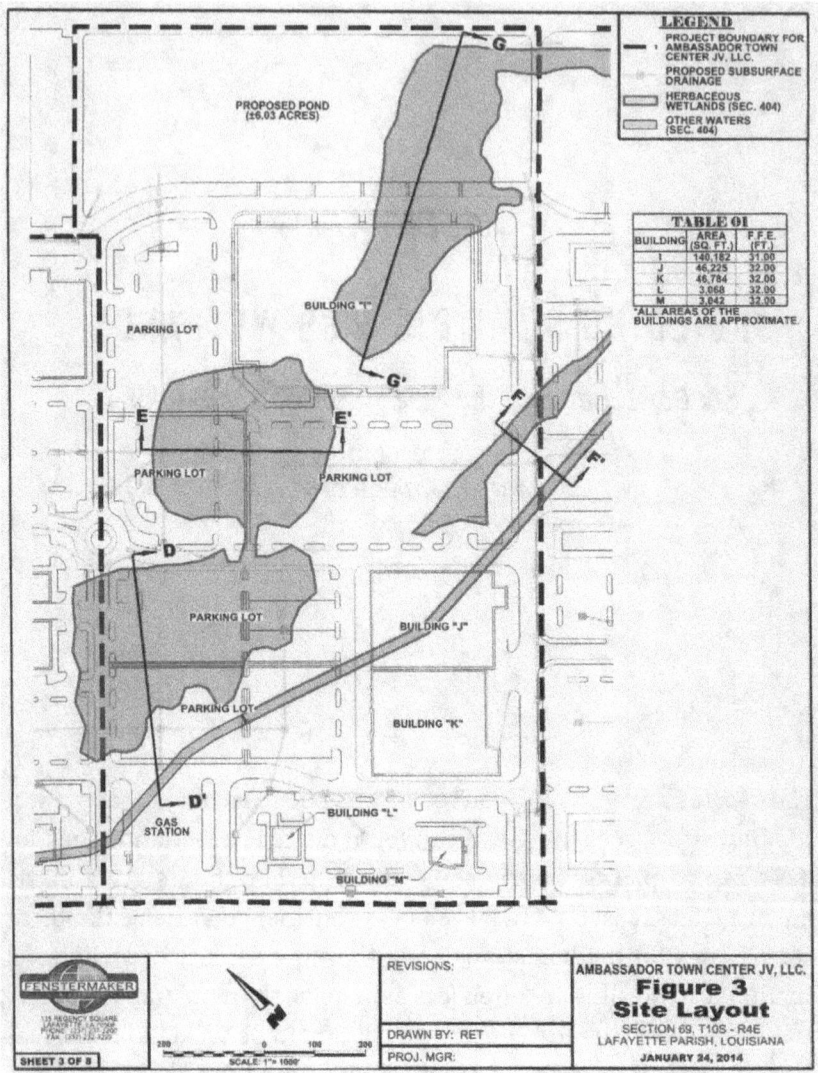

FIGURE 4.1. Site plan for the Ambassador Town Center in Lafayette, Louisiana, with jurisdictional wetlands overlaid.

the vast parking lot of the Ambassador Town Center on a muggy morning in July 2021, we can enter the spacious air-conditioned citadel of a PetSmart, a Marshalls, a HomeGoods, a Costco, or a Dick's Sporting Goods. Had we visited this same site a decade earlier, we would have been standing knee-deep in a marsh.

FIGURE 4.2. Satellite images of marginal swampland in Lafayette, Louisiana (*low resolution, top*), December 1985, which would become the site of the Ambassador Town Center (*bottom*), October 2020. Google Earth.

To build the Ambassador Town Center, Stirling Properties, LLC developed a proposal in 2014 to place approximately 8,600 cubic yards of concrete and 44,600 cubic yards of fill material in a 95-acre site.[2] The development process would erase 13.45 acres of "jurisdictional wetlands," or wetlands regulated under the 1972 Clean Water Act (figures 4.1, 4.2). Under Section 404 of the Clean Water Act, Stirling Properties needed to acquire permits from the US Army Corps of Engineers if it wanted to build. To compensate for this wetland loss, Stirling Properties proposed "to purchase appropriate mitigation credits from an approved Department of the Army mitigation bank to compensate for all project related wetland impacts."[3] Understanding the interplay between "mitigation credits" and "compensate" is critical to understanding the changing geographic distribution and biotic composition of wetlands in the United States and its territories over the last four decades. Big box retailers are consolidating wetlands at the same time they are consolidating commerce. The consolidation of retail and the consolidation of wetlands progressed in parallel and enabled one another. As we will see, wetland mitigation banking also served as the model for the international carbon offsetting market. Offsite mitigation thus reconfigured the geographic distribution of ecosystems along with relations between the global North and the global South, fashioning the latter as a source of "wild" nature.

FROM THREATENING TO THREATENED

The emergence of big box stores in the 1980s is part of a much longer history of retail consolidation that begins with the displacement of independent retailers and downtown shopping districts by shopping centers and chain stores. Land-use patterns changed substantially after the world wars as federal loan programs and subsidies for highway construction gave rise to suburbia and the subsequent birth of big box stores. Lizabeth Cohen argues that in the 1960s, suburban populations increasingly looked to new regional shopping centers for "a new kind of community life—consumption-oriented, tightly controlled, and aimed at citizen-consumers who preferably were white and middle class."[4] In this emerging geography of mass consumption, people were no longer brought together in central marketplaces and the public spaces that surrounded them but instead were separated by class, gender, and race in differentiated shopping spaces. Big box stores emerged in these spaces. In 1963, the American Society of Planning Officials wrote that the new discount stores Kmart, Walmart, and Target were "relieving an 'under-stored' situation in the suburbs."[5] At that time, the nation had about four square feet of retail per American; by 2000, that number had increased to nearly forty square feet.[6] Politicians and planning boards across the country seized upon big box stores and the sales tax dollars they generated as an attractive alternative to raising property taxes.[7]

The reconfiguration and consolidation of wetlands in the United States has an even longer history than that of the consolidation of retail. English settler colonists generally viewed wetlands as wastelands that generated disease, hindered travel, and hampered the production of food and fiber.[8] Hence they drained them or forced enslaved laborers to do so. In what would become the United States, the work of draining initially depended on human and animal labor and gravity, as laborers constructed small open ditches to drain wet spots in fields and reroute streams. In 1835, John Johnson of Seneca County, New York, brought over from Scotland instructions for molding clay drainage tile by hand. The use of underground drainage tile spread rapidly; more than 1,000 tile factories—mainly in Ohio, Illinois, and Indiana—were in operation by 1880. By 1882, more than 30,000 miles of tile had been laid in Indiana alone.[9] Midwestern states were subject to some of the most intensive draining efforts. Wetlands once occupied roughly 30 percent of Indiana's total land area; today that number is less than 1 percent.[10]

Steam power dramatically increased the rate and reach of wetlands draining. Large steam-powered excavating and trenching machines, and then smaller and more nimble machines powered by internal combustion engines, enabled hydrological re-engineering at a massive scale. Draining for agriculture peaked in the 1910s (figure 4.3). By the 1920s, approximately 70 percent of California's Central Valley's original wetland acreage had been modified by levees and drainage infrastructure.[11] In the 1940s, clay tiles gave way to thick-walled plastic pipes, later replaced by PVC and polyethylene tubing in the 1960s.[12]

Along with technological change, state and federal policy encouraged wetlands draining. In 1849, the US Congress passed the first of three Swamp Land Acts, giving 9.5 million acres of federal wetlands in Louisiana over to the state to drain and "reclaim" as agricultural land. In total, the federal government gave multiple states more than 64 million acres of land in this manner. Universities began teaching soil-drainage science in the late 1800s.[13]

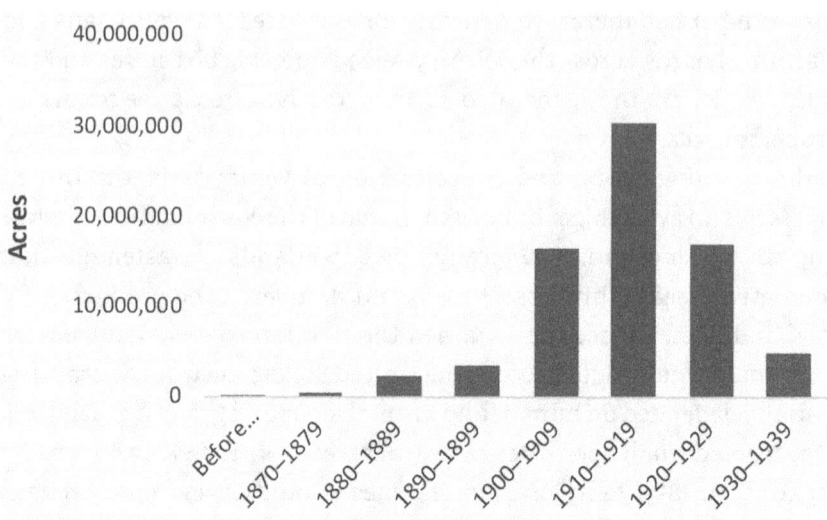

FIGURE 4.3. Total land drained for agriculture by period as reported by the Bureau of the Census. Data from Wooten and Jones, "The History of Our Drainage Enterprises," 478–480.

If wetlands were not drained and filled, they might instead be dredged or channelized to create ports and improve navigation. In 1899, Congress charged the US Army Corps of Engineers (the Corps) with maintaining navigation by regulating the dredging and filling of navigable waters. Severe flooding in Florida in the 1920s and again in the 1940s spurred the Corps to build the Central and Southern Florida Project for flood control. This massive network of levees, channels, and pumps radically changed the ecology of the Everglades.[14] By mid-century, then, the US government was providing free engineering services to drain wetlands and cost sharing with states on these drainage projects. The federal government also directly subsidized wetland drainage through its many public works projects administered by the US Department of Agriculture.

Federal and state sponsorship of wetland destruction continued through the twentieth century. Draining wetlands for agricultural, residential, and commercial development dramatically transformed ecosystems at a national scale. After World War II, the explosion of road and highway construction further transformed wetlands

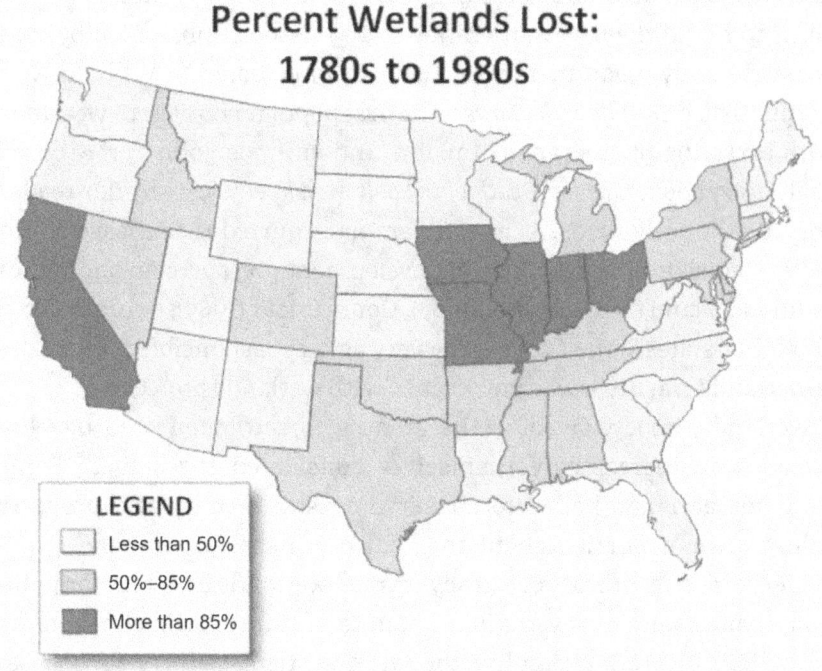

FIGURE 4.4. States that lost more than 50 percent of wetland extent before the 1980s are shaded. Adapted from Dahl and Alford, *Technical Aspects of Wetlands*.

nationwide. Construction crews built roads through the undeveloped, flat wetlands. For example, Interstate 10 crossed the Atchafalaya River swamp in Louisiana with a seventeen-mile bridge completed in 1971.[15] By 1980, only about 47 percent of the original 221 million wetland acres in the conterminous United States remained. Six states lost 85 percent or more of their original wetland acreage: California, Iowa, Missouri, Illinois, Indiana, and Ohio (figure 4.4).[16] The conversion of wetlands to big box stores and vast parking lots is the most recent chapter in this longer history.

Only in the 1960s did journalists and concerned residents begin voicing concern about the rate and extent of wetland loss. In the United States, concern began with coastal wetlands. In 1961, an illustration printed in the *Oakland Tribune* portrayed San Francisco Bay as a narrow channel in the year 2020.[17] According to the Corps, all marsh areas of the bay would be filled if development continued at the astounding rate of more than 2,000 acres per year. The visual prompted local residents to found the Save San Francisco Bay Association, which by 1965 boasted nearly 9,000 members. Then, in 1966, botanist William Niering published *The Life of the Marsh*, the first popular book about wetlands, with arresting photographs of plants and animals. John and Mildred Teal's 1969 book, *Life and Death of the Salt Marsh*, enjoyed similar readership. By the early 1970s, local activism had spurred the passage of protective legislation in response to development pressures on shorelines in Rhode Island (1967), Maine (1967), Connecticut (1969), Georgia (1970), and other states.[18] The Corps—the very agency responsible for decades of wetlands erasure—was now tasked with wetlands protection.

Wetlands, once viewed as threatening to settlement and development, were increasingly themselves considered threatened. Some wetlands activists hoped to conserve coastal scenery and property values. Others worried about the health of fisheries; employing the newly coined term *ecosystem*, they framed wetlands as filters for pollution.[19] Many were newly anxious about the future of wild charismatic animals. Alligators exemplify the late twentieth-century reversal of American attitudes toward wetlands fauna. One 1920 magazine article began: "Consider the alligator! Generally he is supposed to be good for nothing except to furnish the makings of traveling bags—and he can only do that when years have been added to his bulk."[20] But by the 1960s, environmentalists portrayed alligators as maligned and misunderstood, possibly doomed. Florida closed its hunting season on alligators in 1961, and in 1964 the US Fish and Wildlife Service Committee on Rare and Endangered Wildlife Species listed the alligator on the first federal list of native endangered wildlife. In 1967, conservationist Archie Carr wrote in *National Geographic* that "by protecting [the alligator], we will show that we have the sense and soul to cherish a wild creature that was here before any warm-blooded animal walked the earth, and that, given only a little room, would live on with us and help keep up the fading color of our land."[21] This was a consequential shift from the view that alligators were nothing but traveling bag material or that wetlands were without intrinsic value.

The US Congress amended the Federal Water Pollution Control Act in October 1972 (renamed the Clean Water Act in 1977) with the stated purpose of restoring the chemical, physical, and biological integrity of the nation's waters.[22] The Clean Water Act established a structure for regulating pollutant discharges and setting quality standards for surface waters. In doing so, it established what is still one of the federal government's most far-reaching powers to regulate land use. The best-known section of this act is Section 301, which prohibits the discharge of pollutants from point sources—such as factory drain pipes—into navigable waters. Equally important, though less studied by environmental scholars, is Section 404, which established a permit program to regulate the discharge of dredged or fill material into "waters of the United States," defined in 1975—after the Environmental Defense Fund and the Natural Resources Defense Council sued to expand the Corps's regulatory program—to include not only "navigable waters" but also streams, lakes, and wetlands such as marshes, bogs, and swamps.[23] The Corps has administered the permit program since its inception, while the Environmental Protection Agency (EPA) is responsible for establishing environmental guidelines the Corps must use to assess proposed projects when it makes its permitting decisions. The EPA also has the authority to veto permits approved by the Corps—though it rarely exercises this power—and the US Fish and Wildlife Service (FWS), the National Marine Fisheries Service, and the Natural Resources Conservation Service also have the opportunity to review and comment on Corps decisions.

The concept and practice of "compensatory mitigation" emerged unevenly, sometimes inconsistently, across federal agencies administering Section 404 in the 1980s. The idea of mitigation was first introduced with the National Environmental Policy Act of 1969 (NEPA), which required federal agencies to identify the potential adverse environmental impacts of the major actions they proposed to undertake and to consider reasonable alternatives to those actions. President Jimmy Carter's Council on Environmental Quality established a "mitigation sequence" in 1978, an ordered preference for how projects should be modified. Avoiding adverse environmental impacts was the first choice. Minimizing them was second, if avoidance was deemed unreasonable. The third option was to compensate for environmental damage if it could not be minimized.[24]

In their first decade administering Section 404, the Corps and the EPA disagreed about how they expected developers to compensate for or "mitigate" wetlands destruction. Notably, when the EPA issued its Section 404 guidelines in 1975, they did not include a compensatory mitigation option.[25] The guidelines stressed the avoidance of harm and made no mention of mechanisms either to mitigate or compensate for environmental damage. Indeed, the EPA assumed that permits for work that significantly damaged wetlands would either be denied by the Corps or vetoed by the EPA under its Section 404(c) powers.

However, the EPA rarely exercised its veto power over permits approved by the Corps. The Corps, for its part, tended to resolve the most difficult permit decisions by seeking substantial mitigation rather than threatening to withhold permits.[26] Often, the Corps required developers that destroyed wetlands to build small wetlands elsewhere on the development site. These were typically nothing more than holes in the ground, with sides too sloped for wetland vegetation to take hold. The Environmental Working Group in Washington, DC, found that only 0.5 percent of all Section 404 permits on which final action was taken in fiscal year 1995 were denied.[27] According to a report by the *St. Petersburg Times*, the Corps approved more than 12,000 Section 404 permits in Florida between 1999 and 2003 and rejected only one.[28] "Our denial rate is actually seven-tenths of 1 percent. We deny very few," Ted Rugiel of the Corps's Washington, DC, office said to a reporter in 1998. "And that's probably not so strange. That's a last resort. We pretty much go through all sorts of alternatives to try and come up with something so we can issue a permit. An applicant makes a proposal, we suggest something else, the applicant comes back and says, 'How about this?' and it goes back and forth until it's finally realized that in less than 1 percent of the cases, there isn't going to be any meeting of the minds."[29]

The different approaches of the Corps and the EPA played roles in numerous lawsuits and constituted what one analyst called "full-blown, institutional schizophrenia" regarding Section 404 implementation.[30] In the rare instances when the EPA overturned a Corps Section 404 permit, it was national news, often couched in the language of jobs-versus-environmentalists.

CONSOLIDATING WETLANDS

Through the 1980s, the Corps showed a preference for permittee-responsible mitigation: the permittee establishes, restores, or preserves wetlands on the project site or elsewhere to compensate for wetland impacts resulting from a specific project.[31] Indeed, onsite compensatory mitigation projects of this sort were common enough that by the mid-1980s, the Corps claimed to have halted the trend of wetland loss in the United States while continuing to permit development.[32] Between 1983 and 1989, more than 1,000 wetlands were created in Massachusetts alone through the Section 404 permitting process.[33]

But by the late 1980s, it was an open secret among regulators and biologists that permittee-constructed wetlands were no substitute, in acreage or habitat quality, for the wetlands lost to development. A 1992 study, published in 2000, concluded that of Section 404 permits issued in Louisiana, only 8 percent of the filled area was compensated for, and half of the mitigation sites had never been inspected.[34] Ecologists, meanwhile, published papers suggesting that created wetlands functioned nothing like the wetlands being destroyed. Mitigation wetlands contained different and fewer species than those they were meant to replace; they cycled nutrients differently and did not retain storm water as well.[35]

At the same time, a push by developers to make the Section 404 permitting system more "reasonable" and streamlined resulted in a set of policy proposals, gathered under President George H. W. Bush's "No Net Loss of Wetlands" agenda, that promoted a market-based approach. This agenda shaped a 1990 "Memorandum of Agreement" between the Corps and the EPA that formally clarified the procedures to be followed in determining what mitigation is necessary for Section 404 compliance. The memorandum embraced the no net loss of wetlands goal and defined it to mean "no overall net loss of values and functions."[36] Thus, it refrained from requiring acre-for-acre replacement of wetlands damaged or destroyed by development.

Federal promotion of commercial wetland mitigation banks began in earnest with a 1990 EPA workshop on the future of mitigation banking policy.[37] With mitigation banking, a permittee purchases "credits" from a mitigation bank, an entity that has established or restored a wetland somewhere other than the project site. Within a few years, entrepreneurial wetland banks began selling credits.[38] The arrangement was novel: developers could purchase credits in pre-constructed wetlands, and mitigation could be performed "offsite," sometimes hundreds or thousands of miles away. In other words, offsite mitigation detached the site of ecological destruction from the site of ecological care. One contractor in the Chicago area hit on a way to meet Section 404 compliance in 1991. As the contractor later recalled in an interview with geographer Morgan M. Robertson: "I just said, 'Maybe I'll build some big-ass wetlands somewhere, somewhere out there, and build some really good ones, and that ought to make these agencies really happy.'"[39] They floated this idea of a wetlands bank to the project manager at the Chicago Army Corps of Engineers. The project manager approved, and the contractor began constructing a wetland on a former agricultural site. The set of guidelines developed by the Chicago office for this project would become the foundation for the 1995 federal "Guidance" document on wetlands banking policy.[40]

Section 404 of the Clean Water Act was meant to make it difficult for developers to fill wetlands, but the practice of wetlands mitigation made it easy for them to do so. Big box stores and wetland banks proliferated simultaneously in the United States. The George W. Bush and Bill Clinton administrations promoted wetland banking as a "win-win" for environmentalists and developers; it was, in the words of one reporter, "a way to have your K-mart and your wetland, too."[41] Ecologists also supported offsite mitigation banks, as they promised larger and more biodiverse wetlands with better hydrological connectivity and, in theory, better oversight. The belief was that market-based incentives would produce better wetlands than would direct regulatory compulsion.

Along with entrepreneurs, environmental non-government organizations (NGOs) began establishing or managing offsite mitigation projects. In an influential early instance, the Walt Disney World Company paid the Nature Conservancy (TNC) to purchase and restore 11,500 acres of Everglades headwaters to mitigate a proposed 1.5-million-square-foot shopping mall and an exclusive residential community. On April 23, 1993, the governor of Florida, state and federal environmental officials, and representatives of Disney and TNC gathered at the base of a live oak tree to announce the establishment of the Disney Wilderness Preserve mitigation site. Carol Browner, administrator of the EPA, proclaimed that she would like to see consolidated offsite mitigation pursued nationwide. Indeed, it was she who had advocated for the mitigation approach during the permit negotiation phase in her previous role as secretary of the Florida Department of Environmental Regulation. "This is the future of environmental protection," she said.[42]

SEVERING DAMAGE AND CARE

Browner's prediction would prove accurate. The number of commercial wetland mitigation banks increased rapidly, from 46 active banks in 1992 to 330 in 2005.[43] Mitigation banking is changing the spatial distribution of wetlands at a national scale, but in ways few researchers are studying (figure 4.5). Wetland banks consolidated mitigation acreage into a few large sites that were overseen by third parties (i.e., neither the permit-seeking corporation nor the permit-granting agency). Information on acreage is spotty, but the Army Corps of Engineers reported that from 2000 to 2006, an average annual area of 20,620 existing wetland acres were permitted for adverse impacts under the Section 404 program. Over the same time period, the area of required wetlands compensation projects averaged about 47,384 acres per year.[44]

Wetland mitigation banking redistributed wetlands at a national scale in a way social scientists have barely explored. With offsite wetland mitigation, communities harmed by wetland destruction are not compensated with restoration or the building of new wetlands in their community. Rather, a different community benefits from the mitigation. This raises clear environmental equity and justice concerns. The literature on the geography of wetland redistribution is sparse. The first attempt to quantify wetland relocation compared the population densities of areas in which wetlands were restored or lost in Florida between 1992 and 1997. The data indicated that wetland banking policy was driving a migration of wetlands from urban to rural areas.[45] In the most comprehensive such study to date, regional planning scholar

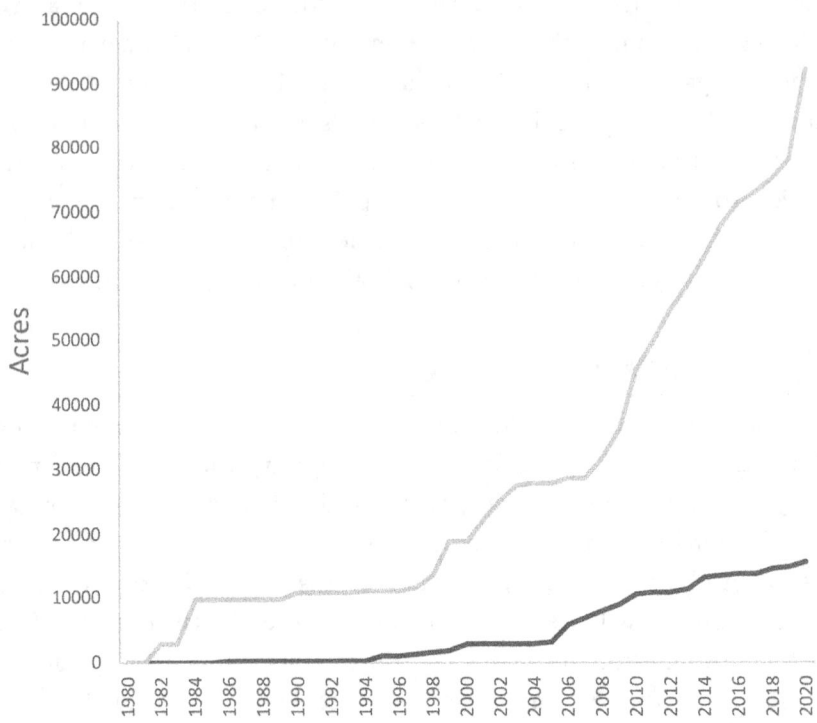

FIGURE 4.5. Total acres in wetland mitigation banks in Louisiana (gray line) and California (black line) by year. Data source: US Army Corps of Engineers Regulatory In-lieu Fee and Bank Information Tracking System.

Todd BenDor and colleagues analyzed the spatial pattern of wetland mitigation in the Chicago region between 1993 and 2004. They found a wide range of displacement distances. One mitigation banking transaction compensated for a wetland more than seventy miles away. They also found that areas surrounding impact sites had, on average, larger Black and Hispanic populations, lower levels of home ownership, and lower average household incomes than areas surrounding mitigation sites.[46] At a national scale, is wetlands mitigation policy disproportionately benefiting white or higher-income communities? Should wetlands mitigation—and other ecosystem markets—be considered under federal environmental justice regulations?

This brings us back to the Ambassador Town Center developers' proposal to "purchase appropriate mitigation credits from an approved

Department of the Army mitigation bank to compensate for all project related wetland impacts." In December 2014, Stirling Properties purchased 13.5 acres of bottomland hardwood mitigation credits from Cypremort-Teche Mitigation Bank for "unavoidable impacts associated with proposed work" on the Ambassador Town Center. The Cypremort-Teche Mitigation Bank is located in St. Mary Parish, thirty-eight miles southeast of the Ambassador Town Center. The 759-acre site received federal approval as a private commercial mitigation bank in 2012. J. M. Burguières Co. Ltd. owns and operates the mitigation bank. The company, founded in 1877 from three sugar plantations, is a land acquisition and holding company with the slogan "building value in land" that now operates eleven wetlands mitigation banks in Louisiana, Florida, and Texas. The Cypremort-Teche Mitigation Bank sells credits for "bottomland hardwoods," "cypress/tupelo gum swamp," and "fresh marsh-tidal." Embedded within Louisiana's fossil fuel extraction and processing landscape, the Cypremort-Teche property includes pipeline easements for Shell Oil, the United States of America, and Louisiana Intrastate Gas Company as well as mineral leases to Humble Oil and Refining Company and the Exxon Corporation.[47]

In addition to reconfiguring wetlands and retail districts at a regional scale, wetland mitigation banking paved the way conceptually and procedurally for carbon offsetting and other commodity markets in ecosystem services.[48] The idea behind carbon offsetting is that emissions generated in one location can be "offset" by removing greenhouse gases from the atmosphere somewhere else, through tree planting, say, or underground carbon storage. Today, entities as various as big box stores, cities, universities, and even individuals who wish to offset their air travel pay for projects elsewhere to compensate for greenhouse gas emissions. Many environmental organizations that manage carbon offsetting projects, including the Nature Conservancy, began by managing wetland banking sites.

The places that "offset" are increasingly remote from the sources of ecological damage, even further apart than the Ambassador Town Center is from the Cypremort-Teche Mitigation Bank. In a global market, purchasers of carbon offsets are able to appreciate the benefits of offsetting while continuing to emit greenhouse gasses and outsourcing the possible negative social and ecological impacts of mitigation. At present, the greatest number of voluntary carbon credit buyers is found in the United States, France, the United Kingdom, Germany, and Switzerland. The major offset-producing countries include Peru, Brazil, Kenya, Zimbabwe, Bolivia, Indonesia, and Cambodia. In 2010, Europe purchased 10.6 MtCO$_2$e in the carbon markets and contracted to supply only 0.2; in contrast, Latin America contracted to supply 16.9 MtCO$_2$e and purchased just 4.5.[49] Indeed, the global carbon market incentivizes the privatization and commodification of land and forest resources in developing regions, and it is not difficult to see forest- and land-use–based carbon offsetting as a mode of appropriating land in the global South for the alleged "universal" environmental end of solving climate change. In the emerging carbon economy, the global North continues to pollute, while communities in the global South lose land and sovereignty.

Carbon offsetting appeals to big box retailers for the same reasons wetland mitigation banking appeals: it enables the continuation of business as usual for a small price. Offsite mitigation requires no changes to onsite behavior: the wetland can still be filled and the fossil fuels can still be burned. In 2005, Walmart announced that it would begin voluntary offsite wildlife habitat mitigation. In partnership with the National Fish and Wildlife Foundation, Walmart launched Acres for America "with the goal to permanently protect one acre of important wildlife habitat in the United States for every acre of land developed by Walmart." The program was meant to "completely offset the company's land footprint in the United States." As of 2020, the program had put under legal protection more than 1.6 million acres across forty-two states, the District of Columbia, and Puerto Rico. Retailers like Walmart are reshaping ecosystems far beyond the reaches of their parking lots.[50]

In the United States, the consolidation and marginalization of retail came with the consolidation and marginalization of wetlands. This was part of a much larger story of environmental governance turning from regulation to market-based solutions. In administering Section 404, the Corps gave developers great latitude in setting the terms of wetlands compensation. Governance of wetlands fell somewhere between federal agencies and the private sphere. As big box stores shutter across the country or are repurposed into restaurants, online retail distribution centers, and even churches, what will happen to wetlands? When the development company Lormax Stern purchased a former Kmart store in Acme, Michigan, in 2019, it presented a proposal that would include restaurants, office space, indoor self-storage, and a plan to maintain existing wetlands, retention ponds, and woods on the property and to build green buffers around "specific stormwater infrastructure to improve water quality and to preserve and enrich the wildlife habitat."[51]

The compensatory wetland is the twin of the store, yet visiting one, you would never know the connection to the other. In 1986, for instance, the EPA vetoed a proposal by Pyramid Companies to build a shopping mall on top of Sweedens Swamp in Attleboro, Massachusetts. The Corps had determined that the project should be allowed to proceed, as Pyramid Companies had offered to create thirty-six acres of artificial marsh to compensate for the loss of Sweedens Swamp. The case is well-known among the small community of scholars who study wetlands policy, as it led to the development of federal compensatory mitigation guidelines in 1990.[52] The EPA's veto, however, did not kill the project; it simply moved it elsewhere. After much negotiation, Pyramid Companies was given the go-ahead to build the mall in the residential community of North Attleboro, three miles to the north. The Emerald Square Mall opened in 1989, anchoring further commercial development in North Attleboro. "It was like a bomb had been dropped on Route 1, and the shock waves are still being felt," a local reporter later recounted. That bomb cleared the way for the establishment of a district of big box stores. "Now there's Toys 'R' Us, Kids R Us, Wal-Mart, Target," the Emerald Square Mall general manager mused in 1999. "All of this will definitely help this area continue to grow and become even more of a destination."[53]

Of course—as is the case across the country—these big box stores would contribute to the decline of local malls. As I write this, the Emerald Square Mall has been placed in receivership by a federal court.[54] I witnessed this global trend personally; as a teenager in the 1990s, I spent my afternoons at Emerald Square Mall, roaming the aisles of Hot Topic and eating food court French fries. Returning home in the 2020s,

I accompanied my mother to Route 1 to go to the Walmart Supercenter, Lowe's, Best Buy, Dick's Sporting Goods, and Target. This is a rare case of Section 404 working as it was intended: Sweedens Swamp was spared, somewhere else was not. The same cannot be said for the bottomland hardwood wetlands that are now a conglomeration of big box stores and parking lots in Lafayette, Louisiana.

NOTES

1. A slight modification of the joke as recounted by Gardner, *Lawyers, Swamps, and Money*, 96.
2. Stirling Properties, LLC is a real estate brokerage firm licensed in Louisiana, Mississippi, Alabama, Florida, Texas, Arkansas, and Kentucky.
3. US Army Corps of Engineers and State of Louisiana Department of Environmental Quality, Joint Public Notice, 1.
4. Cohen, "From Town Center to Shopping Center," 1068. See also Jackson, "All the World's a Mall."
5. American Society of Planning Officials, "Discount Stores," Planning Advisory Service, Chicago, IL, March 1963, quoted in Press, "Dr. StrangeBox," 22.
6. Holeywell, "Welcome to Walmart."
7. Lewis, "Retail Politics."
8. Dahl and Alford, *Technical Aspects of Wetlands*; Nash, *Inescapable Ecologies*.
9. Wooten and Jones, "The History of Our Drainage Enterprises."
10. McCorvie, and Lant, "Drainage District Formation and the Loss of Midwestern Wetlands," cited in Baeten, "Making Wet Places Drier."
11. Dahl and Alford, *Technical Aspects of Wetlands*, 22.
12. Valipour et al., "The Evolution of Agricultural Drainage."
13. Heimlich and Langner, Swampbusting.
14. McCally, *The Everglades*.
15. Vileisis, *Discovering the Unknown*, 207.
16. Dahl and Alford, *Technical Aspects of Wetlands*; Vileisis, *Discovering the Unknown*; Lewis, *Wetlands Explained*.
17. "Our Shrinking Bay," *Oakland Tribune*, April 23, 1961, C-1.
18. Vileisis, *Discovering the Unknown*, chapter 11.
19. For more on this, see Martin, *Wild by Design*.
20. Dix and Macgonigle, "The Everglades of Florida"; "Mr. Alligator Cleans Sewers," *The Independent* 103 (September 18, 1920): 347.
21. Carr, "Alligators." See Barrow, "Dragons in Distress."
22. An Act to Amend the Federal Water Pollution Control Act, 1972, 816.
23. Stine, "Regulating Wetlands in the 1970s."
24. Neal, "Paving the Road to Wetlands Mitigation Banking."
25. Hough and Robertson, "Mitigation under Section 404 of the Clean Water Act."

26. Race and Fonseca, "Fixing Compensatory Mitigation."
27. Environmental Working Group, "Swamped with Cash."
28. Cited in Pittman and Waite, *Paving Paradise*, 293.
29. Melinda Roth, "Of Wetlands and Wal-Marts," Riverfront Times, November 25, 1998, https://www.riverfronttimes.com/stlouis/of-wetlands-and-wal-marts/Content?oid=2481551.
30. Houck, "Hard Choices."
31. In 1980, the §404(b)(1) guidelines were adopted as final regulations. On the legal basis of mitigation, see chapter 3 of Wilkinson et al., "The Next Generation of Mitigation."
32. Tiner, *Wetlands of the United States*.
33. Dobberteen, "Scientific Analysis and Policy Evaluation of Wetland Replication in Massachusetts."
34. Mitsch and Gosselink, *Wetlands*, 680–681.
35. Zedler, "Ecological Issues in Wetland Mitigation."
36. Memorandum of Agreement between the Department of the Army and the Environmental Protection Agency.
37. Robertson, "Emerging Ecosystem Service Markets"; Wilkinson, *Status Report on Compensatory Mitigation*.
38. Hough and Robertson, "Mitigation under Section 404 of the Clean Water Act." The first commercial sale of Section 404 compensation credits occurred at the LaTerre Bank in southern Louisiana in February 1986. Robertson, "Emerging Ecosystem Service Markets"; Wilkinson, *Status Report on Compensatory Mitigation*.
39. Robertson, "The Neoliberalization of Ecosystem Services," 363.
40. Robertson, "Emerging Ecosystem Service Markets"; "Federal Guidance for the Establishment, Use, and Operation of Mitigation Banks."
41. Roberts, "Wetlands Trading Is a Loser's Game," 1890.
42. "Disney Deal Sets Healthy Precedent," *Tampa Tribune*, May 14, 1993, clipping in Folder 22, Box 160, TNCR.
43. Wilkinson, *Status Report on Compensatory Mitigation*.
44. As reported in Wilkinson et al., "The Next Generation of Mitigation."
45. King and Herbert, "The Fungibility of Wetlands." See also Ruhl and Salzman, "The Effects of Wetland Mitigation Banking on People."
46. BenDor, Brozovic, and Pallathucheril, "Assessing the Socioeconomic Impacts of Wetland Mitigation in the Chicago Region."
47. Martin FOIA request; FP-22-003169; FA-22-0040; US Army Corps of Engineers to Mr. Quebedeaux, 12/11/2014.
48. Robertson, "The Neoliberalization of Ecosystem Services"; Martin, *Wild by Design*, chapter 8.
49. Diaz, Hamilton, and Johnson, *State of the Forest Carbon Markets 2011*.
50. "Wal-Mart Grant Helps Protect over 16,000 Acres of California Forestland," Walmart corporate website, https://corporate.walmart.com/newsroom/2008/01/29/wal-mart-grant-helps-protect-over-16-000-acres-of-california-forestland; "Walmart's Acres for America Program Aims to Protect an Additional 113,500+ Acres of Wildlife

Habitat through New Grants," Globe Newswire, https://www.globenewswire.com/en/news-release/2020/12/10/2143290/32340/en/Walmart-s-Acres-for-America-Program-Aims-to-Protect-an-Additional-113-500-Acres-of-Wildlife-Habitat-Through-New-Grants.html.

51. Beth Milligan, "Development Group Proposes Major Project for Former Acme Kmart Site," The Ticker, September 21, 2019, https://www.traverseticker.com/news/development-group-proposes-major-project-for-former-acme-kmart-site/.
52. Zallen, "The Mitigation Agreement."
53. Rick Thurmond, "A Decade On, Mall's Influence Profound," Sun Chronicle (Attleboro, MA), August 7, 1999.
54. Mark Stockwell, "Emerald Square Mall in North Attleboro Placed in Receivership," Sun Chronicle (Attleboro, MA), November 13, 2020.

BIBLIOGRAPHY

An Act to Amend the Federal Water Pollution Control Act. Public Law 92-500. US Statues at Large 86 (1972).

Baeten, John. "Making Wet Places Drier: Mapping the Evolution of Drainage Technology in the U.S." 2020. https://niche-canada.org/2020/07/14/making-wet-places-drier-mapping-the-evolution-of-drainage-technology-in-the-u-s/.

Barrow, Mark V., Jr. "Dragons in Distress: Naturalists as Bioactivists in the Campaign to Save the American Alligator." *Journal of the History of Biology* 42 (2009): 267–288.

BenDor, Todd, Nicholas Brozovic, and Varkki Pallathucheril. "Assessing the Socioeconomic Impacts of Wetland Mitigation in the Chicago Region." *Journal of the American Planning Association* 73 (2007): 263–282.

Carr, Archie. "Alligators: Dragons in Distress." *National Geographic* 131 (October 1967): 133–148.

Cohen, Lizabeth. "From Town Center to Shopping Center: The Reconfiguration of Community Marketplaces in Postwar America." *American Historical Review* 101 (1996): 1050–1081.

Dahl, Thomas E., and Gregory J. Alford. *Technical Aspects of Wetlands: History of Wetlands in the Conterminous United States*. Washington, DC: US Geological Survey, 1996.

Diaz, David, Katherine Hamilton, and Evan Johnson. *State of the Forest Carbon Markets 2011: From Canopy to Currency*. Forest Trends, 2011. https://www.forest-trends.org/wp-content/uploads/imported/state-of-forest-carbon-markets_9292011_web-pdf.pdf.

Dix, Edwin Asa, and John Nowry Macgonigle. "The Everglades of Florida: A Region of Mystery." *Century Illustrated Magazine* LXIX (February 1905): 512–527.

Dobberteen, Ross A. "Scientific Analysis and Policy Evaluation of Wetland

Replication in Massachusetts." PhD dissertation, Tufts University, Medford, MA, 1989.

Environmental Working Group. "Swamped with Cash." 2022. https://www.ewg.org/research/swamped-cash.

"Federal Guidance for the Establishment, Use, and Operation of Mitigation Banks." *Federal Register* 60 (1995): 58605–58614.

Gardner, Royal C. *Lawyers, Swamps, and Money: US Wetland Law, Policy, and Politics.* Washington, DC: Island Press, 2011.

Globe Newswire. "Walmart's Acres for America Program Aims to Protect an Additional 113,500+ Acres of Wildlife Habitat through New Grants." Washington, DC. December 10, 2020. https://www.globenewswire.com/en/news-release/2020/12/10/2143290/32340/en/Walmart-s-Acres-for-America-Program-Aims-to-Protect-an-Additional-113-500-Acres-of-Wildlife-Habitat-Through-New-Grants.html.

Heimlich, Ralph E., and Linda L. Langner. *Swampbusting: Wetland Conversion and Farm Programs.* Agricultural Economic Reports 308005. Washington, DC: US Department of Agriculture, Economic Research Service.

Holeywell, Ryan. "Welcome to Walmart: Big Cities Learn to Love the Big Box." *Governing* (June 2012): 47–50.

Houck, Oliver. "Hard Choices: The Analysis of Alternatives under Section 404 of the Clean Water Act and Similar Environmental Laws." *University of Colorado Law Review* 60 (1989): 773–840.

Hough, Palmer, and Morgan Robertson. "Mitigation under Section 404 of the Clean Water Act: Where It Comes From, What It Means." *Wetlands Ecology and Management* 17 (2009): 15–33.

Jackson, Kenneth T. "All the World's a Mall: Reflections on the Social and Economic Consequences of the American Shopping Center." *American Historical Review* 101 (1996): 1111–1121.

King, Dennis M., and Luke W. Herbert. "The Fungibility of Wetlands." *National Wetlands Newsletter* 19 (1997): 10–13.

Lewis, Paul G. "Retail Politics: Local Sales Taxes and the Fiscalization of Land Use." *Economic Development Quarterly* 15 (2001): 21–35.

Lewis, William. *Wetlands Explained: Wetland Science, Policy, and Politics in America.* New York: Oxford University Press, 2001.

Martin, Laura J. *Wild by Design: The Rise of Ecological Restoration.* Cambridge, MA: Harvard University Press, 2022.

McCally, David. *The Everglades: An Environmental History.* Gainesville: University Press of Florida, 1999.

McCorvie, Mary, and Christopher Lant. "Drainage District Formation and the Loss of Midwestern Wetlands, 1850–1930." *Agricultural History* 67 (1993): 13–39.

"Memorandum of Agreement between the Department of the Army and the Environmental Protection Agency: The Determination of Mitigation under the Clean Water Act Section 404(b)(1) Guidelines." Signed February 6, 1990, Washington, DC.

Mitsch, William J., and James G. Gosselink. *Wetlands*. 3d edition. New York: John Wiley and Sons, 2000.

Nash, Linda. *Inescapable Ecologies: A History of Environment, Disease, and Knowledge*. Berkeley: University of California Press, 2007.

Neal, Jennifer. "Paving the Road to Wetlands Mitigation Banking." *Boston College Environmental Affairs Law Review* 27 (1999): 161–192.

Niering, William. *The Life of the Marsh*. New York: McGraw-Hill, 1966.

Pittman, Craig, and Matthew Waite. *Paving Paradise: Florida's Vanishing Wetlands and the Failure of No Net Loss*. Gainesville: University Press of Florida, 2009.

Press, Jared H. "Dr. StrangeBox or: How I Learned to Stop Worrying and Love Urban Big Box Retail." Master's thesis, Massachusetts Institute of Technology, Boston, 2013.

Race, Margaret, and Mark Fonseca. "Fixing Compensatory Mitigation: What Will It Take?" *Ecological Applications* 6 (1996): 94–101.

Roberts, Leslie. "Wetlands Trading Is a Loser's Game, Say Ecologists." *Science* 260 (1993): 1890–1892.

Robertson, Morgan M. "Emerging Ecosystem Service Markets: Trends in a Decade of Entrepreneurial Wetland Banking." *Frontiers in Ecology and the Environment* 4 (2005): 297–302.

Robertson, Morgan M. "The Neoliberalization of Ecosystem Services: Wetland Mitigation Banking and Problems in Environmental Governance." *Geoforum* 35 (2004): 361–373.

Ruhl, J. B., and James Salzman. "The Effects of Wetland Mitigation Banking on People." *National Wetlands Newsletter* 28 (2006): 9–14.

Stine, Jeffrey K. "Regulating Wetlands in the 1970s: U.S. Army Corps of Engineers and the Environmental Organizations." *Journal of Forest History* 27 (1983): 60–75.

Teal, John, and Mildred Teal. *Life and Death of the Salt Marsh*. New York: Little, Brown, 1969.

Tiner, Ralph. *Wetlands of the United States: Current Status and Recent Trends*. Washington, DC: US Fish and Wildlife Service, 1984.

US Army Corps of Engineers and State of Louisiana Department of Environmental Quality. Joint Public Notice, "Commercial Development in Lafayette Parish." February 24, 2014.

US Army Corps of Engineers Regulatory In-lieu Fee and Bank Information Tracking System. N.d. https://ribits.ops.usace.army.mil/.

Valipour, Mohammad, Jens Krasilnikof, Stavros Yannopoulos, Rohitashw Kumar, Jun Deng, Paolo Roccaro, Larry Mays, Mark E. Grismer, and Andreas N. Angelakis. "The Evolution of Agricultural Drainage from the Earliest Times to the Present." *Sustainability* 12 (2020). https://doi.org/10.3390/su12010416.

Vileisis, Ann. *Discovering the Unknown: A History of America's Wetlands*. Washington, DC: Island Press, 1999.

Walmart. "Wal-Mart Grant Helps Protect over 16,000 Acres of California Forestland." Roseville, CA. December 12, 2007. https://corporate.walmart.com/newsroom/2008/01/29/wal-mart-grant-helps-protect-over-16-000-acres-of-california-forestland.

Wilkinson, Jessica B., James M. McElfish Jr., Rebecca Kihslinger, Robert Bendick, and Bruce A. McKenney. "The Next Generation of Mitigation: Linking Current Plans and Future Mitigation Programs with State Wildlife Action Plans and Other State and Regional Plans." White Paper, Environmental Law Institute and the Nature Conservancy, 2008. https://www.eli.org/sites/default/files/eli-pubs/d19_08.pdf.

Wilkinson, Thompson J. 2005. *Status Report on Compensatory Mitigation in the United States*. Washington, DC: Environmental Law Institute, 2006.

Wooten, Hugh, and Lewis Jones. "The History of Our Drainage Enterprises." *Yearbook of Agriculture* 1955: 478–480.

Zallen, Margot. "The Mitigation Agreement—a Major Development in Wetland Regulation." *Natural Resources and Environment* 7 (1992): 19–21.

Zedler, Joy B. "Ecological Issues in Wetland Mitigation: An Introduction to the Forum." *Ecological Applications* 6 (1996): 33–37.

Section III

Attention Shoppers

CREATING CONSUMER MIND-SETS

5

BOXING IN THE OUTDOORS

Cabela's, REI, and the Growth of Specialty Retailers

RACHEL S. GROSS

In 2017, American retail giant Walmart acquired a niche outdoor industry brand called Moosejaw. While this acquisition made waves within the outdoor industry, where Moosejaw was known as both an online retailer and a limited brick-and-mortar presence, the impact was otherwise slight.[1] The following year, Walmart opened a "curated by Moosejaw" online store with brands more common at upscale specialty stores including Deuter, a German pack company, and Black Diamond Equipment, a Utah-based climbing equipment manufacturing company.[2] Essentially, the new store within a store was meant to introduce Walmart customers to premium outdoor brands.

The outdoor industry's response was immediate and angry.[3] Within a few days, Deuter, LEKI, Therm-a-Rest, and other outdoor brands pulled out of the Moosejaw agreement. Black Diamond sent a cease and desist order to Walmart, claiming the retail giant was not authorized to use its brand.[4] The pushback from brands that had previously sold on the Moosejaw website often critiqued the quality of the goods associated with Walmart. "When's the last time you bought something nice from Walmart?" asked Wes Allen, the owner of a specialty outdoor store in Cody, Wyoming.[5] Rich Hill, president of the Grassroots Outdoor Alliance, added that because of the lack of expertise on the part of both customers and sellers, "a store like Amazon or Walmart is going to get someone killed."[6] The Moosejaw CEO responded forcefully to these criticisms. He suggested that the new Walmart.com site had the potential to be more inclusive and to reach younger, female, and non-white markets.[7]

The dramatic reaction was decades in the making. Walmart was hardly the first big box store to touch the outdoor industry. Indeed, the biggest players for more than two decades preceding the Moosejaw fallout were all big box stores. And yet, the special ire this iteration drew is instructive because it reveals how the big box model had long existed in creative, uncomfortable tension with the outdoor industry. Moosejaw was a well-respected company, but for many in the outdoor industry, Walmart represented a threat to small, independent retailers and to the brand identity outdoor companies had so carefully cultivated over decades. At the core of this concern was the threat big box stores posed to specialty retail, both economically and culturally. Walmart, as the largest and best-known big box store, was a direct threat and represented a broader shift in the outdoor industry. The outdoor industry's negative reaction to the Moosejaw Walmart collaboration was that Walmart was an outsider in the outdoor space.[8]

The outdoor press in the twenty-first century likes to hark back to a golden age of the industry, when independent mountain shops outfitted a generation of outdoorsmen. Reporter Daniel Duane's 2017 telling in *Outside* magazine was a common one: "Before Amazon and big-box stores eviscerated brick and mortar retail," there were small mountain shops all over the American West.[9] For manufacturers, the narrative was similar: either you were specialized and sold to small shops, or you weren't and you sold to the big boxes.[10] The trajectory of some of the largest outdoor retailers of recent years highlights this narrative. Both Cabela's, a hunting and fishing store founded in Nebraska in 1961, and Recreational Equipment, Incorporated (REI), founded in Seattle as a cooperative in 1938, began as small family-run shops but became behemoths of the industry by the end of the twentieth century—as much a threat to Duane's small mountain shops as any Walmart. These stores were marked by their large size and inventory—they often manufactured house-brand products, and they could undercut the prices of smaller stores.

Forgotten in this narrative of the spectacular growth of REI, Cabela's, and similar outdoor companies since the 1970s is that Walmart *was* the outdoor industry. More people bought camping goods at stores such as Walmart, Sears, Kmart, and Target than anywhere else. This matters because in the narratives about the demise of specialized retail, there is rarely a longer view of history that includes discount stores as central players in the equipment market since the middle of the twentieth century. Walmart and its large-format discount store competitors matter to the outdoor industry's history in two ways. First, despite being disregarded by the outdoor press, they were a part of the outdoor industry. Second, Walmart and other big box retailers influenced the outdoor industry's structure. A process I call Walmartization explains how the outdoor industry at the end of the twentieth century grew its reach and its market and the way it sold to mimic discount large-scale retailers even as industry insiders shunned the comparison. National chains such as Bass Pro Shops, Cabela's, Eastern Mountain Sports, and REI all began to fit into the big box model starting in the 1990s.[11] Despite the importance of folksy origin stories to contemporary outdoor retailers, there is one story of economic progress the industry prefers even more: the outdoors represents nearly 2 percent of gross domestic product (GDP), which is only possible because of large-scale retail.[12] Essentially, the outdoor industry today is a product of the Walmartization of the economy, the very reflection of what the industry claims to despise.

This chapter traces the growth of the outdoor industry since the early twentieth century. It highlights two issues: first, the relationships of big box stores to small specialty shops, and second, the relationships of specialty big box stores to general discount retailers. In the first half of the century, we see the origins of large-format specialty stores, though far from the contemporary association with big box stores. In the post–World War II era, there have been two important phenomena in the outdoor world. First, the biggest purveyors of outdoor goods were mass merchandisers. Second, by the 1970s, the specialty outdoor industry was booming. The 1980s saw the rise of the big box format for discount stores and the 1990s for outdoor retailers. By the early 2000s, many outdoor chains were clearly big boxes in Walmart's vein, but they rejected the term for cultural reasons and strove to create an experience distinct from Walmart. In each era, the core of debate in the outdoor industry was who the outdoors is for. Affordable, mainstream, family, and beginner meant big box stores. Premium, athlete, adventure, expert, and expensive meant specialty shops. This terminology reflects the same debate that came to the fore with the Walmart Moosejaw announcement. To understand the deep ambivalence about the big box label in the outdoor specialty retail world, we have to look at the long history of the industry debating just who the outdoors is for.[13]

BIG BUSINESS AND THE OUTDOOR INDUSTRY, 1920S–1970S

Bass Pro, Cabela's, and REI were not the innovators of the big box experience of the outdoors. Indeed, to understand what makes the specialty retail big box distinctive, we must go back to the early twentieth century, when a twelve-story building at Madison Avenue and Forty-fifth Street in New York City boasted the company name of Abercrombie and Fitch (A&F) in large lettering. If they had read a catalog prior to visiting, shoppers would know that this mecca was the self-proclaimed "greatest sporting goods store in the world."[14] Abercrombie and Fitch was neither as large nor as grand as famous department stores such as Macy's and Marshall Field's.[15] Nonetheless, A&F drew on similar strategies as those embraced by its more famous counterparts to entice a mostly male customer base into the store to make a purchase.[16] With ornate window decorations and in-store displays of merchandise, A&F developed a new visual language for selling nature to the American public.[17]

The A&F retail sales department boxed in the outdoors with a range of strategies. As store images that survive from an early catalog show, under the large set of windows at the back of the sales floor stood a fully erected tent, at least seven feet by ten feet. In one image, two young men sit in two camp chairs under the tent, perhaps waiting for their father to finish the purchase of a pair of skis that lean against the framed tent. Nearby, a camp hammock and cozy fur blanket beckon.

The scene the company set mattered as much as the goods themselves for turning customers into consumers who maintained allegiance to the A&F brand.[18]

With game adorning the walls, a miniature pond on the roof, fully erected tents on the shop floor, and log cabin paint colors, the store created a spectacle that announced that nature itself was for sale. In this building, catalog copywriters would have Americans imagine, the "blazed trail crosses the boulevard." The outdoor store brought the experience of the blazed trail—and its sense of human conquest of wild lands—to the boulevard, which might have otherwise seemed disconnected from nature. As an advertisement in *Country Life in America* in 1920 explained, "There is one spot in the metropolis which always remains green in your memory, even when you're out among the fields and the links and the lakes." A&F copywriters framed the store itself as a green respite from city life.[19]

A&F in Manhattan was one of the first mega-outdoor stores, but despite its shape, it was not a "big box" in the late twentieth-century notion of the term. A&F's shopping experience was closer to that of a department store than a big box store, for a few reasons. One was the interaction with shopkeepers and the role of service in shaping how people bought. Another was the fact that it was not a discount store. Indeed, A&F served an elite clientele. With only a few outposts, A&F was not a national chain. Nonetheless, A&F's model of creating a nature experience in the store would shape future iterations of outdoor retail as the industry expanded in the decades that followed.

ADDRESSING THE PARADOX OF AN OUTDOOR INDUSTRY

As the outdoor industry and outdoor market grew in the 1970s—from the elite A&F to surplus or veteran-run shops such as the Co-op, Holubar, and Kelty to brands such as Sierra Designs, Patagonia, and the North Face—the biggest paradox for both sellers and buyers was addressing the size of the industry, its structure, and its impact on the environment. Using metaphors of department stores and supermarkets, executives confronted the changes to retail space and concluded that the size was worth it, given the impact.[20]

Outdoor recreation had been becoming more popular since World War II, but its appeal grew exponentially in the late 1960s. By the 1970s, the popularity of hiking "exploded like an overheated camp stove."[21] Guidebook authors attested to packed trails and commented that it seemed like the "entire nation began carrying rucksacks."[22] Government studies supported these observations. In 1962, 9 million Americans went camping. Only ten years later, that number had increased to 40 million.[23] Retail sales of new gear such as internal frame packs and domed tents increased in tandem, with Americans spending $3 billion on outdoor equipment and recreational trips in 1972.[24]

Was this the golden age of the outdoors or the beginning of the end? Many industry retrospectives celebrated the democratic access to the outdoors the 1970s boom in activity and entrepreneurship brought.[25] The evolution of a Seattle-based outdoor company reveals some of the larger, fundamental issues at stake in the growth of the outdoor industry in the 1970s that would ultimately shape its relationship to the big box concept. The Co-op, later known as REI, began in 1938 when a group of climbers imported Austrian ice axes for themselves and their friends. After World War II, the Co-op sold military surplus goods before shifting to goods manufactured in-house. The business evolved from a side project of founders Lloyd and Mary Anderson to a full-time job requiring new floor space and a larger roster of employees. Membership in the cooperative grew from the twelve founding members to more than a quarter million in 1972, with sales nearing $12 million that year.[26]

This growth felt like a mixed blessing to some consumers and industry professionals. They saw the expansion of REI as promoting a more anonymous shopping experience, with fewer experts helping customers in the stores. They also worried about selling everyday products to casual outdoorspeople who might misuse the goods or, worse, mistreat beloved wild landscapes. Defenders of REI's growth took a different tack. As the general manager at the time, Jim Whittaker, explained, a "supermarket of the outdoors" approach was well worth it if it meant getting more people into the woods.[27] While Whittaker didn't define precisely what he meant by supermarket, the shift toward a broad membership with less expertise and stores in more cities was part of the evolution of REI under his leadership. REI was one of many outdoor companies that grew rapidly in this era, but its shift in thinking epitomizes industry changes generally. REI was only one example of the supermarket approach, as many companies tried to present themselves as separate from it. For better or, as many would eventually argue, for worse, the supermarket era fundamentally changed outdoor recreation in the United States.

THE BIG TENT OF DISCOUNT RETAILERS

A growing outdoor industry alone does not necessarily signal Walmartization, of course. But the biggest reason the outdoor industry drew on Walmart's example in the second half of the twentieth century was that Walmart and its counterparts *were* the outdoor industry. Coleman and Sears, Roebuck were the biggest players in camping equipment in the 1960s, as the outdoor industry boom was beginning.[28] Throughout the 1980s, despite the tremendous growth of retailers such as REI, the biggest purveyors of outdoor products were mass merchandisers such as Kmart, Target, Montgomery Ward, and Sears, Roebuck.[29] By the 1990s, according to the National Sporting Goods Association, a majority of Americans bought their camping equipment at Walmart.[30] Kmart and Walmart had combined sales of outdoor equipment of around $1 billion in 1994.[31]

The dominance of mass merchandisers matters because discussions of just *who* was buying equipment at big box stores compared with specialty retailers reflected a core debate within the outdoor world. Mass consumerism, industry insiders presumed, undermined the outdoor industry in two ways. First, they argued, the Walmarts of the world were a threat to the small, regional outdoor shops that struggled to survive the competition. "Never sell to the big guys" seemed to be the baseline assumption of specialty gear manufacturers, even as their equipment appeared on the shelves at Target or Costco.[32] Second, disdain for Walmart and Target as purveyors of outdoor goods reflected disdain for non-elite consumers themselves. Any consumer who bought from Costco would be fine with second-tier goods from last season and probably wasn't engaging in any *real* outdoor activity anyway.

The spread of outdoor clothing as fashionable attire supported the retail transition away from smaller-format, specialized, high-performance equipment stores. The more clothing outsold equipment, the less it mattered what kind of equipment retailers stocked and the more likely it became that consumers would find what they wanted at Walmart or Dick's Sporting Goods rather than at a specialty store. Fleece, also known by the brand name Polartec, is a good example of this trend.[33] In the 1990s, fuzzy polyester vests that had been a mainstay of outdoor product lines spread far beyond the packing lists of mountain climbers. Malden Mills, the producer of Polartec, expected to sell $500 million in fleece and similar fabrics in 1995. Of that amount, 80 percent, estimated one product manager, was for the mass of consumers who embraced the trekking archetypes in advertisements but were unlikely to go trekking themselves.[34] Mainstream consumers' use of fleece paralleled their shopping habits. How special could a specialty store be if fleece was available at Kmart, Costco, and Old Navy?[35]

Other industry reports suggested that any outdoor equipment for sale at a discount store was out of date. One gossipy report from 1993 suggested that the North Face (TNF) line on sale through a onetime deal with Costco was a "melange of . . . old pack designs, old tent designs," and Polarguard sleeping bags. The implication in this insider news report was that TNF was sending its older, back-of-the-shelf items to Costco while keeping newer, top-of-the-line products for other retailers. The official word from Costco, though, was that TNF gear was "the upper end of the spectrum" targeting its climbing and skier customers.[36] Other reports affirmed that big boxes sold "closeouts" even two or three years old.[37] The undertone of these reports was clear: old equipment was inferior, and shoppers who couldn't recognize that probably were too.

Big box retailers didn't just sell the equipment; they also owned the brands that sold the most: Hilary (Sears), Ozark Trail (Walmart), American Camper and Greatland (Target). In 1997, Coleman and American Camper surpassed both Kelty and TNF.[38] Despite the difference in product offerings, this was a problem for the outdoor industry. A 1979 issue of the *National Outdoor Outfitters News* "warn[ed]" of discount store activity selling sportswear in 1979, suggesting that it was a threat.[39] Frank Hugelmeyer, president of the Outdoor Recreation Coalition of America, asserted that deeply discounted goods at big box stores undercut specialty retailers.[40] Debates over where people ought to shop also reflected ideas about outdoor expertise and the economy. The industry consensus was that big boxes were for beginners. Consumers could save at big box stores buying Ozark Trail or Greatland products, but for "key items" where features mattered, they should opt for "proven" equipment.[41] Another widely held belief was that shoppers were likely to go to big boxes for apparel but to specialty stores for hard goods.[42]

Big boxes participated in the outdoor industry not just with a single aisle dedicated to camping but rather with a concerted effort, complete with multi-channel advertising and product tie-ins. One example is the traveling truck exhibit Target created as part of its sponsorship of an international expedition. In 1989, Target Stores, a division of Dayton-Hudson Corporation, had 392 discount chain stores around the country, with plans to expand to 400 by January 1990. That same year, Target signed on to a sponsorship deal to promote a global outdoor adventure, once again highlighting the close ties between big box stores and the outdoor industry and how they took their cues from one another. Adventurer and activist Will Steger and his counterpart in France, Jean-Louis Etienne, led a small team on a long-planned ski traverse of Antarctica in 1989–1990. Called the Trans-Antarctica Expedition, the team cultivated international press coverage and multi-million dollar-sponsorships in an effort to draw attention to an expiring international treaty, in addition to the fact that the team members sought that kind of adventure. To the outdoor world, this was an important event for equipment and clothing designers. For W. L. Gore and Associates (the manufacturers of the waterproof breathable laminate Gore-Tex) and DuPont's fiberfill division (which manufactured synthetic down filling), the expedition was a chance both to test equipment and to push design and marketing further.[43] Drawing its patterns from the outdoor industry, which had been a dedicated sponsor of extreme adventures at the poles and on high peaks for decades, Target signed up alongside these larger sponsors in an effort to draw American consumers to its stores to buy spin-off products.[44]

While the other sponsors negotiated logos on jackets and toured schools with sled dogs, Target was at work planning a different kind of boxing in of the outdoors. The company created a traveling exhibit inside a large moving truck, decorated on the outside with snow-covered mountains and a map of the team's 4,000-mile journey across the continent. On the inside, more maps, photographs, and a 3-D camp scene—complete with mannequins of the expedition leaders in "authentic expedition clothing"—awaited visitors. The truck made stops around the country throughout the summer and fall of 1989. Drivers took the truck from Minnesota to Texas to California and back, pausing for a few days at different Target locations. Along with the exhibit itself, the stores developed a curriculum guide about the expedition—including lesson plans—to be distributed to schools "in all Target markets."[45] Most telling was the list of the clothing and equipment Target expected to sell as part of this promotion. The list of products included more than 100 items under the Greatland/Will Steger label, named after the co-leader and person responsible for many of the sponsorship deals. The products included camping equipment, skis, polar fleece clothing, and boots of all kinds. Beyond the outdoors, Greatland products included office supplies, school lunch boxes, bed sheets, and stuffed animals.[46]

TV commercials that ran during the expedition underlined Target as a purveyor of outdoor goods. The "Steger-inspired" Greatland gear included parkas, sleeping bags, and flashlights because, as the narrator of the commercial explained, "Will Steger won't be the only one braving the elements this winter." As of September 1989, over 10,000 people had visited the truck as it toured the western and central US.[47] John Pellegrene, senior vice president of marketing for Target, explained, "we believe that our customers, drawn by the excitement of the expedition, will respond with enthusiasm to the many lines of merchandise that Trans-Antarctica has inspired at Target."[48] For its part, the outdoor industry shunned the big box association even as it began to draw on similar strategies of product tie-ins and multi-channel advertising.

By the turn of the millennium, the line between specialty retail and big box was less clear than ever. "It used to be simple," one reporter wrote. "You were a specialty brand, or you weren't. You advertised in *Backpacker* and *Outside* and ran clinics at the small stores that were loyal to your product, or you wore a suit and sold to the big boxes."[49]

Despite purists' admonitions to avoid discount retailers, a Kelty external frame pack was spotted for sale at Costco in 1993.[50] Ultimately, even as the broad tent of outdoor goods distribution led to Walmart, Target, and Costco, the outdoor industry maintained a deep suspicion of the big box model. When the trends that Walmart and its competitors shaped began to influence the outdoor world as well, outdoor executives sought to develop ways to create their own distinctive, less threatening version of the big box store.

THE RISE OF THE BIG BOX FORMAT IN THE OUTDOOR INDUSTRY

With the wide popularity of outdoor clothing and sportswear more broadly across regions and demographics, outdoor wear continued to spread. In the 1990s, catalog giants Eddie Bauer and L. L. Bean remained close to the top of sales lists for sporting goods retailers, beating out more traditional sporting goods stores (meaning they also sold baseball mitts and football cleats) such as the Sports Authority, Champs Sports, and Sportmart. For the first time, in 1994 Eddie Bauer sales surpassed L. L. Bean's, at $850 million to Bean's $775 million. The success of these brands as mall outposts and catalog distributors, respectively, allowed for national reach in a way smaller, regionally based outdoor companies such as REI ($400 million in sales) and Bass Pro Shops ($200 million) could not match.[51] Nonetheless, the regional hunting and fishing companies Bass Pro Shops and Cabela's began to make inroads, mainly by building something the likes of which American consumers hadn't seen since the closure of Abercrombie and Fitch in 1976: an outdoor superstore and tourist magnet (figure 5.1).

Outdoor retailers began building bigger boxes for their stores in the 1980s, and by the 1990s a full-fledged big box model arrived. No company better exemplified the new format than Cabela's, a Nebraska-based outdoor retailer that got its start as a direct-mail catalog business. Cabela's mimicked the Walmart model of large-store footprints sited in small towns or along transit corridors. Cabela's sold a culture and an ethos, much as Walmart did. But the outdoor retailer differed in one important way: whereas Walmart was spare, even austere, inside, Cabela's created a nature experience indoors.

FIGURE 5.1. Displays of political T-shirts and other pieces of merchandise unrelated to the outdoors in this Cabela's reflect a shift among large outdoor retailers away from a specialized market to a broader, "lifestyle"-centered one. *Courtesy*, Keira Richards.

Cabela's was a small company in the 1980s, selling regionally when Eddie Bauer and L. L. Bean were becoming national models for how to run an outdoor company retailer through catalogs or mall shops. Founders Dick and Jim Cabela opened the first retail store in the company headquarters of Sidney, Nebraska, which boasted a population of 6,000 in 1991. Their vision was to make a kind of showcase for the catalog, to put on display fun items that would bring people in. They had visited Freeport, Maine, and, as many had done before them, thought they could become a kind of L. L. Bean of Nebraska. For them, that meant making their small town of Sidney a tourist destination and making shopping at their store an "experience."[52]

Cabela's stores operated with the ethos of bringing the outdoors indoors. Rather than skimping on costs and opting for bare walls or harshly lit fluorescent lighting in wide aisles, the Cabela brothers invested in the Sidney store. The outdoors store looked like a midcentury Abercrombie and Fitch on steroids, for a television age: stuffed deer, yes, but also stuffed polar bears, waterfalls, and a stream with trout.[53] Disneyland would have been a closer comparison. Their efforts paid off as their store drew traffic to Sidney. The year it opened, the store attracted 1.2 million visitors.[54]

A central component of Cabela's growth was clear statements about America's outdoor past, though the conservative politics of the company founders, the location, and demographic differences between hunters and climbers meant that Cabela's heritage was decidedly different from that of other outdoor companies. The history presented in Cabela's Nebraska store shows a mishmash of eras that complemented the notion of heritage it strove to create. The mannequins near the entrance, for instance, donned attire and equipment that appeared to be dated to the mid-twentieth century, at least a decade before Cabela's existed. The mid-twentieth-century objects served to remind visitors of the cutting-edge products currently on sale and how these technologies built on past ones. Black-and-white photographs of hunters and antique game bags highlighted a bygone pre-Cabela's entirely. The photographs linked the store to a nineteenth-century white past, with the colonial era presented as hardscrabble pioneers, and suggested that those actors' values had passed on.[55] Of course, Cabela's "heritage" did not simply appear in photos. It had been built by sports authors in the nineteenth century and expanded by popular press and media in the twentieth century to teach Americans about the sportsman as exemplifying three strands: conservationist, naturalist, and rugged frontiersman.[56] Cabela's in-store display augmented that larger mythology, helping to create and teach a heritage in which, historically speaking, Cabela's did not exist.

The experience of two ordinary Cabela's consumers illustrates what it was like to walk into the big box store. In 2002, when two ranchers and friends, Darrell Roush and Gene Markin, drove 350 miles from Gillette, Wyoming, to Sidney, Nebraska, the idea of selling an outdoor lifestyle as opposed to outdoor products was firmly ingrained in Cabela's corporate strategy. Although they called themselves "lifelong haters" of shopping, they were headed to Cabela's outdoor store to browse, to gawk, and to buy. Rousch's purchases were emblematic of the outdoor lifestyle: he bought a new gun case for himself and candles, candies, and a mirror for his girlfriend. Rousch and Markin were typical visitors to the Sidney store, which boasted a museum-like wildlife display and giant aquariums. They came as both consumers and tourists, along with busloads of schoolchildren and entire families on vacation in search of the outdoor lifestyle.[57]

In the wake of Cabela's success, other outdoor retailers began to build bigger boxes over the course of the 1990s. Some, like the New Hampshire–based Eastern Mountain Sports, explicitly took cues from discount retailers Sears and Kmart in how to run these larger-format stores.[58] Others, like Bass Pro Shops, focused more on how to create an outdoor destination indoors, a clear means of differentiating the outdoor big box from the general merchandise market (as Sherri Sheu details in chapter 6 of this volume). Overall, the largest outdoor companies began to reposition both their product lines and their marketing toward more casual and less sport-specific "lifestyle" attire. The very critique they had directed at Walmart—selling non-specialized goods to the non-expert—could be applied just as easily to these new stores.

RESHAPING THE BOX

In the early 2000s, many category-killing big box stores were failing, including Circuit City, Borders, and Linens 'n Things. Outdoor retailers, for the most part, evaded these bankruptcies because of the ways they differed from traditional big box discount stores. Outdoor stores were creating experiences that could not be repeated online. The displays, classes, events, and service projects were the model of success in boosting store traffic and brand appeal.[59] Consumers saw big boxes such as REI and Cabela's as significant destinations for those seeking outdoor expertise and quality merchandise.[60]

An REI mega-store in Denver, Colorado, illustrates how the shape of the box continued to evolve in the outdoor industry in the twenty-first century (figure 5.2). The REI flagship store is a 90,000-foot conversion of a powerhouse (and former museum) adjacent to downtown, built as a public-private partnership with millions of dollars in subsidies and intended to be a tourist destination as well as a retail center. The Denver REI is an example of an ornate, beautiful box in concert with the

FIGURE 5.2. The REI flagship store in Denver, Colorado, leans into the aesthetic of the repurposed historic building in which it is located, pushing back against perceptions of large retailers as purveyors of low-quality goods in big, bland warehouses. *Courtesy*, Keira Richards.

landscape. It reflects how REI responded to claims that it was too big, too much of a category killer. The Denver REI reflects a corporate pushback against the process of Walmartization while still embracing its scale and size.

The REI plan to purchase the Forney Transportation Museum adjacent to the South Platte River and Cherry Creek confluence in downtown Denver began in the late 1990s. It was part of a larger trend of big box outdoor retailers opening stores in the Denver metro area. Bass Pro's 186,000-square-foot retail store near I-70 in Denver's Stapleton area opened in 2005.[61] Gander Mountain opened a 91,000-square-foot store in Aurora. Cabela's had a plan in 2005 for a store three times the size of a Walmart that was billed as half-retailer, half-museum.[62] REI's initial plans called for creating a 70,000-square-foot retail space in the location where the museum had been. The Denver Urban Renewal Authority approved $5 million in tax breaks for the project.[63] The Denver effort paralleled a slightly earlier model of an REI flagship store in

Seattle, which became a kind of entertaining, educational superstore and a "leading tourist attraction" after it was built in 1996.⁶⁴

Skepticism about how big box stores fit into outdoor culture continued even as some in the industry insisted that the relationship between big box chain stores and specialty shops was a "happy marriage."⁶⁵ One Colorado customer, Brian Bordelon, said that with "some of the big box stores"—perhaps the very ones that had recently arrived in Colorado—"I feel like I'm shopping at Kmart. I'm looking for the highest quality and expertise and I'm willing to spend more for that."⁶⁶ Bordelon's preferred specialty shop in Englewood, Colorado—Mountain Miser—closed in 2006, just as all the big box outdoor stores were arriving in the metro area.⁶⁷

Different models of specialty big boxes persist, as does the suspicion of Walmart as both a cultural influence and a touchstone for how to build retail spaces. Business reporters have been predicting the end of big box stores for decades.⁶⁸ The reasons they offer vary and include warmer winters, competition from online retailers, and continued buyouts, bankruptcies, and closures. The latter include Cabela's being bought out by Bass Pro and Gander Mountain declaring bankruptcy. But American consumers' flexible schedules and mobility during the pandemic led to a thriving outdoor industry, suggesting that the predictions of demise are premature. The line between Walmart and Walmartized outdoor stores continues to shrink as small retailers go out of business and big ones become larger. The growth of outdoor specialty stores helps us trace not only the shifting geography of shopping but also the capacity corporations have to shape consumer mind-sets.

NOTES

1. "Walmart Announces the Acquisition of Moosejaw, a Leading Online Outdoor Retailer," Walmart, 2017, https://corporate.walmart.com/newsroom/2017/02/15/walmart-announces-the-acquisition-of-moosejaw-a-leading-online-outdoor-retailer.
2. Amelia Arvesen, "Moosejaw Is Curating a Premium Outdoor Store for Walmart.com," *Outside Business Journal*, August 27, 2018, https://www.outsidebusinessjournal.com/retailers/online-retailers/moosejaw-curates-outdoor-premium-store-for-walmart-online/.

3. Amelia Arvesen, "Why Brands Quickly Changed Their Minds about Selling on Walmart.com," *Outside Business Journal*, September 8, 2018, https://www.outsideonline.com/business-journal/brands/why-brands-changed-their-minds-about-selling-through-walmart/.
4. Amelia Arvesen, "Black Diamond Sends Cease and Desist Notice to Walmart," *Outside Business Journal*, August 28, 2018, https://www.outsidebusinessjournal.com/brands/black-diamond-equipment-sends-cease-and-desist-to-walmart/.
5. Arvesen, "Why Brands Quickly Changed Their Minds."
6. Tracy Ross, "The End of Elite," *Outside Business Journal*, January 30, 2019, https://www.outsideonline.com/business-journal/brands/the-end-of-elite-walmart-moosejaw/.
7. Eoin Comerford, "Walmart Outdoor Manager Pens Open Letter to Outdoor Industry," *Gear Junkie*, September 7, 2018, https://gearjunkie.com/news/walmart-moosejaw-eoin-comerford-open-letter-outdoor-industry.
8. Ross, "End of Elite."
9. Daniel Duane, "The Greatest Mountain Shop in America," *Outside Online*, November 21, 2017, https://www.outsideonline.com/outdoor-adventure/climbing/retail-experience/.
10. Leigh Gallagher, "Natural Selection," *Sporting Goods Business*, January 6, 1998.
11. For a broader history of big box stores, see Howard, *From Main Street to Mall:*; Hyman, *Borrow*; Lichtenstein, *Retail Revolution*; Lichtenstein, "Wal-Mart: A Template for Twenty-First-Century Capitalism"; Moreton, *To Serve God and Wal-Mart*; Stobart and Howard, *Routledge Companion to the History of Retailing*.
12. Outdoor Recreation Satellite Account, Bureau of Economic Analysis, 2021, https://www.bea.gov/data/special-topics/outdoor-recreation.
13. Ross, "End of Elite." On big box backlash, see Newman and Kane, "Backlash against the 'Big Box.'"
14. *Abercrombie and Fitch* catalog, 1922, Trade Catalog Collection, National Museum of American History Library, Washington, DC.
15. Leach, *Land of Desire*, 9, 20.
16. Leach, *Land of Desire*, 9.
17. Store descriptions drawn from *Abercrombie and Fitch* catalog, 1922.
18. On the transformation of customers into consumers, see Strasser, *Satisfaction Guaranteed*, 17.
19. *Country Life in America*, May 1920, 139, Winterthur Library, Wilmington, DE.
20. On the outdoor industry in the 1970s, see Alagona and Simon, "Contradictions at the Confluence of Commerce, Consumption, and Conservation"; Simon and Alagona, "Beyond Leave No Trace"; Young, *Camping Grounds*; Young, *Heading Out*.
21. Rob Carson, "The R.E.I. Card: Quintessential Northwest," *Pacific Northwest*, March 1987.
22. Manning, *REI*; Abel, *Backpacking Made Easy*.
23. B. Drummon Ayres, "Today's Campers Bring the Comforts of Home to the Out-of-Doors," *New York Times*, August 13, 1972.
24. Joan Cook, "Jerseyans Taking to Camping in Increasing Numbers," *New York Times*, August 3, 1972.

25. "Outdoor Pioneers, 1900–1970," *Outdoor Retailer*, 1992, Boulder Public Library, Boulder, CO.
26. On the expansion of store space, see Klindt Vielbig to Harvey Manning, March 9, 1987, Harvey Manning Papers, Acc. 2097-003, Box 19, University of Washington Special Collections, Seattle. For memebership, see "The Co-op Story," REI catalog 1968, University of Washington Special Collections, Seattle. For sales, see "Record of Sales—Total Sales," Box 1, Recreational Equipment, Inc., Acc. #3129-2, and "Recreational Equipment, Inc.—Net Income and Income Tax Projection for Year Ending 12/31/72," Box 1, Recreational Equipment, Inc., Acc. #3129-2, University of Washington Special Collections, Seattle.
27. Cited in Timothy Egan, "REI: Three Initials That Changed Life in the Northwest," *Pacific, Seattle Times/Seattle Post-Intelligencer*, March 6, 1988, 4, Harvey Manning Papers 2097, Box 20, UWSC.
28. Edward Kulkosky, "Camping in Woods: Comforts Increase and So Do the Profits," *New York Times*, June 18, 1967.
29. Eric Schmitt, "Surge in US Sales of Outdoor Goods," *New York Times*, July 21, 1986.
30. Kristin Hostetter, "Attention Shoppers," *Backpacker* (August 1999): 44.
31. John Merwin, Ken Schultz, Bob Saile, Bob Gwizdz, Ted Leeson, and William G. Tapply, "The Sportsman's Dollar," *Field and Stream [West ed.]* (May 1994): 41+.
32. SNEWS 10, no. 6, July 1993, Periodicals, Outdoor Recreation Archive, Utah State University Special Collections and Archives, Logan.
33. Robin Wood, "Outdoor Gear Retailers Face Tough Climb," *Capital District Business Review*, October 2, 2000.
34. Hal Espen, "Fleeced," *New York Times Magazine*, February 15, 1998.
35. Leigh Gallagher, "Natural Selection," *Sporting Goods Business*, January 6, 1998.
36. SNEWS 10, no. 6, July 1993.
37. Wood, "Outdoor Gear Retailers Face Tough Climb."
38. Kristin Carpenter, "Family Ties," *Sporting Goods Business*, November 6, 1998.
39. "NOON Warns Outfitters," *National Outdoor Outfitters News* 4 (April–May 1979), Outdoor Recreation Archive, Utah State University Special Collections and Archives, Logan.
40. Cited in Wood, "Outdoor Gear Retailers Face Tough Climb."
41. Hostetter, "Attention Shoppers"; Billy Brown, "Save on Gear at Big Box Stores," *Backpacker*, March 6, 2016, https://www.backpacker.com/gear-reviews/save-on-gear-at-big-box-stores/.
42. Bryan Chitwood, "Rough Outing," *Sporting Goods Business*, January 1996.
43. "Trans-Antarctica Traveling Exhibit Kicks off US Tour," press release, July 31, 1989, 14418 Polar Expedition Promotional Materials Target Stores 1, Box 4, International Polar Expedition, Minnesota Historical Society, St. Paul.
44. For more on the history of commercial sponsorship of expeditions, including the Trans-Antarctica Expedition, see Gross, "Logos on Everest."
45. "Target Plays Leadership Role in Educating Nation . . . ," press release, n.d., 14418 Polar Expedition Promotional Materials Target Stores 1, Box 4, International Polar Expedition, Minnesota Historical Society, St. Paul.
46. "Target Plays Leadership Role in Educating Nation."

47. "Attendance Log for Trans-Antarctica Traveling Exhibit, September 12, 1989," 14418 Polar Expedition Promotional Materials Target Stores 1, Box 4, International Polar Expedition, Minnesota Historical Society, St. Paul.
48. Fax, Chuck Swenson to Cathy de Moll, March 24, 1989, 14418 Polar Expedition Promotional Materials Target Stores 1, Box 4, International Polar Expedition, Minnesota Historical Society, St. Paul.
49. Gallagher, "Natural Selection."
50. SNEWS 10, no. 6, July 1993.
51. "SGB Retail Registry '94," *Sporting Goods Business*.
52. On the origin story of Cabela's, see Amy Merrick, "How Dick Cabela Sold the Great Outdoors," New Yorker, February 21, 2014, https://www.newyorker.com/business/currency/how-dick-cabela-sold-the-great-outdoors and Cabela, Cabela's.
53. Kevin Helliker, "Hunter Gatherer: Rare Retailer Scores by Targeting Men Who Hate to Shop," *Wall Street Journal*, December 17, 2002.
54. Helliker, "Hunter Gatherer."
55. I draw on Lee McGuigan for the description of Cabela's, as well as of the assessment of the retail setting as amplifying a construction mythology of heroic sportsmen. McGuigan, "The Hunting Industry."
56. McGuigan, "The Hunting Industry."
57. Helliker, "Hunter Gatherer." On lifestyle, see Binkley, *Getting Loose*; Featherstone, "Lifestyle and Consumer Culture"; Ozyurtcu, "Living the Dream."
58. Glenn A. Bischoff, "The Outdoors Specialists," *National Outdoor Outfitters News*, October 1984, Outdoor Recreation Archive, Utah State University Special Collections and Archives, Logan.
59. Denise Lee Yohn, "Big-Box Retailers Have Two Options if They Want to Survive," *Harvard Business Review*, June 22, 2016.
60. Matt Powell, "Retail Report Card: An Overview of the Results," *Sporting Goods Business*, October 2006.
61. Kristi Arellano, "Shop Makes Colo. Splash," *Denver Post*, October 29, 2005, https://www.denverpost.com/2005/10/29/shop-makes-colo-splash/.
62. Kristi Arellano, "Outdoor Retailers Hunting Denver," *Denver Post*, August 18, 2004.
63. Dina Bunn, "The Outside Story: REI Brings Much of Great Outdoors under One Roof to Grab Customers," *Rocky Mountain News*, May 17, 1998.
64. Bunn, "Outside Story."
65. Jason Blevins, "Gear Biz Has Room for All: Outdoor Industry Open to Big, Small," *Denver Post*, January 24, 2001.
66. Blevins, "Gear Biz."
67. Admin, "Mountain Miser Shuts Doors without Warning," *Outside Business Journal*, January 18, 2006, https://www.outsidebusinessjournal.com/brands/mountain-miser-shuts-doors-without-warning/.
68. Paige Yowell, "Canfield's Sporting Goods to Close after 71 Years in Business," *Daily Nonpareil*, December 6, 2017, https://nonpareilonline.com/business/canfield-s-sporting-goods-to-close-after-71-years-in-business/article_7076afa4-dac4

-11e7-af85-c7d53da5b234.html; Bob Calandra, "Growing Pains," *Sporting Goods Business*, July 1996.

BIBLIOGRAPHY

Abel, Michael. *Backpacking Made Easy*. Happy Camp, CA: Naturegraph, 1975 [1972].

Alagona, Peter S., and Gregory L Simon. "Contradictions at the Confluence of Commerce, Consumption, and Conservation; or, an REI Shopper Camps in the Forest, Does Anyone Notice?" *Geoforum* 45 (2013): 325–336.

Binkley, Sam. *Getting Loose: Lifestyle Consumption in the 1970s*. Durham, NC: Duke University Press, 2007.

Cabela, David. *Cabela's, World's Foremost Outfitter: A History*. Forest Dale, VT: Paul S. Ericksson, 2001.

Featherstone, Mike. "Lifestyle and Consumer Culture." *Theory, Culture and Society* 4, no. 1 (February 1987): 55–70.

Gross, Rachel S. "Logos on Everest: Commercial Sponsorship of American Expeditions, 1950–2000." *Enterprise and Society* 22, no. 4 (December 2012): 1067–1102.

Howard, Vicki. *From Main Street to Mall: The Rise and Fall of the American Department Store*. Philadelphia: University of Pennsylvania Press, 2015.

Hyman, Louis, *Borrow: The American Way of Debt*. New York: Vintage, 2012.

Leach, William. *Land of Desire: Merchants, Power, and the Rise of a New American Culture*. New York: Pantheon Books, 1993.

Lichtenstein, Nelson. *The Retail Revolution: How Wal-Mart Created a Brave New World of Business*. New York: Picador, 2010.

Lichtenstein, Nelson. "Wal-Mart: A Template for Twenty-First-Century Capitalism." In *Wal-Mart: The Face of Twenty-First-Century Capitalism*, edited by Nelson Lichtenstein, 3–30. New York: New Press, 2006.

Manning, Harvey. *REI: 50 Years of Climbing Together*. Seattle: Recreational Equipment, Inc., 1988.

McGuigan, Lee. "The Hunting Industry: Exploring the Marriage of Consumerism, Sport Hunting, and Commercial Entertainment." *Journal of Consumer Culture* 17, no. 3 (2017): 910–930.

Moreton, Bethany. *To Serve God and Wal-Mart: The Making of Christian Free Enterprise*. Cambridge, MA: Harvard University Press, 2009.

Newman, Benjamin J., and John V. Kane. "Backlash against the 'Big Box': Local Small Business and Public Opinion toward Business Corporations." *Public Opinion Quarterly* 78, no. 4 (Winter 2014): 984–1002.

Ozyurtcu, Tolga. "Living the Dream: Southern California and the Origins of Lifestyle Sport." *Journal of Sport History* 46, no. 1 (Spring 2019): 20–35.

Simon, Gregory L., and Peter S. Alagona. "Beyond Leave No Trace." *Ethics, Place, and Environment* 12, no. 1 (March 2009): 1–34.

Stobart, Job, and Vicki Howard, eds. *The Routledge Companion to the History of Retailing*. London: Routledge, 2020.

Strasser, Susan. *Satisfaction Guaranteed: The Making of the American Mass Market*. New York: Pantheon Books, 1989.

Young, Phoebe S. K. *Camping Grounds: Public Nature in American Life from the Civil War to the Occupy Movement*. New York: Oxford University Press, 2021.

Young, Terence. *Heading Out: A History of American Camping*. Ithaca, NY: Cornell University Press, 2017.

FIGURE 6.1. The Memphis Pyramid Bass Pro Shops is a major Memphis tourist attraction inside one of the world's largest pyramid structures. Author photo, November 2021.

6

BASS PRO SHOPS

Selling Conservative Conservation

SHERRI SHEU

Bass Pro Shops founder Johnny Morris made one of the biggest gambles of his career on November 10, 2005. For over a decade, the gigantic $54 million Memphis Pyramid sat empty, ever since the Memphis Grizzlies professional basketball team abandoned the distinctive building—by some accounts the tenth-largest pyramid in the world. As a result, Memphis had a boondoggle on its hands: the gleaming city icon on the banks of the Mississippi River now served as home to cobwebs and dust bunnies. Legendary angler and television host Bill Dance eyed Morris as the person who could restore life to the Pyramid. Tennessee native Dance lobbied his billionaire friend hard. To support the efforts, the city of Memphis reportedly offered $100 million in incentives for the retailer to set up shop in the building (figure 6.1).[1]

Morris hemmed and hawed, unable to make a decision. Even with city funding, he would need to invest millions in the space to make it usable. Finally, Morris decided to let nature make the decision. He took a fishing trip with Dance on the Tennessee River, agreeing to make the investment deal based on one condition: a member of the fishing party had to catch a monster catfish, at least a thirty-pounder, or the deal was off. Ten minutes before a self-imposed deadline, one of the anglers felt a pull on the end of his line. Almost in the shadow of the Pyramid, the river gave the billionaire the sign he needed, gifting the party with a thirty-four-pound whiskered beauty of a fish.[2]

While other chapters in this collection delve into the supply-chain and ecological transformations of big box stores, this chapter considers how Bass Pro cultivates spaces that support the political and cultural inclinations of its shoppers. The arguments that Bart Elmore (chapter 1), Laura J. Martin (chapter 4), and Johnathan Williams (chapter 2) make about the environmental impact of big box stores apply to Bass Pro as well. From paving new roads and parking lots to supply-chain impacts and traffic and sound pollution, Bass Pro joins other big box retailers in having substantial impacts on both local and global environments. Like Rachel S. Gross's chapter (chapter 5), this chapter examines the outdoor industry and the selling and packaging of the outdoors inside the big box.

This chapter, however, looks beyond these material and business impacts to understand how a retailer constructs cultural spaces within the big box. It takes seriously Bass Pro's claim of "leading North America's largest conservation movement."[3] This essay examines how Bass Pro uses retail spaces, museums, and catalogs as three sites where the retailer both promotes conservation and delineates what types of people belong in outdoor recreational spaces. Who are these spaces made for? Who is left out? This chapter posits that the immersive environments created by Bass Pro support the cultural and political identities of its shoppers. By doing so, it uniquely positions the corporation to enfold people into the conservationist cause who might otherwise reject the politics of the environmental movement. The chapter concludes with a case study of the proposed Pebble Mine in Alaska that Bass Pro helped stop.

THE ECOLOGICAL ROOTS OF BASS PRO

The rise of Bass Pro Shops is inextricably tied to the environmental transformation of the United States. The eponymous fish became much more widespread in the United States during the postwar period as federal and state governments built hydroelectric dams across the country. Hundreds of new dams and lakes replaced native waterways in a bid for both electrification and flood control. The new reservoirs tended to be deep, cold, and still—a disaster for any native species that relied on warm, moving water. In place of native species, reservoir managers stocked billions of bass. *Salmonides micropetrus* (largemouth bass) and *Micropterus dolomieu* (smallmouth bass) are resilient, adaptable species almost ideally suited to the constraints of the reservoir. They can survive and thrive in a wide range of environments and will eat anything from insects to small ducklings. Just as important, they have an ardent fanbase of anglers who prize their willingness to fight the hook.[4]

One of these dams was Table Rock Dam, built in 1958 just a few miles outside the boundaries of Branson, Missouri. A schoolboy named Johnny Morris watched the opening of Table Rock Dam with his grandfather and witnessed the first water that spilled over it. By 1971, Morris had grown into a young man competing in the newly created sport of competitive bass fishing. His enthusiasm outstripped his success on the bass fishing circuit. However, Morris's journeys to distant competition sites afforded him a national view of the fishing lure market, an unusual perspective at a time when lures tended to be made for local markets and environments. As Morris traveled, he gathered many of the popular lures used by his fellow competitors, filling a U-Haul trailer.[5]

Back home in Springfield, Missouri, his father owned a chain of businesses, including liquor stores and dry cleaners. Johnny persuaded his father to allow him to use the back of one of his Brown Derby Liquor Stores to sell equipment to traveling anglers driving down to Table Rock Lake, just fifty miles away. The micro-enterprise opened in 1972, taking up just eight square feet. Morris had found a niche. Weekend warrior anglers took quickly to the new lures, and many called in purchases when they returned home.[6]

Although the eventual retail stores grew much larger than the back of a liquor store, the stores remained places designed to appeal to Morris's Missouri customers. Morris positioned himself as an enthusiast selling to other enthusiasts, a position that later became a slogan for the company: "sportsmen for sportsmen." Morris appeared less a savvy businessman than a knowledgeable friend. The slogan combined the down-home familiarity of a country tackle store with evoking the elite clubiness of nineteenth-century hunting and fishing clubs populated by titans of industry.

BRINGING THE OUTDOORS INSIDE: THREE SITES OF BASS PRO SHOPS CULTURAL TRANSMISSION

Bass Pro Shops uses three main sites to transmit its messaging: retail outlets, catalogs, and museums. Alongside catalogs and stores, Bass Pro also operates several museums connected to its retail spaces. These spaces largely appeal to white men. As one reporter put it, "It's a mecca for men, a temple of testosterone, where homage is paid to man's history as hunter and gatherer."[7] Through these three types of spaces, Bass Pro has ample room to support and promote its consumers' cultural and political identities. The sites delineate Bass Pro's vision of who belongs in the world of its stores and in outdoor recreational spaces more broadly.

RETAIL STORES

A large network of big box retail stores forms the most conspicuous part of the Bass Pro empire. On a trip to Maine with his sister, Johnny Morris toured the L. L. Bean Factory Store, which inspired him to create a destination travel experience to convert people who shopped from Bass Pro catalogs into customers willing to make a pilgrimage to a "fairytale" space.[8] Like Filene's in another era, the store itself became a destination. While the austere, fluorescent surroundings of Walmart in the 1970s and 1980s differentiated it from up-market retailers and shopping malls, Bass Pro made the display the destination—much as REI did for its consumers, as Rachel Gross illustrates in chapter 5. In

1981, the first flagship Bass Pro Shops opened in Springfield, Missouri. Bass Pro did not expand outside of Missouri until the mid-1990s. The corporation's footprint expanded slowly at first, adding just a store or two each year. In the early 2000s, the retailer's expansion began picking up steam, with the company opening as many as 9 stores per year. In 2017, the store acquired its biggest competitor, Cabela's, creating a network that numbered 171 Bass Pro and Cabela's locations by 2023.[9]

Despite its massive footprint, a spokesperson claimed in 2014 that Bass Pro was "not a big box store" but instead was "a destination that specializes in providing entertainment and education through our aquariums, mounts, and murals." The store was "a great shopping experience" with "opportunities to learn how to use the gear." The company touted its ability to draw and keep customers, noting that an average customer drove over fifty miles to spend two-and-a-half hours at each store.[10]

The effect of entering a Bass Pro Shops mimics the experience of an amusement park with a carnivalesque atmosphere. At some locations, customers enter through turnstiles. As one store's general manager explained in 1997, the stores "create an entrance into an entertainment area. You are entering an atmosphere that is not like anything you've ever experienced."[11] A visit could prove mind-boggling. Angler and *Washington Post* travel writer Bill Heavey narrated his experience of a visit to the flagship Springfield location in 1998: "After three hours in the store, I'm paralyzed by the abundance. Numbly strolling through the crankbait aisles, I come upon an old standby bass lure, the Rat-L-Trap. When I started fishing, it came in two sizes and three colors, I think. Now it comes in six sizes and 47 colors, from Bleedin' Shiner to Firetiger. If you bought one in each size and color, your boat would sink, all the lures would catch on your clothing and then they'd drag you down to Lunker Land."[12] Every Bass Pro store features extensive design details, including plastic rock walls and trees, tanks of fish large enough for fishing demonstrations, and museum-grade taxidermy displays. Most try to evoke the feeling of an old hunting lodge, with simulated log and stone details.

The apotheosis of the Bass Pro shopping experience is the Memphis Pyramid, now a veritable cathedral to fishing and hunting cultures. Customers approach the store from a grass-lined driveway suggestive of a well-manicured park. They drive under a stone arch that evokes the famous Roosevelt Gate at the north entrance of Yellowstone National Park. "Welcome to Sportsman's Paradise," it declares. A sharp-eyed pedestrian walking from their car to the store might notice that the reverse sides of stop signs in the lots, typically just bare metal, contain quotes about conservation and nature from well-known figures. "Conservation is the state of harmony between men and land" reads one sign with a possum hanging down, quoting pioneering ecologist and wildlife manager Aldo Leopold. Another sign with a skunk cutout above the text presents advice from the ornithologist John James Audubon: "A true conservationist is a man who knows that the world is not given by his father, but borrowed from his children." Albert Einstein also proffers wisdom about the natural world: "Look deep, deep into nature, and then you will understand everything better" (figure 6.2). More than likely, customers walking through the parking lots will overlook Leopold, Audubon, and Einstein.

Retail is almost secondary to the plethora of experiences available at the store. The store offers valet parking next to a row of gleaming metallic Tracker bass boats. Customers can eat at several restaurants, watch schools of fish swim through tanks, and take the Sky High Ride to an observation deck to see the Memphis skyline and the Mississippi River. In the middle of the store, live ducks cluster in a corner of a pond as fish dart in and out of the submerged fake cypress knees. A separate enclosed tank houses live alligators relaxing on fake rocks under heat lamps. It is a spectacular replica of the natural world, although none of it feels particularly real. A group of feral pigs frozen in taxidermized time charges across a tiny island, a neon sign for lady's T-shirts flickering behind them. Should a few hours not suffice, customers can stay inside the Pyramid at the Big Cypress Lodge, where the comfortable hotel rooms have balconies overlooking the retail floor.

The spaces of Bass Pro, largely subsidized by public taxpayers, present a view of a bucolic, abundant, well-managed nature.[13] Yet this nature is not one that is open to all. Bass Pro codes itself not just through the implicit assumptions about race, hunting, and fishing that often erase the long histories of people of color in the outdoors but also through the ancillary products sold at its stores. Some offerings hint at the intended

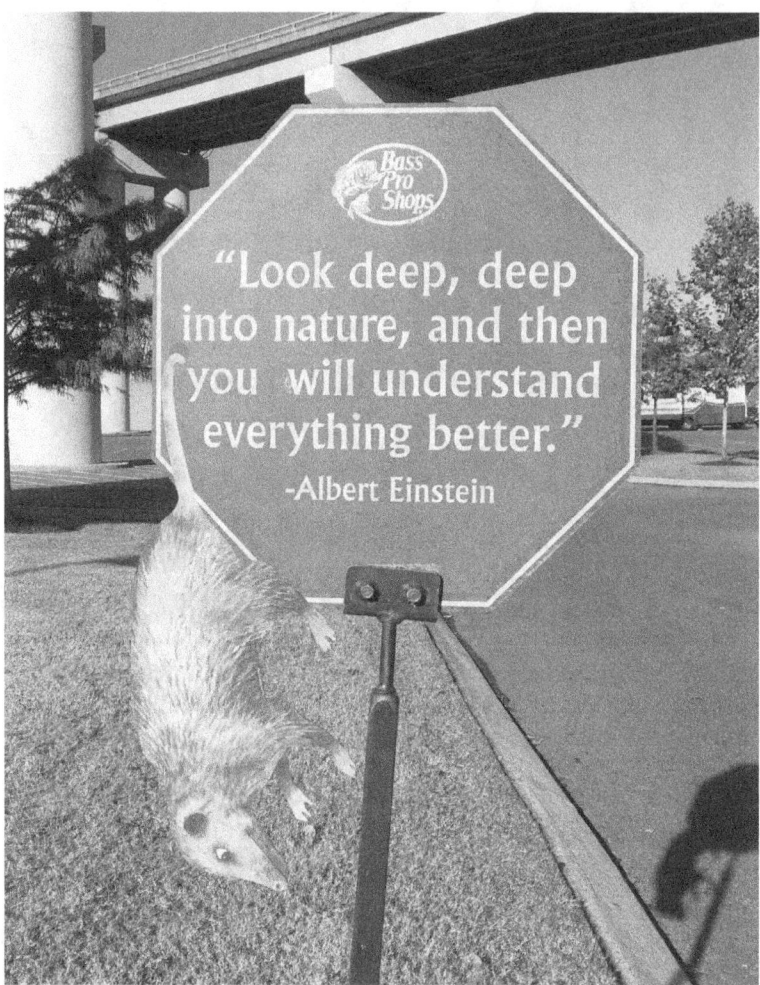

FIGURE 6.2. Albert Einstein: "Look deep, deep into nature, and then you will understand everything better." Outside Bass Pro Shops retail locations, signs such as this one underscore the corporation's self-portrayal as a leader in conservation. Author photo, November 2021.

audience's political tendencies. For example, on a recent visit to the Memphis Pyramid, a customer could buy doormats reading "This Place Is Politically Incorrect. We Say Merry Christmas, One Nation under God and Give Thanks to Our Troops. If This Offends You, LEAVE." The back of a vintage pickup truck hawked a mountain of Black Rifle Coffee Company coffee beans (figure 6.3). On the garment racks, a Grunt Style

FIGURE 6.3. Displays selling non-fishing products such as this Black Rifle Coffee Company coffee bean arrangement reflect the cultures sold at Bass Pro Shops. Author photo, November 2021.

display lets consumers pick from their choice of American flag bullet shirts or a "Family, Faith, Friends, Flag, Firearms" design.[14] These two brands connote a particular political sensibility often invisible to outsiders: both Grunt Style and Black Rifle Coffee were brands popular among rioters at the January 6 insurrection at the US Capitol in 2021. Kyle Rittenhouse, who infamously shot into a crowd that was protesting the murder of a Black man by police, was also reportedly a fan of the two companies.[15] These items, unrelated to hunting or fishing on their own, quietly demarcate who belongs and who does not in the spaces of Bass Pro and, by extension, in outdoor recreation.

CATALOGS

For shoppers who cannot travel to a retail location, Bass Pro Shops comes to their mailboxes, even in the age of e-commerce. Johnny Morris launched the first Bass Pro mail-order catalog in 1974 after customers called in their orders to his store. The first catalog contained 1,400 items across 180 pages. Subsequent editions became veritable doorstops. They quickly earned a national following. If the concurrent growth of Walmart as explained by Bart Elmore (chapter 1, this volume) represented the growth of mass retail—that of many diverse types of goods under one roof—the growth of Bass Pro represented a different sort of retail: that of one type of good with endless permutations. By the late 1990s, Bass Pro was sending out 40 million catalogs a year, with many products developed and manufactured exclusively for the company.[16]

In 2022, the company issued nine catalogs by July. Bass Pro used the catalogs to connect across generations. Its customers may have received copies in the mail for many years or remembered it as a staple in a relative's home. "Generations of sportsmen grew up reading these pages," explains one page. "It is an anchor from memories and times long ago—time spent outside with mothers and uncles, fathers and grandparents." The free publication represents something more than just consumption: "This is more than a catalog, it's a dream book."[17] Such language echoes the language used in older Sears, Roebuck catalogs.

As a "dream book," the pages of the catalog depict the people who recreate outdoors as almost exclusively white. The 2022 Spring Master Fishing catalog, at 300 pages, contains hundreds of photographs of people recreating in the outdoors. Of these, only a handful of images depict people of color. One depicts a Black family relaxing on a pontoon boat (21), another is a headshot of the professional bass fisherman Mark Daniels Jr. endorsing a fishing rod, one shows a Black man releasing a smaller bass, and two are images of young Latinx girls advertising the Bass Pro Outdoor Access Fund (65).[18] One image shows a Black man modeling a generic Bass Pro Henley shirt (274), while another image depicts a Black father and son at the Wonders of Wildlife Museum (288). Notably, people of color are not in positions of expertise—they are not shown using equipment or reeling in fish, even in the case of Mark Daniels. Although the sport of fishing is less diverse than the country as a whole, Bass Pro depicts an even whiter world. The US Fish and Wildlife Service and US Census Bureau's *2016 National Survey of Fishing, Hunting, and Wildlife-Associated Recreation* figures found that African Americans made up 9 percent of anglers.[19]

The shorter 2022 Western Big Game Hunting Specialist catalog does only slightly better in terms of representation. Of twenty-two images featuring people in the thirty-seven-page catalog, three images depict people of color, one of which shows a male Asian employee assisting a racially ambiguous customer with binoculars. The second shows a Black woman with a gun slung on her back on a page advertising women's performance clothing, and the final image shows a Black woman riding in an all-terrain vehicle (ATV).[20] The hunting catalog accurately reflects the paltry number of minorities involved in hunting, a sport whose participants are 97 percent white.[21] In contrast, the fifty-five-page Camping catalog shows only one person of color in the outdoors—a glaring omission when the camping industry's research finds that, as a group, non-whites account for 39% of campers.[22] The sole representation in the Camping catalog of a person of color is that of a Black man with dreadlocks lying on his stomach sucking from a pool of dirty water with a water filtration straw. Other images on the same page show white models sitting relaxed and upright, using handheld pump filters. Especially in the context of these images of white models at leisure, the image of a dreadlocked Black man drinking out of a survival straw is borderline offensive, evoking visual tropes of desperate Africans in primitive circumstances. Across the catalogs, Black men are largely denied the privilege of recreational action, particularly those involving firearms.[23]

In contrast to the homogeneous world of Bass Pro catalogs, the REI summer 2022 catalog shows many people of color and highlights their names and backgrounds. Lydia is described as "a soil scientist, runner, REI Co-op Member and citizen of Huichol and Pascua Yaqui Nations." A two-page spread is dedicated to Dr. Tiffany Gayle Chenault, a Black sociology professor and runner. The text explained the challenges of running for Black women. "Why is running so white?" asked Chenault. Her story had a happy ending, as she "found people who looked like me" when running. Of the twenty-five photographs in the catalog that contain pictures of people or parts of people (such as legs running to show shoes), at least sixteen photographs contain people of color, often featuring racially mixed groups performing outdoor activities together. By contextualizing the challenges people of color face in participating in outdoor activities and modeling people of color doing so,

REI creates a parallel fantasy catalog world where people of color are well-represented in the outdoors and feel comfortable participating as experts and equals.[24]

At a time when other outdoor retailers such as REI and Patagonia make concerted—if sometimes problematic—efforts to put people of color in their promotional materials, Bass Pro does so rarely.[25] The specialty Marine and Fly Fishing editions of Bass Pro catalogs seemingly use only white models. As a way of policing and representing who does and who does not belong in outdoor recreation, then, the world of the Bass Pro catalog portrays the outdoors as a place with very few people of color.

MUSEUMS

Beyond the spaces of the catalogs and retail stores, Bass Pro also operates several museum spaces, including the Johnny Morris Wonders of Wildlife National Museum and Aquarium, the National Rifle Association's (NRA) National Sporting Arms Museum, the Archery Hall of Fame and Museum, and the Ducks Unlimited National Waterfowl Heritage Center. These museums present a chance for Bass Pro to reach its consumers with a longer, more sustained message of conservation. The history these spaces purport to teach is one skewed heavily toward a nostalgic view of the American past, where white men conquered the wilderness and the West before saving nature for future generations.

Wonders of Wildlife is the largest of the museum spaces and is one of the largest museums and aquariums in the Midwest at 350,000 square feet, with impressive live aquarium exhibits, reptile habitats, and a penguin enclosure. Although operated as a separate entity on paper, Wonders of Wildlife is deeply intertwined with the retailer. The museum and aquarium are located next to the company's flagship store in Springfield, Missouri, and customers can enter the Wonders of Wildlife exhibits from the store. The museum space offers visitors an experience that "celebrates those who hunt, fish and act as stewards of the land and water."[26]

Some of the most admired stewards include Lewis and Clark and Theodore Roosevelt. Exhibit spaces include a replica of Theodore Roosevelt's hunting cabin and a Lewis and Clark room with paintings depicting scenes from the expedition leaders' journals. In the Native American Hall, visitors can "see the story of North America's first people of conservation." By "illustrating the deep connection between mankind and nature," the "reverent space" teaches "the value of being one with our land."[27] The conservation history taught in the Wonders of Wildlife museum elevates visitors to potential heroes if they also become hunter-angler conservationists. The narrative it pushes relies on framing Native Americans as mystical figures while underplaying the processes that subjugated them.[28]

If a visitor wanders into the Springfield Bass Pro from Wonders of Wildlife, they can find the NRA's National Sporting Arms Museum inside the store. The NRA museum "celebrates the history of hunting, conservation and freedom," reinforcing some of the messaging of Wonders of Wildlife. The collection contains more than 900 guns, including guns that once belonged to Lewis and Clark, Jesse James, and Annie Oakley. A Colt revolver owned by Bass Reeves, an African American US marshal who was born enslaved, is also featured in the collection. Reeves served in Indian Territory during the late nineteenth century.[29] Theodore Roosevelt again gets a room of his own, the Theodore Roosevelt Conservation Room. A "21 Gun Salute to our 2nd Amendment" display of rifles is placed against an American flag backdrop.[30] Visitors might also explore the Archery Hall of Fame and Museum in the store, where they can view a bow and arrow set made by the Apache leader Geronimo in Florida when the US Army imprisoned him.[31]

The museum spaces operated by Bass Pro give customers a heritage they can adopt as their own, affording them access to an ongoing genealogy of American conservation stretching back to include precontact Indigenous Americans, Lewis and Clark, and Theodore Roosevelt. The consumer's position as a hunter or an angler makes them the rightful heirs of the conservation tradition. The history taught in these spaces glorifies a traditional narrative of American history and great men. Though Native Americans might be highlighted in the displays, they are not active participants in history; instead, they exist in an ethereal "before" time—or, in the case of Geronimo, are reduced to making souvenirs for sale. The processes of conquest, colonialism, and empire that empowered conservationists such as Theodore

Roosevelt go largely untold. It is, at its heart, a depiction of an uncomplicated American history.

Through its catalogs, retail locations, and museums, Bass Pro delineates the consumers who belong in the world of outdoor recreation and the ones who do not. It creates an environment where white consumers—particularly men—expect to see their histories and politics celebrated, commercialized, and reified.[32] Bass Pro is careful to present itself as conservationist, not environmentalist. It traces its lineage through leaders who saw natural landscapes and waterways as resources, not those who wanted the environment protected for its own sake. The company has little to say about the threat of climate change, and it does not work toward environmental justice.[33] Instead, it presents a vision of the outdoors in which hunters and anglers pass on their hobbies to infinite generations, with many trophy bucks, ducks, turkeys, and bass in-between. It is a vision of conservation that would not be lost on Theodore Roosevelt.

BASS PRO AND THE LABOR OF THE RETAIL COUNTER

By both reference and design, Bass Pro presents a vision of nature reliant on the image of the customer as the conservationist angler-hunter. What is sold at Bass Pro is less fishing and hunting supplies than an identity, much like the well-known example of Whole Foods Market.

The image extends to hiring and employment practices. These identities, in theory open to all who buy into the fishing and hunting culture, carry social and political weight. As demonstrated by a series of class action lawsuits, not everyone can assume the mantle of Theodore Roosevelt in the world of Bass Pro. According to the federal Equal Employment Opportunity Commission (EEOC), the retailer engaged in a long-standing practice of discriminating against Black and Hispanic job applicants. During a lawsuit first filed against Bass Pro in September 2011 by the EEOC, the EEOC argued that if Bass Pro had followed fair hiring practices, the company would have employed 1,097 additional Black employees and 187 additional Hispanic employees.[34]

The EEOC lawsuit documented a pattern of behavior in stores that discriminated against Black and Hispanic job applicants and prevented their advancement in the organization. In court, the EEOC accused Bass Pro of using a "nationwide standard operating procedure of denying employment to Black and Hispanic applicants for many hourly and salaried positions at their retail stores, because of their race."[35] Of 600 managers at Bass Pro retail stores across the country, only 10 to 15 were Black.[36] The EEOC listed nearly 200 Black and Hispanic job applicants denied employment by Bass Pro.[37] The EEOC further alleged that Bass Pro retaliated against employees who opposed the discriminatory practices.[38]

At stores across the country, senior employees felt empowered to discriminate and to use racially vitriolic language. In the summer of 2006, an assistant general manager at a store in Louisiana told the human resources manager that a qualified Black candidate "really doesn't fit our profile." Pressed for clarification, the assistant general manager curtly explained that at Bass Pro, "We don't hire [n-word]s." One lead employee told the EEOC that the Destin, Florida, store had a policy of not hiring Black or Hispanic employees.[39]

In 2005, a general manager of the store in Katy, Texas, told the human resources manager, "It is getting a little dark in here; you need to hire some white people." The Katy general manager also pejoratively referred to people of Hispanic descent as "'wetback,' 'Pedro,' and 'Mexican.'" A department lead employee in Clarksville, Indiana, destroyed an employment application, saying that the applicant has what "sounded like a '[n-word] name'" and that "[n-word]s steal." At the same store, a lead employee also declared that "Hispanics should be shot at the border by border patrol."[40]

Employees at stores who reported cases of discriminatory behavior became subjects of retaliation. When Velecia Cruse—a Black woman with years of experience in human resources—began working at the Katy, Texas, location, she saw that managers forced Black applicants to take a test not required of white applicants, hired less qualified white applicants over more qualified Black applicants, and assigned undesirable work shifts to Black employees. Cruse complained, which led to retaliation by the company. She was fired from her position after the regional human resources manager—whom she had complained to—accused her of payroll irregularities.[41]

The EEOC alleged that the discrimination came from Johnny Morris himself, arguing that Morris told a meeting of Bass Pro general managers that "this company will never have a [racial] quota system because that's not the kind of people I want working in my store." Morris's preferences became known as "the Profile," which human resources managers used to preferentially hire white candidates.[42] The judge on the case found that Morris's comments reflected "racial animus" and "a discriminatory attitude."[43]

Mike Rowland, vice president of human resources for Bass Pro, went on the attack against these allegations of discrimination. Rowland insisted that the "investigation and the EEOC's conduct demonstrate a troubling tendency by the EEOC to stereotype those who love outdoor sports and support conservation as people who unlawfully discriminate or oppose equal opportunity for all," subtly suggesting that the federal government discriminated against camo wearers. Rowland inadvertently underscored the lack of diversity within Bass Pro by stating that "EEOC staff investigators have suggested on several occasions that because Bass Pro sponsors a NASCAR race team the company is more likely to discriminate against minorities."[44] Famously, NASCAR is one of the least diverse sports in the country. At the time of the lawsuit, fans still commonly displayed Confederate flags at NASCAR races.[45] The statement has a strong undertone of accusing the EEOC of so-called reverse discrimination. Rowland was himself named in the lawsuit as someone who disseminated the discriminatory hiring policies to other managers in the company.[46]

In 2011, Bass Pro settled the lawsuit for $10.5 million without admitting guilt. The company agreed to appoint a director of diversity and inclusion, hold affirmative outreach efforts, and update hiring practices.[47]

The fact that Bass Pro's audience is white and male is indicative of a broader problem. In a rapidly diversifying country, the conservation movement and its attendant spaces are coded white and often male. On the other side of the hunter/hiker divide, REI and Patagonia have struggled with this same question of audience. Retail often serves as the first point of contact for neophytes entering the outdoor world. An aspiring hunter, angler, birdwatcher, hiker, or kayaker who enters the big box outdoor retail world may find themselves turned off from these activities when they see no one who looks like them reflected there.

The potential environmental impact of Bass Pro Shops reaches far beyond the physical supply linkages or the impacts of building large shopping centers. Recreation forms the gateway for many consumers to better understand the threats to the natural world around them. Viewed in this light, discriminatory exclusionary behavior toward staff and customers actively works against Bass Pro Shops' stated goal of leading "North America's largest conservation movement." Each customer lost is a customer who could have become a conservationist. Especially at risk are people without a family background of outdoor recreation. In this sense, consumption and consumer behavior—not a family heritage of outdoor recreation—might form the first step in creating environmental awareness and forming a conservationist inclination.

Bass Pro does not face this challenge alone; the outdoor recreation industry at large has a well-documented whiteness problem. However, perhaps more than any other mainstream outdoor retailer, Bass Pro has seemingly doubled down on preserving its locations, retail channels, and the outdoors as sanctuaries for white participants.

SELLING CONSERVATION IN RED AMERICA: STOPPING PEBBLE MINE WITH FOX NEWS

As a business decision, excluding new audiences in an increasingly diverse nation seems to constitute poor business. Yet the chain has become successful precisely because it crafts an environment designed to support a very specific demographic. Because the Bass Pro environment feels unthreatening by design, the firm can press its conservationist messaging among its core audience without setting off alarm bells about leftist environmentalists. Indeed, the conservationist messaging likely elicits sympathy and support. The hunters and anglers who shop at Bass Pro may not ever explicitly identify themselves as conservationists, much less environmentalists, but they likely support catch limits on fish and bag limits on game. Anglers and hunters also likely support limitations on water pollution in the rivers and

Donald Trump Jr.
@DonaldJTrumpJr

Thanks #Iowa. Amazing crowd last night in Des Moines at the @bassproshops talking to outdoorsmen/women in the area

8:04 AM · Nov 7, 2016

FIGURE 6.4. A Trump presidential rally before the 2016 election inside a Bass Pro Shops reflected and reinforced the expected political tendencies of BPS consumers. Twitter screenshot.

lakes they boat and fish in, as well as the preservation of public lands for hunting.

Bass Pro operates a cultural space in which its core audiences of rural and suburban white men feel welcome and supported, often at the expense of other groups. The very success of these spaces, in turn, constrains the ability of Bass Pro to reach out to new audiences, including people of color and many women. However, in a politically fractured country where outdoor spaces are increasingly seen as red or blue, Bass Pro has a unique cultural ability to disseminate the message of conservation and to flex its social muscles. Bass Pro's involvement in stopping the Alaskan Pebble Mine development provides clues to what this brand of corporate activism might look like.

On November 6, 2016, Donald Trump Jr. held a rally for his father at the Bass Pro Shops outside Des Moines, Iowa, just before the presidential election (figure 6.4).⁴⁸ The image of the event the candidate's son posted on Twitter showed a large crowd inside the store. The big box in Iowa could have been any Bass Pro in the United States. A flock of taxidermized birds hung above the crowd, which stood between posts made to resemble large tree trunks. Leaves and other foliage hung down between the fake trunks. In the upper left corner of the photo, the rumps of large mammals were visible, part of a taxidermy display above a store fitting room. In effect, the presidential candidate's son held a rally at a location where many of his father's supporters would feel at home.

The relationship between Bass Pro and Don Jr. would become significant toward the end of the Trump presidency during a controversy over the proposed Pebble Mine in southwest Alaska. As late as the end of July 2020, the Trump administration supported the proposed 8,400-acre open-pit gold mine that threatened the salmon stock in Bristol Bay. However, Donald Trump, Sr. began receiving significant social pressure from quarters that mattered to him. Don Jr. reportedly lobbied his father hard at a fundraiser and publicly voiced his opposition in a Twitter post.⁴⁹ In a response on the platform, Bass Pro Shops thanked the younger Trump for speaking out against the Pebble Mine project and "once again, standing up for your fellow sportsmen and women and steadfastly supporting conservation."⁵⁰

On August 14, 2020, Johnny Morris appeared on *Tucker Carlson Tonight* to speak out against the mine. President Trump was known as a voracious watcher of the show. Carlson, himself an avid angler, dedicated a segment to "The Case against Pebble Mine." Carlson set up his interview with Morris by noting that opposition to the mine had amassed a bipartisan coalition, with "a number of Republicans, including some prominent ones, including some very conservative ones, saying, 'Hold on, maybe Pebble Mine is not a good idea, maybe you should do whatever you can not to despoil nature, and maybe not all environmentalism is about climate.'"⁵¹

Carlson introduced Morris as the founder of Bass Pro Shops, "probably the greatest outdoor retailer in the history of the world." For many viewers of the show, Bass Pro needed no introduction. Both Carlson and Morris noted that they did not see opposition to the mine as a political issue. As Carlson interviewed Morris, the stock footage beside the two on-screen showed the spectacular scenery of Bristol Bay, replete with grizzly bears and their cubs and aerial shots of bright blue waterways darkened by teeming schools of fish.[52] Carlson presented Morris as an apolitical figure who only cared about conservation, although Federal Election Commission records show that Morris had made sizable contributions to Republican candidates and the Republican National Committee, including a $100,000 contribution to Donald Trump in 2016 and one of $200,000 in 2020.[53]

Morris spoke against the mine and in favor of the 14,000 jobs that relied on both commercial and sport fishing in the region, telling the audience that "conservation should be a uniter of people." The billionaire business owner quoted Theodore Roosevelt, a Trump favorite, on conservation. Morris made sure to applaud Trump's other policies, praising the president's energy and security policies. Carlson then closed out the segment by drawing a contrast between environmental debates and the one in Bristol Bay. The host claimed that "anybody who doesn't spend a good part of his life outdoors is not a credible voice on conservation and the environment," casting Morris as a more than credible authority. The host linked conservation of natural environments with hunters and anglers, telling viewers that "Trout Unlimited and a lot of other conservation groups with actual sportsmen in them, people who hunt and fish and use the outdoors," also opposed the mine.[54]

The *Tucker Carlson Tonight* segment achieved almost immediate success. On August 24, opponents of the mine declared victory. The *Washington Post* credited Carlson and others with successfully delaying the project.[55] Since the Trump administration was willing to let the mine die under bureaucratic red tape and then-presidential candidate Joe Biden did not support the project, it was effectively shuttered. In January 2023, the US Environmental Protection Agency blocked the project under the Clean Water Act. Although the firms involved in the mining project have threatened legal action, the mine was unlikely to be built as this book went to press.[56]

Bass Pro's campaign against the Pebble Mine that resulted in protecting the salmon fisheries and waterways of Bristol Bay succeeded because of the company's legacy of promoting conservation in a manner culturally attuned for conservatives. By operating in a cultural space where its name carried power and weight, the company influenced a conservation decision at a time when other organizations and businesses such as the Sierra Club and Patagonia—also vociferous opponents of the mine—had been ignored.[57] Bass Pro had the social and cultural capital and the leverage to carry out its goal of conserving Bristol Bay. Left-leaning environmentalists will find many faults with both the message and the messenger: they may find the company's lack of resolve for diversifying the outdoors or its support of the National Rifle Association unpalatable. However, the commercial and political successes of Bass Pro suggest that the company will play a major role in the future in shaping the nation's outdoor spaces.

To an observer, the indoor swamps, alligator tanks, and taffy factories of a Bass Pro can seem kitschy, if not tacky. For a large segment of American consumers, however, a Bass Pro is a space of acceptance: a place where camouflage pants and blaze orange shirts are de rigueur, where parking lots are sized for pickup trucks towing boats, and where NASCAR sponsorship engenders brand loyalty. Bass Pro has carved out a niche in which its shoppers feel supported and seen by the multi-billion-dollar corporation. The spaces of Bass Pro are designed around shoppers and their political and cultural identities, unlike the more generic spaces of big box mass-market retailers. Bass Pro's close proximity to, if not outright alliance with, conservative politics raises issues of discrimination and exclusion. To wit, supporting Bass Pro's core audience comes at the expense of marginalized groups that are not reflected in the corporation's retail outlets, advertising, historical displays, or employees. In the long run, Bass Pro may be robbing Peter to pay Paul if it wants to advance the mission of conservation.

Bass Pro presents a complicated case study about the entanglements of retail, identity, politics, and environment. In some ways, Bass Pro represents both an evolution and a revolt: it is a big box chain that evokes not the fluorescent lights of mass-market retailers but the extravagance of Jazz Age department store displays. Yet it also resists the idea that all consumers are fit for its wares or that workers at its tills and counters are essentially fungible. Bass Pro promotes not the democratizing effect of having access to a global marketplace of goods but rather its customers' inclusion in an exclusive space. It arbitrates the historical lineages of ethical outdoor users. By yoking its customers' identities to the message of conservation, Bass Pro suggests a model of gatekeeper outdoor retail, where the corporation plays an outsized role in determining who gets to recreate in the outdoors.

NOTES

1. Kriston Capps, "Is Memphis Making (Another) Massive Mistake With Its Pyramid," *Bloomberg CityLab* (December 4, 2014), https://www.bloomberg.com/news/articles/2014-12-04/is-memphis-making-another-massive-mistake-with-its-pyramid; Sills, "Unbelievable True Story."
2. Sills, "Unbelievable True Story."
3. Bass Pro, https://about.basspro.com/conservation/.
4. For more on the natural history of bass, see Long, et al., "A Historical Perspective of Black Bass Management in the United States."
5. Waszczuk, "The Johnny Morris Story."
6. Waszczuk, "The Johnny Morris Story."
7. Bill Bowden, "Bass Pro Shop a Mecca for Men," *Arkansas Business*, March 17, 2003, https://www.arkansasbusiness.com/article/56349/bass-pro-shop-a-mecca-for-men.
8. Wes Johnson, "Bass Pro Founder Johnny Morris Receives Excellence in Business Award," *Springfield News-Leader*, March 26, 2016, https://www.news-leader.com/story/news/business/2016/03/24/bass-pro-founder-johnny-morris-receives-excellence-business-award/81912690/.
9. Brian Brown, "Bass Pro Blitz," *Springfield Business Journal*, March 25, 2013, https://sbj.net/stories/bass-pro-blitz,17556. On the Bass Pro acquisition of Cabela's, see Debter, "Outdoor Retailer Bass Pro Shops Is Buying Cabela's.," Store count as of June 2023; https://stores.basspro.com/.
10. Thomas Gounley, "During Tough Times for Sector, Bass Pro Is Opening Seven Stores in 2014," *Springfield News-Leader*, March 22, 2014, https://www.news-leader.com/story/money/2014/03/23/during-tough-time-for-sector-bass-pro-is-opening-seven-stores-in-2014/6741089/.
11. Jodie Jacobs, "Outdoors Indoors," *Chicago Tribune*, November 23, 1997, https://www.chicagotribune.com/news/ct-xpm-1997-11-23-9711230322-story.html.
12. Bill Heavey, "It's A Bass World after All," *Washington Post*, August 16, 1998, https://www.washingtonpost.com/archive/lifestyle/travel/1998/08/16/its-a-bass-world-after-all/787cface-5336-44e4-99ff-827500ae10dd/.
13. The economics of Bass Pro are beyond the scope of this chapter. For more information, see Reeder, "Why Have So Many Cities and Towns Given Away So Much Money to Bass Pro Shops and Cabela's"; Stecker and Connor, "Fishing for Taxpayer Cash." For more on the visual culture inside Bass Pro, see Colvin, "Bass Pro Shops."
14. Patterson, "From Grunt Style to 'Warcore.'"

15. Brandon Lingle, "Rioters Wore Black Rifle Coffee, Grunt Style Gear at Capitol Siege," *San Antonio Express-News*, January 18, 2021, https://www.expressnews.com/business/local/article/Rioters-wore-Black-Rifle-Coffee-Grunt-Style-gear-15878210.php#photo-20504942. See also Jason Zengerle, "Can the Black Rifle Coffee Company Become the Starbucks of the Right," *New York Times*, July 14, 2021, https://www.nytimes.com/2021/07/14/magazine/black-rifle-coffee-company.html.
16. Bridges, "Bass Pro," 20.
17. Bass Pro Shops, 2022 Master Fishing Catalog, 6.
18. The Outdoor Fund was created in 2011 to promote fishing in Hispanic and other multi-cultural communities. The fund seems to have been created after the EEOC began investigating the company for discrimination.
19. US Fish and Wildlife Service and US Census Bureau, *2016 National Survey of Fishing, Hunting, and Wildlife-Associated Recreation*, 19.
20. Bass Pro Shops, 2022 Western Big Game Hunting Specialist Catalog.
21. Kampgrounds of America Research, "North American Camping & Outdoor Hospitality Report 2023," 54.
22. US Fish and Wildlife Service and US Census Bureau, 2016 National Survey of Fishing, Hunting, and Wildlife-Associated Recreation, 33.
23. Bass Pro Shops, 2022 Camping Catalog. For more on the advertising and representation, see Martin, "Apartheid in the Great Outdoors"; Frazer and Anderson, "Media Representations of Race, Ability, and Gender."
24. REI Summer 2022 Catalog, https://catalogs.rei.com/2022-Summer-Catalog/1/#.
25. See Martin, "Is Diversity Just a Marketing Strategy for Gear Brands"; Aleem, "REI's Union-Busting Podcast."
26. Wonders of Wildlife, "About," https://wondersofwildlife.org/about/.
27. Description taken from Wonders of Wildlife website, https://wondersofwildlife.org/wildlife-galleries/.
28. See O'Brien, *Firsting and Lasting*.
29. The NRA's member publication, *American Rifleman*, published an article on Reeves and the Colt revolver. See Wilson, "Frontier Lawman."
30. https://www.basspro.com/shop/en/nra-museum.
31. https://www.basspro.com/shop/en/archery-hall-of-fame-and-museum. Other corporations also have company museums, such as the World of Coca Cola in Atlanta. See Hollenbeck, Peters, and Zinkhana, "Retail Spectacles and Brand Meaning."
32. For more on Bass Pro's appeal to men, see Hirschman, *Branding Masculinity*, chapter 9. See also Bowden, "Bass Pro Shop a Mecca for Men."
33. For the complexities and critiques of the conservation and environmental movements, see Taylor, *Rise of the American Conservation Movement*.
34. Equal Employment Opportunity Commission, "Bass Pro Failed to Hire Blacks and Hispanics"; *Equal Employment Opportunity Commission, Plaintiff v. Bass Pro Outdoor World, LLC, et al. Defendants*, Document 99, filed in Southern District of Texas on March 18, 2013, 19.
35. *Equal Employment Opportunity Commission, Plaintiff v. Bass Pro Outdoor World, LLC, et al. Defendants*, Document 99, 5.

36. *Equal Employment Opportunity Commission, Plaintiff v. Bass Pro Outdoor World, LLC, et al. Defendants*, Document 99, 16.
37. *Equal Employment Opportunity Commission, Plaintiff v. Bass Pro Outdoor World, LLC, et al. Defendants*, Document 99, 5.
38. *Equal Employment Opportunity Commission, Plaintiff v. Bass Pro Outdoor World, LLC, et al. Defendants*, Document 99, 2.
39. *Equal Employment Opportunity Commission, Plaintiff v. Bass Pro Outdoor World, LLC, et al. Defendants*, Document 99, 2.
40. *Equal Employment Opportunity Commission, Plaintiff v. Bass Pro Outdoor World, LLC, et al. Defendants*, Document 53, filed in Southern District of Texas on May 31, 2012, 2–3.
41. *Equal Employment Opportunity Commission, Plaintiff v. Bass Pro Outdoor World, LLC, et al. Defendants*, Document 99, 13.
42. *Equal Employment Opportunity Commission, Plaintiff v. Bass Pro Outdoor World, LLC, et al. Defendants*, Document 99, 6.
43. *Equal Employment Opportunity Commission, Plaintiff v. Bass Pro Outdoor World, LLC, et al. Defendants*, Document 99, 7–8.
44. Kimberly Quillen, "EEOC Files Suit against Bass Pro That Alleges Discriminatory Practices," *Times-Picayune* (New Orleans), September 21, 2011, https://www.nola.com/news/business/eeoc-files-suit-against-bass-pro-that-alleges-discriminatory-hiring-practices/article_7c9fbc88-990b-5db7-9474-5aae35d5e274.html; see also Jim Forsyth, "Bass Pro Shops Accused of Discrimination, Racial Slurs," *Reuters*, September 22, 2011, https://www.reuters.com/article/us-race-bassproshops/bass-pro-shops-accused-of-discrimination-racial-slurs-idUSTRE78L4K820110922.
45. For NASCAR fans' resistance to removing Confederate flags, see Andrew Shain, "'This Is My Tradition': Confederate Flags Still Fly at Darlington Race," *The State* (Columbia, SC), September 6, 2015, https://www.thestate.com/news/state/article34262640.html; Busbee, "NASCAR's Thorny Throwback Problem." The Confederate flag's connection to NASCAR and southern white male identity has also received considerable academic attention. See Newman, "Old Times There Are Not Forgotten"; Shackleford, "NASCAR Stock Car Racing"; Lee, Bernthal, Whisenant, and Mullane, "NASCAR."
46. *Equal Employment Opportunity Commission, Plaintiff v. Bass Pro Outdoor World, LLC, et al. Defendants*, Document 99, 2.
47. Equal Employment Opportunity Commission, "Bass Pro to Pay $10.5 Million."
48. Donald Trump Jr., Twitter post, November 7, 2016, 8:04 a.m., https://twitter.com/donaldjtrumpjr/status/795612811141464064.
49. Dino Grandoni with Alexandra Ellerbeck, "The Energy 202: How Pebble Mine Opponents Used Fox News [to] Push Trump to Delay the Alaska Project," *Washington Post*, October 24, 2020, https://www.washingtonpost.com/politics/2020/08/24/energy-202-how-pebble-mine-opponents-used-fox-news-push-trump-delay-alaska-project/; Donald Trump Jr., Twitter post, August 4, 2020, 2:58 p.m., https://twitter.com/DonaldJTrumpJr/status/1290723762523045888.
50. Bass Pro Shops, Twitter post, August 5, 2020, 5:29 p.m., https://twitter.com/bassproshops/status/1291124167761371136.

51. *Tucker Carlson Tonight*, Fox News, August 14, 2020, https://video.foxnews.com/v/6181326417001#sp=show-clips.
52. *Tucker Carlson Tonight*, Fox News, August 14, 2020.
53. Federal Election Commission, https://www.fec.gov/data/receipts/individual-contributions/?contributor_name=morris%2C+john&contributor_employer=bass+pro&two_year_transaction_period=2016&two_year_transaction_period=2020.
54. *Tucker Carlson Tonight*, Fox News, August 14, 2020.
55. Colman and Guillén, "Trump Set to Block Controversial Alaska Gold Mine"; Grandoni with Ellerbeck, "The Energy 202."
56. Timothy Puko, "EPA May Have Dealt Final 'Nail in the Coffin' to Alaska's Pebble Mine," *Washington Post*, January 31, 2023, https://www.washingtonpost.com/climate-environment/2023/01/31/epa-may-have-delivered-knock-out-blow-alaskas-pebble-mine/.
57. See Jones, "Pebble Mine Threatens One of the Last Great Salmon Rivers"; Hed, "Everything Old Is New Again."

BIBLIOGRAPHY

Aleem, Zeeshan. "REI's Union-Busting Podcast Shows How Diversity Programs Can Be Abused." *MSNBC*, February 11, 2022. https://www.msnbc.com/opinion/msnbc-opinion/rei-s-union-busting-podcast-shows-how-diversity-programs-can-n1288965.

Bass Pro Shops 2022 Camping. Catalog.

Bass Pro Shops 2022 Fly Fishing. Catalog.

Bass Pro Shops 2022 Marine. Catalog.

Bass Pro Shops 2022 Spring Master Fishing. Catalog

Bass Pro Shops 2022 Western Big Game Hunting Specialist. Catalog.

Bowden, Bill. "Bass Pro Shop a Mecca for Men." *Arkansas Business*, March 17, 2003. https://www.arkansasbusiness.com/article/56349/bass-pro-shop-a-mecca-for-men.

Bridges, Toby. "Bass Pro: A Transcendental Marketer." *Direct Marketing* 55, no. 6 (1992): 20–26.

Brown, Brian. "Bass Pro Blitz." *Springfield Business Journal* (Springfield, MO), March 25, 2013. https://sbj.net/stories/bass-pro-blitz,17556.

Busbee, Jay. "NASCAR's Thorny Throwback Problem: The Confederate Flag." *Yahoo Sports*, September 7, 2015. https://sports.yahoo.com/blogs/nascar-from-the-marbles/nascar-s-thorny-throwback-problem--the-confederate-flag-004046532.html.

Capps, Kriston. "Is Memphis Making (Another) Massive Mistake with Its Pyramid?" *Bloomberg CityLab*, December 4, 2014. https://www.bloomberg.com/news/articles/2014-12-04/is-memphis-making-another-massive-mistake-with-its-pyramid.

Colman, Zack, and Alex Guillén. "Trump Set to Block Controversial Alaska Gold Mine." *Politico*, August 22, 2020.

Colvin, Christina M. "Bass Pro Shops, Environmental Thought, and the Anima(l)tronic Dead." *Evental Aesthetics* 4, no. 2 (2015): 105–115.

Debter, Lauren. "Outdoor Retailer Bass Pro Shops Is Buying Cabela's for $5.5 Billion." *Forbes*, October 3, 2016. https://www.forbes.com/sites/laurengensler/2016/10/03/bass-pro-shops-to-buy-cabelas-for-5-5-billion/?sh=100428382157.

Equal Employment Opportunity Commission. "Bass Pro Failed to Hire Blacks and Hispanics at Its Stores Nationwide, EEOC Says in Suit." Press release, September 21, 2011. https://www.eeoc.gov/newsroom/bass-pro-failed-hire-blacks-and-hispanics-its-stores-nationwide-eeoc-says-suit.

Equal Employment Opportunity Commission. "Bass Pro to Pay $10.5 Million to Settle EEOC Hiring Discrimination and Retaliation Suit." Press release, July 25, 2017. https://www.eeoc.gov/newsroom/bass-pro-pay-105-million-settle-eeoc-hiring-discrimination-and-retaliation-suit.

Equal Employment Opportunity Commission. *Plaintiff v. Bass Pro Outdoor World, LLC et al., Defendants*. United States District Court, Southern District of Texas, Houston Division. Equal Employment Opportunity Commission, Case no. 4:11-cv-03425, filed May 31, 2012.

Forsyth, Jim. "Bass Pro Shops Accused of Discrimination, Racial Slurs." *Reuters*, September 22, 2011.

Frazer, R. Lee, and Kelsey Anderson. "Media Representations of Race, Ability, and Gender in Three Outdoor Magazines: A Content Analysis of Photographic Images." *Journal of Outdoor Recreation, Education and Leadership* 10, no. 3 (2018): 270–273.

Hed, Scott. "Everything Old Is New Again: Bristol Bay and the Pebble Mine." Patagonia.com, no date. https://www.patagonia.com/stories/everything-old-is-new-again-bristol-bay-and-the-pebble-mine/story-33103.html.

Hirschman, Elizabeth C. *Branding Masculinity: Tracing the Cultural Foundations of Brand Meaning*. New York: Routledge, 2016.

Hollenbeck, Candice R., Cara Peters, and George M. Zinkhana. "Retail Spectacles and Brand Meaning: Insights from a Brand Museum Case Study." *Journal of Retailing* 84, no. 3 (September 2008): 334–353.

Jones, Brendan. "Pebble Mine Threatens One of the Last Great Salmon Rivers." *Sierra*, March 2, 2018. https://www.sierraclub.org/sierra/2018-2-march-april/grapple/pebble-mine-threatens-alaska-salmon-bristol-bay.

Kampgrounds of America Research. "North American Camping & Outdoor Hospitality Report 2023: The Ninth Annual Survey of the General Population. Conducted by Cairn Consulting Group." 2023.

Lee, Jason W., Matthew J. Bernthal, Warren A. Whisenant, and Susan Mullane. "NASCAR: Checkered Flags Are Not All That Are Being Waved." *Sport Marketing Quarterly* 19, no. 3 (2010): 170–179.

Long, James M., Micheal S. Allen, Wesley F. Porak, and Cory D. Suski. "A Historical Perspective of Black Bass Management in the United States." *American Fisheries Society Symposium* 82 (2015): 99–122.

Martin, Claire. "Is Diversity Just a Marketing Strategy for Gear Brands?" *Outside*, July 23, 2018. https://www.outsideonline.com/culture/opinion/outdoor-industry-getting-more-diverse-slowly/.

Martin, Derek Christopher. "Apartheid in the Great Outdoors: American Advertising and the Reproduction of a Racialized Outdoor Leisure Identity." *Journal of Leisure Research* 36, no. 4 (2004): 513–535.

Newman, Joshua I. "Old Times There Are Not Forgotten: Sport, Identity, and the Confederate Flag in the Dixie South." *Sociology of Sport Journal* 24, no. 3 (2007): 261–282.

O'Brien, Jean. *Firsting and Lasting: Writing Indians out of Existence in New England.* Minneapolis: University of Minnesota Press, 2010.

Patterson, Troy. "From Grunt Style to 'Warcore,' Civilians Are Embracing Military Fashion." *New Yorker*, March 6, 2019. https://www.newyorker.com/culture/on-and-off-the-avenue/from-grunt-style-to-warcore-civilians-are-embracing-military-fashion.

Reeder, Scott. "Why Have So Many Cities and Towns Given Away So Much Money to Bass Pro Shops and Cabela's?" *Bloomberg*, August 13, 2012. https://www.bloomberg.com/news/articles/2012-08-13/why-do-these-towns-give-away-so-much-to-big-box-stores.

REI summer 2022. Catalog.

Shackleford, Ben. "NASCAR Stock Car Racing: Establishment and Southern Retrenchment." *International Journal of the History of Sport* 28, no. 2 (2011): 300–318.

Sills, Joe. "The Unbelievable True Story of How the Memphis Pyramid Became a Bass Pro Shops." *Forbes*, August 26, 2020. https://www.forbes.com/sites/joesills/2020/08/26/the-unbelievable-true-story-of-how-the-memphis-pyramid-became-a-bass-pro-shops/.

Stecker, Andrew, and Kevin Connor. "Fishing for Taxpayer Cash: Bass Pro's Record of Big-League Subsidies, Failed Promises, and the Consequences for Cities across America." Public Accountability Initiative Report, June 2, 2010. https://public-accountability.org/report/fishing-for-taxpayer-cash/.

Taylor, Dorceta E. *The Rise of the American Conservation Movement: Power, Privilege, and Environmental Protection.* Durham, NC: Duke University Press, 2016.

US Fish and Wildlife Service and US Census Bureau, *2016 National Survey of Fishing, Hunting, and Wildlife-Associated Recreation*. Washington, DC: US Fish and Wildlife Service and US Census Bureau.

Waszczuk, Savannah. "The Johnny Morris Story." *417 Magazine*, November 2014. https://www.417mag.com/issues/november-2014/the-johnny-morris-story/.

Wilson, Jim. "Frontier Lawman: Deputy U.S. Marshal Bass Reeves." *American Rifleman*, February 12, 2015. https://www.americanrifleman.org/content/frontier-lawman-deputy-u-s-marshal-bass-reeves/.

CONCLUSION

SHANE HAMILTON

Is the big box store a peculiarly American phenomenon? In one sense, no; giant retailers exist, indeed thrive, outside North America. Shoppers in the United Kingdom routinely fill their car boots with goods bought in bulk at out-of-town "superstores." The French invented the *hypermarché*, with Carrefour's mega-format serving as a direct inspiration for Sam Walton's vision for Walmart Supercenters. Australians have Kmarts and Targets. India rejects multinational retailers but has homegrown Big Bazaar and Saravana stores. Chinese consumers frequent mega-retailers such as Sun Art—previously a joint venture with Western corporations but now majority-owned by the China-based conglomerate Alibaba.

But even if giant retail formats are hardly unique to the United States, big box stores undeniably dominate—and in many ways define—the contemporary American economic landscape. America's big box stores are reliant on global flows of capital, commodities, technologies, and business practice; but those flows are very uneven. Seven of the world's top ten retailers (by revenue) are based in the United States, including big box pioneers Walmart, Costco, Home Depot, Kroger, and Target.[1] Domestically, of the ten top US retailers (by sales), only one (Amazon) is not primarily a big box format (if by "big box" one refers to retail space as distinct from distribution space, a point to which I return).[2] Big boxes loom larger in the US than elsewhere. Retail space occupies more square footage per capita in the United States than in any other country: nearly twice as much as in Australia, five times as much as in Japan, and seven times that in Spain.[3] For much of the twentieth century, the most important industrial space of the American economy was the factory—such as Ford's monstrous River Rouge automobile plant, photographed and painted in reverent awe by the Precisionist artist Charles Sheeler. Today, manufacturing takes up only a third as much industrial space (3.5 billion square feet) in the US as warehousing and distribution (10.2 billion square feet).[4] It remains to be seen whether paintings of distribution centers will ever hang on the gallery walls of the Museum of Modern Art, eliciting ambiguous sensations of beautiful menace as does the industrial pastoralism of Sheeler's 1930 *American Landscape*.[5]

The outsized role of the big box store in American consumer culture is a product not of destiny but of choice. India has big box stores, to be sure, but it also enforces strict limits on retailer expansion to protect the livelihoods of independent shop owners. Approximately 12 million family-owned *kiranas*, densely distributed in every Indian city, consequently account for 95 percent of the country's grocery sales.[6] In much of Europe, local, regional, national, and European Union regulations limit retailer size—whether measured in physical terms or in degree of economic concentration—and most such regulations emerged in the 1990s as a direct response to the perceived threat of American-style retailing to European ways of working and consuming.[7]

If the American big box store is a product of choice, *whose* choice is it? Until the late 1970s, American shoppers spent more than half of their retail dollars at single stores, not big chains.[8] In aggregate, the decisions of millions of consumers to frequent general merchandise chains such as Walmart or Home Depot, rather than independent local dry goods or hardware stores, created the demand that has enabled the big box format to expand dramatically since the 1970s. But the consolidation of the US retail sector in the hands of a shrinking number of corporations meant that American shoppers had fewer choices of where they *could* shop after the 1970s. To claim that consumers were "sovereign"—for example, all-powerful determinants of how retail businesses operated—is an unconvincing economic theory and has historically served primarily as a means of deflecting deeper inquiry into the structures of power in modern retailing.[9] Furthermore, the fact that no other country has anything like the same concentration and scale of big box retailers as the United States suggests that the choices supporting the rise of the big box have been more structural than individual.

This point highlights the first of three major themes that recur throughout this volume: *governance*. Governance, particularly as conceptualized in global value chains (GVC) theory, refers not so much to government institutions (e.g., states and courts) but instead to how the concrete practices and decisions of actors in a network of interrelated organizations establish hierarchies of power. The fact that a cotton T-shirt is available for an "always low price" at a 155,774-square-foot store in Dodgeville, Wisconsin, is the result of choices made by a bewildering array of organizational actors—spanning South Asian textile manufacturers, trans-Pacific container-shipping firms, and North American logistics firms, as well as big box retailers. The choices made by any of the actors in the value chain are fundamentally structured by traditional governments. When one of the actors in that chain is a multinational retailer with a budget larger than that of most nations in the world, however, one must acknowledge that power relations are inherently asymmetrical and that traditional notions of private versus public governance have become increasingly blurred in the past three decades. In the context of retailer-driven value chains, the choices made by any individual consumer are therefore framed by a set of possibilities and limitations disproportionately established by those firms that occupy the "strategic heights of the economy."[10]

The big box retailers' rise to commanding power is one episode in a much longer history of incessantly changing organizational forms in American consumer culture. Waves of "modernization" and "rationalization" have repeatedly swept through the business of getting goods to customers, as entrepreneurs and managers have seized opportunities provided by technologies of transportation and communication to rewrite the rules of the industry. The grand department stores of late nineteenth-century urban America offered "luxury for the masses," while mail-order catalogs provided rural Americans with access to an astounding array of items from faraway manufactories. Both organizational innovations were built on the new technological infrastructures of national rail transportation and telegraph communications networks and advancements in mass production and specialized manufacturing.[11] Chain hardware stores, self-service grocers and supermarkets, and discount general merchandisers such as Woolworth's likewise drew on the technological infrastructures of their time to drive out competitors and "middlemen" in their supply chains, perhaps not occupying the "commanding heights" of an entire globe's value chains but certainly calling shots more powerfully than could an atomized set of independent and often uncoordinated retailers and wholesalers.[12]

Widespread and sometimes violent resistance often accompanied these transformations in the structure of retailing, as when small-town residents gathered in town squares to burn mail-order catalogs or when populists inside and outside government denounced the "chain store menace" of the 1930s.[13] What was touted as "rationalization" by consolidated retailers, in other words, looked very different to those for whom the new organizational structures entailed loss of livelihoods. Yet despite oft-repeated language of "removing middlemen," the incessant transformation of organizational structures in American retailing has primarily been about setting new rules and power relations for the processes of moving goods from production to consumption. "Middlemen" do not disappear; they get absorbed into a different (usually larger) organization. The terms of governance in the value chain are rewritten, generally with a strategic goal to reduce margins and increase stock turns—the most essential numbers for any business seeking to profitably sell goods to the masses. Indeed, around the turn of the twentieth century, warehouse operators—later to be written off as hidebound "middlemen" wedded to an inefficient past—touted themselves as quintessential modernizers, capable of stretching, saving, and commodifying time to even out the unpredictable flows of credit and goods on which any retailer depends.[14]

The history of American retailing, both before and after the arrival of big box stores, has thus been consistent with economist Joseph Schumpeter's conception of "creative destruction." Retailing entrepreneurs repeatedly found creative ways of doing what had been done before but more efficiently, such as replacing independent high-margin food shops staffed by owner-proprietors with chain stores offering national brands at low margins. Although more efficient, the process of creating new opportunities for consolidated retailers and the producers of nationally advertised goods also entailed the destruction of existing businesses, buildings, jobs, and cultural norms and social practices. Much as the Parisian food markets of Les Halles have been repeatedly razed and rebuilt over multiple centuries to conform to the retailing fashions of the time, the definitions of what counts as "modern" in retailing can write some places onto the economic map—for example, Bentonville, Arkansas—while writing others off it. This can include the same structures erected by the creative destroyers themselves; "ghost" Walmarts populate many of the towns and cities where the retailer first disrupted local trade before moving on to other shopping plazas or nearby towns with lower tax rates, leaving empty cavernous buildings and giant parking lots behind with few options for repurposing the space. Although Silicon Valley entrepreneurs often overlook Schumpeter's dark vision when uncritically touting the possibilities of "creative destruction," Schumpeter himself understood that the long-term consequences of incessant technological change included undermining the institutions and values on which the initial entrepreneurial act was predicated.[15]

Governance in retailing, in other words, is the means by which certain organizational forms—whether downtown palaces offering glittering luxuries or exurban boxes filled with fluorescent-lit racks of polyester—structure the choices any individual actor can make in the network of production, distribution, and consumption. As this volume makes clear, the incessant restructuring of retail governance in the big box era has reshaped both economic value and cultural and social values for everyone from consumers to shareholders.

For managers and investors, one key question of governance involves the specific choices involved in constructing a big box business model. At core, all big box retailers share assumptions about the value proposition to be made: a wide range of goods on offer; margins set low enough to encourage bulk/repeat purchasing and hence rapid stock turnover; and a primary focus on goods, not services ("no frills"). Providing access to a wide range of goods is built into the defining physical feature of the individual big box but is also tightly linked to the network effect enabled by a chain of big boxes embedded in a technologically sophisticated distribution system: one study estimates that for every 10 percent increase in the number of individual stores in a big box chain, the firm can add 100 more items to product lines across all its stores.[16] Economies of scale and scope thus produce a seemingly endless positive feedback loop, with boxes and chains and distribution centers all expanding in concert—increasingly raising barriers to entry for smaller retail firms that simply cannot provide the same diversity of products at consistently low margins.

The other half of the business model equation is the value architecture, or how the firm captures profit from the value proposition. Here the model varies somewhat by sector and firm, but generally the assumption is that low margins require vigilant cost cutting, which most managers take as a cue to push down worker wages and fight efforts at unionization—both inside the store and further upstream in the supply chain.[17] This approach contradicts increasing evidence that mass retailers can in fact increase profitability and productivity by improving worker wages and working conditions, boosting employee skill sets and customer satisfaction—specific examples include Costco, Trader Joe's, and Mercadona (Spain's largest supermarket chain). These exceptions, however, prove the rule.[18] Workers who seek to collectively assert a stake in the governance of the American big box business model are routinely denied opportunities to do so.

The big box business model would not be possible without the "logistics revolution" of the second half of the twentieth century.[19] As Johnathan Williams explores in chapter 2 of this volume, big box retailers depend on the technologies and deregulatory politics of a fast-paced, low-wage distribution system. Strategic management consultants coined the term *supply-chain management* in the 1980s to conceptualize this logistics-enabled network as a new form of business enterprise: governed not by the demands of vertically integrated manufacturers—as had been the case in the mid-twentieth century—but instead by a set of "partnerships" among multiple firms. In these idealized supply chains, far-flung suppliers, distributors, and retailers would share information—about costs, inventories, and so on—to avoid bottlenecks and "bullwhips" in the process of getting huge volumes of low-priced goods into the hands of affluent consumers.[20] Technologies such as the UPC barcode and the internet surely enabled unprecedented information sharing across supply chains. But while the rhetoric of supply-chain management has historically emphasized equal "partnerships," the reality has more often reflected unequal hierarchies, with big retailers setting the rules of engagement.[21]

From the choices made in establishing a big box business model, then, a host of governance implications flow: retail and supply-chain workers become fungible commodities rather than employees invested in the business's success; nominally independent manufacturers become beholden to big buyers' demands for ever lower costs and ever tighter delivery schedules. As Williams's and Aaron Van Neste's chapters (2 and 3, respectively) in this volume further emphasize, the ability of local, state, and national governments to harness the power of multinational corporations to serve a public interest beyond that of "always low prices" seems to have waned in recent decades. Not that governments have disappeared; as both Williams and Van Neste make clear, government power—whether in the form of action or inaction—is often quite useful for big box firms in setting favorable terms for taxation, worker safety standards, and environmental regulations. Public-private hybrid collaborations, in fact, may be a defining feature of this neoliberal approach to corporate governance—for although "free markets" are upheld as a theoretical ideal, when something like a market for sustainable seafood does not exist, a multi-stakeholder initiative funded by multinational retailers and supported by multiple government agencies can force such a market into existence. Historical precedents for such private-public collaborations—such as the American supermarket industry's 1940s alliance with the US Department of Agriculture to create an entirely new mass market for fresh chicken[22]—suggest the need to critically interrogate the assumptions on both the political left and the political right that abstract "market" forces of neoliberalism are responsible for erasing the state. Markets are very much the product of governance choices; when business models are predicated on corporate tax breaks, taxpayer-supported research and development into transportation and distribution technologies, and lax regulation of environmental quality, worker safety, and labor rights, calling those markets "free" borders on the farcical.

In historical perspective, the outsized economic power that has come to be concentrated in the hands of American big box retailers is not in and of itself an issue. For almost two centuries, American corporations of one sort or another have maintained extraordinary power to shape the working lives and consumption possibilities of citizens around the world.[23] A key question this volume helps to highlight, however, is how the power of the big box might be more effectively harnessed to broader, more socially and environmentally sustainable visions of corporate *responsibility* for the choices made in the value chain. History can provide important lessons in this regard; indeed, this volume can be read as a call for further historical analysis of the governance implications of the rise of big box retailing.

A second theme that permeates this volume is that of *experience*. Many of this book's readers will have spent time in big box stores, perhaps quite a bit of time. Most readers will furthermore presumably have spent most of that time in such stores as shoppers, not employees; indeed, this volume—in keeping with nearly all works in retail history—focuses primarily on the experiences of customers, managers, and owners rather than those of shop-floor employees (with the notable exception of Sherri Sheu's [chapter 6] examination of discriminatory hiring practices).[24] At the core of this volume's intellectual framework, as a work in environmental history, is the premise that in emotional and sensory terms, the shopping experience of a typical big box consumer is inherently and problematically divorced from the physical environments that enable the abundance they perceive on the shelves. Obfuscations and half-truths occupy the distance between material reality and emotional experiences in this big box moral economy. Big box shoppers do not buy merely a dead fish, they buy certified "sustainable seafood"; they do not buy merely waterproof breathable laminate outerwear, they buy the imaginary of an "authentic expedition" to mountains they will probably never set foot on; they do not buy merely a box of fishing tackle, they buy affirmation of their conservative worldviews.

It is tempting, then, to caricaturize the big box experience as one of soul-crushing sameness, devoid of authentic meaning. The term *big box*, which first came into widespread use in the 1990s (as Williams rightly notes in chapter 2, this volume), clearly carried a derogatory connotation; early uses of the term in mass publications routinely characterized the retail format as unpleasant, inauthentic, and harmful to local communities and physical environments.[25] Big boxes were often contrasted to the department stores of a century before; although a Macy's or an Abercrombie and Fitch could also be very big and very much in the shape of a cube, the items on offer in those stores evoked delight, longing, and magic. The attraction of affordable yet luxurious goods that in previous decades would have been too costly for middle-class consumers drove many to kleptomania, while in Theodore Dreiser's novel *Sister Carrie* the magnetic pull of glittering goods in Chicago's department stores ensnares the title character into a life of insatiable longing.[26] Department stores may have raised moral quandaries about the nature of consumption, but even their harshest critics would not have deemed them boring or unpleasant. Sister Carrie wandered into a department store in a bustling, pedestrian-focused retail district—a distinctly different experience from that of a modern big box shopper, forced to drive a car on a suburban "stroad" into a giant, hot parking lot that leads to a fluorescent-lit cavern of metal and plastic.[27]

More charitably, one could see the architecture of the big box as a product of many decades of effort to replace "traditional" retail formats with more "modern" spaces of consumption. Independent retailers in the late nineteenth and early twentieth centuries were often the first to develop new technologies and store designs to improve the shopping experience for customers, but chain stores learned from (or copied) the independent's experiments.[28] Early chain stores selling ordinary goods—tea, groceries, and household necessities—routinely advertised their spaces as distinctively clean, efficient, and nondiscriminatory. For Black and immigrant customers, chain stores often appealed as places where what counted most was the number of dollars in one's checkbook, not one's color of skin or proficiency in speaking English. Customers accustomed to being cheated by discriminatory clerks appreciated the written price tags, cash registers, sanitary standards, and effective lighting that smoothed transactions in a chain store in ways that could often feel liberating. Chain stores, to be sure, continued to maintain unequal structures of race, class, and gender, but they did so in increasingly subtle ways as their architecture became increasingly depersonalized and standardized over the course of the twentieth century.[29]

Not all big boxes are monotonous, austere, and devoid of personal meaning. As Sheu and Rachel S. Gross (chapter 5) reveal in this volume, outdoor gear chain stores routinely seek to evoke sensory delight and surprise—selling not only hunting, fishing, and camping gear but also imaginaries of a wilderness far removed from any stroad. As Gross's chapter highlights, the big box consumer experience is often characterized by irony: while purists may disdain the stripped-bare aesthetic and cost-cutting fixation of a discount chain, it is only through that no-frills portal that the majority of consumers gain access to the goods and experiences prized by the affluent. Both Walmart and REI, in their divergent ways, offer a democratic shopping experience for outdoor gear. Much like Allen Ginsberg, strolling through the aisles of a mid-twentieth-century supermarket looking for the spirit of Walt Whitman, contemporary customers may surprise the elitists by finding deeper meanings—perhaps even dreams—in the "open corridors" of a big box store.[30] (I, for one, distinctly remember having repeated hallucinatory dreams after visiting the first Walmart to arrive in my rural, working-class neck of the woods in the late 1980s.)

Sheu and Gross rightly point to the limits of democracy in big box outdoor retailing, highlighting racist and gendered notions that permeate the industry, such as the idea that white men who "hate to shop" as much as they hate multiculturalism will inherently love an outdoor store like Cabela's. And for decades, discount chains such as Walmart have deservedly come under public censure for discriminatory practices. Yet as chains become increasingly dependent for profitability on embracing more diverse customer bases, their shareholders have pushed firms to present the big box shopping experience as politically neutral. In 2018, for instance, Walmart's corporate headquarters implemented voluntary restrictions on gun sales, including background checks and bans on high-capacity magazines.

No matter whether emphasizing standardization or diversity, the orchestrators of the big box store shopping experience present the consumer as the sovereign of the brightly lit domain. Sister Carrie was attracted to consumer goods by "magnetic forces," illustrating Dreiser's naturalist portrayal of a world in which industrialization and urbanization restricted the possibilities of free will. By contrast, free will is lionized in a big box store; Sheu notes in this volume (chapter 6) how Bass Pro Shops upholds hunter-customers as heroic contributors to conservation, while Bart Elmore (chapter 1) recounts how Walmart's introduction of the UPC barcode to link point-of-sale information to supply chains enabled the firm to respond more effectively to consumers' specific demands than any retailer had before it. Customers in a big box store consequently assume that the shelves will be filled with precisely what they expect to find there. Occasional disruptions, such as those that occurred during the hoarding and supply-chain breakdowns experienced in Covid-19 lockdowns, can trigger a sense of panic and disbelief when, say, toilet paper or bags of flour are suddenly conspicuously absent. Such moments of breakdown, though rare, potentially open a window for consumers onto the broader consequences of their shopping choices. When toilet paper and bags of flour appear to flow, uninterrupted, from some distant and unknown location, a big box customer need not think about the material waste, unfair labor conditions, and reliance on fossil fuels that make that "flow" possible.

As a work rooted in the concerns and methods of environmental history, this book goes a long way toward revealing those consequences, often summed up by economists as "externalities." More work can be done, however, for, as noted above, this volume focuses primarily on the experiences of consumers, managers, and investors rather than the workers in the stores and supply chains of the big box political economy. An understanding of the historical experiences of workers in the factories that supply big box chains—or those of the workers who recycle, upcycle, dismantle, and dispose of the waste of global commodity chains—would reveal important truths about the lived experiences of big box capitalism.[31] Much as the histories in this volume have revealed surprises and ironies in the big box shopping experience, future histories that take into account the meaning of big box capitalism for workers in warehouses and distribution centers may produce startling insights—as does Heike Geissler's semifictional portrayal of the absurdities and inefficiencies embedded in the work routines of a supposedly ultra-rationalized distribution center.[32]

Space is a third key theme resonating throughout the chapters in this volume. An environmental history perspective reveals the extent to which big box retailing radically distorts space, capitalizing on the transformation of *places*—context-specific, meaning-rich locations of human experience—into abstract blank slates primed for profit maximization.[33] Big box stores inherently lengthen the distance between home and shop; Sister Carrie walked to her department stores, while we learn from Sheu's chapter that the average Bass Pro Shops customer drives over fifty miles. Perhaps sitting in a car on a traffic-jammed stroad meets some individuals' perceptions of a meaningful experience, but urbanists are keen to ridicule the suburban shopping trip as a boring and unhealthy waste of time, built on the wasted space of inefficient highways and parking lots.[34]

The key spatial distortion of the big box is that it transforms what can reasonably be understood as "wasted space" into highly profitable space. As architectural critic Jesse LeCavalier has argued, the logic of how to best use space in a big box business model is an inversion of how retailers approached urban space a century before: whereas the architect of New York's Woolworth Building declared a high-rise "merely the machine that makes the land pay," in the big box economy, a giant store "is not a machine for making the land pay but instead pays the land to be part of the machine."[35] As Laura J. Martin insightfully demonstrates in chapter 5 of this volume, the sites for big box stores are often located on what was once the "periphery" of urban space: wetlands, exurbs, economically faltering hinterlands. In the early decades of the rise of the big box, from the 1960s to the 1980s, those peripheries were often created by the demolition attendant on suburbanization—bulldozing land for interstate highways and suburbs exposed precisely the kinds of locations Sam Walton famously scouted from airplanes, seeking out seemingly blank places on the retail map where he envisioned future development anchored by mass merchandisers (cf. Elmore, chapter 1, this volume).[36] Even more important than store location, however, was the location of the rural distribution centers that anchored the chain's logistics network. Interstates and long-haul trucking provided the flexible transportation required to pump high volumes of goods out to the widely distributed stores of this commercial periphery.

By the 1990s, with the big box model well established, the pattern reversed: rather than capitalizing on spaces that had already been made peripheral, big box stores increasingly drove the process of creating new peripheral spaces. Martin's chapter explains how previously unvalued wetlands, having been re-valued as locations for big box stores yet also recognized as ecologically beneficial, have been re-created as "banked" wetlands in locations that, for now, are far removed from any major population centers or big box real estate agents' plans. Martin reveals the cold legal logic and regulatory framework in which this wetland banking makes sense, although in LeCavalier's terms, one wonders how the heads would spin of the architects of the early twentieth century for whom space became valuable when it was transformed into a place worthy of being experienced and imbued with meaning.

Whether logical or not, the spatial distortions of the big box are deeply embedded in contemporary American life. As noted, American boxes are very big by any objective measure. So are their parking lots, which are typically three times the size of the stores themselves. The designers of the popular video game *SimCity* wanted to simulate contemporary urban life as accurately as possible, but the designers realized that "our game was going to be really boring if it was proportional in terms of parking lots"; consequently, the software developers put most of their virtual parking lots underground, wishing away the unpleasant aspects of urban space premised on individual car ownership.[37] Shoppers at big box stores tend not to think about how much space is taken up by big box parking lots, though they probably think even less about the stroads, highways, distribution centers, ports, container ships, factories, landfills, and hazardous waste centers that occupy even vaster spaces yet are geographically and mentally distant from the point of consumption. There are, as Aaron Van Neste emphasizes in chapter 3 of this volume, millions of "ghost acres" in the spatial empire of the big box. Any complete mapping of this empire would include not only the distribution centers and inland ports, however, but also the millions of acres of agricultural space where cotton is grown for big box textiles and soya and maize are raised for the processed foods sold in supercenters, as well as the landfills where 99 percent of big box goods end up within six months of purchase. The internal space of the big box store, as cavernous as it may seem, is relatively small compared to the space consumed by the wider distribution system in which the box is just the endpoint of a globe-spanning supply chain.

Yet as Williams rightly notes in this volume, the once peripheral elements of the big box economy are increasingly moving closer to city centers. With distribution centers relocating to metropolitan areas and some big box stores opening in urban centers, the environmental consequences of the big box model may start hitting closer to home for many. Perhaps expectations for how best to use urban, suburban, and rural space for retailing and distribution will fundamentally transform in coming years. Consumers may realize, for instance, that for many years they have been providing big box retailers with free labor by transporting themselves and their goods over the ultra-expensive "last miles" of the distribution system, scanning their own UPC codes at self-checkout machines, and providing marketers with valuable data along the way.

This history of the American big box surely serves as a useful guide in rethinking both the past and the future of retailing. The most crucial lesson of big box history is that these cinderblock-and-parking-lot edifices are a product of choices rather than fate and that the entrepreneurship that created them will also surely destroy the current system for one deemed more efficient. It is hoped that feeding into that definition of "efficiency" will be serious considerations of the environmental impacts produced by the modes of governance, values of experience, and approaches to space that have made Big Box USA what it is today.

NOTES

1. Deloitte, "Global Powers of Retailing."
2. National Retail Federation, "Top 100 Retailers."
3. Peterson, "The Retail Apocalypse Is Still in Its 'Early Innings.'"
4. Statista, "Big-Box Real Estate in North America,"
5. Lucic, *Charles Sheeler and the Cult of the Machine.*
6. Gent, "The Battle for India's Street Corner," 59.
7. Sanchez-Vidal, *Retail Shocks and City Structure.*
8. Basker, Klimek, and Hoang Van, "Supersize It."
9. Hamilton, *Supermarket USA*, chapter 5.
10. Gereffi, Humphrey, and Sturgeon, "The Governance of Global Value Chains"; Bair, "Global Capitalism and Commodity Chains"; Lichtenstein, "Supply Chains, Workers' Chains, and the New World of Retail Supremacy," quote on 17.
11. Kline, *Consumers in the Country*; Howard, *From Main Street to Mall*; Scranton, *Endless Novelty.*
12. Levinson, *The Great A&P*; Deutsch, *Building a Housewife's Paradise.*
13. Schlereth, "Country Stores, County Fairs, and Mail-Order Catalogues," 5; Scroop, "The Anti-Chain Store Movement."
14. Orenstein, *Out of Stock*; Tangires, *Movable Markets.*
15. McCraw, *Prophet of Innovation.*
16. Basker, Klimek, and Hoang Van, "Supersize It."
17. Lichtenstein, "Two Cheers for Vertical Integration."
18. Rahmandad and Ton, "If Higher Pay Is Profitable, Why Is It So Rare."
19. Bonacich and Hardie, "Wal-Mart and the Logistics Revolution"; Bonacich and Wilson, *Getting the Goods.*
20. Oliver and Webber, "Supply-Chain Management"; Harland, "Supply Chain Management"; Fawcett and Magnan, "The Rhetoric and Reality of Supply Chain Integration"; Sheffi, *The Resilient Enterprise.*
21. Ballou, "The Evolution and Future of Logistics and Supply Chain Management."
22. Hamilton, *Supermarket USA*, 38–40.
23. Gomory and Sylla, "The American Corporation"; Enstad, *Cigarettes, Inc.*; Lamoreaux and Novak, *Corporations and American Democracy.*
24. A handful of important exceptions that do investigate the historical experience of ordinary retail workers includes Benson, *Counter Cultures*; Moreton, *To Serve God and Wal-Mart*; Ikeler, *Hard Sell.*
25. A sample of headlines from the ProQuest Historical database of major US newspapers (https://about.proquest.com/en/products-services/pq-hist-news/): "Here's to

the Town That Wasn't Afraid to Shove Wal-Mart" (1994); "They Came, They Conquered, They Closed" (1995); "Megastores, Bargain Hunting, and Life's Little Indignities" (1995); "The Box Stops Here" (1999).
26. Abelson, *When Ladies Go A-Thieving*; Dreiser, *Sister Carrie*.
27. Stroad is an intentionally derogatory portmanteau describing a space that is unsafe for pedestrians yet so broken up by intersections leading to giant parking lots that it functions well neither as a *street* (for pedestrians and businesses) nor as a *road* (for moving traffic).
28. Spellman, *Cornering the Market*.
29. On consumer appreciation of chain stores as cleaner and less discriminatory than independent retail shops: Cohen, *Making a New Deal*; Tolbert, "The Aristocracy of the Market Basket"; Levinson, *Great A&P*; Cochoy, Hagberg, and Kjellberg, "The Technologies of Price Display." On the entrenchment of social inequalities in "modern" retail spaces, see Deutsch, *Building a Housewife's Paradise*.
30. Ginsberg, "A Supermarket in California."
31. To date, most of this sort of work has been done by anthropologists and geographers; see, for example, Herod, Pickren, Rainnie, and Champ, "Global Destruction Networks, Labour and Waste"; Tsing, *Friction*.
32. Geissler, *Seasonal Associate*.
33. Tuan, *Space and Place*.
34. See, for instance, the work of Strong Towns, a nonprofit organization advocating "for cities of all sizes to be safe, livable, and inviting"; https://www.strongtowns.org/bigbox.
35. LeCavalier, *The Rule of Logistics*, 3.
36. Rome, *The Bulldozer in the Countryside*; Ammon, *Bulldozer*.
37. Manaugh and Twilley, "The Philosophy of SimCity."

BIBLIOGRAPHY

Abelson, Elaine S. *When Ladies Go A-Thieving: Middle-Class Shoplifters in the Victorian Department Store*. New York: Oxford University Press, 1989.

Ammon, Francesca Russello. *Bulldozer: Demolition and Clearance of the Postwar Landscape*. New Haven, CT: Yale University Press, 2016.

Bair, Jennifer. "Global Capitalism and Commodity Chains: Looking Back, Going Forward." *Competition and Change* 9, no. 2 (2005): 153–180.

Ballou, Ronald H. "The Evolution and Future of Logistics and Supply Chain Management." *European Business Review* 19, no. 4 (2007): 332–348. https://doi.org/10.1108/09555340710760152.

Basker, Emek, Shawn Klimek, and Pham Hoang Van. "Supersize It: The Growth of Retail Chains and the Rise of the 'Big-Box' Store." *Journal of Economics and Management Strategy* 21, no. 3 (2012): 541–582. https://doi.org/10.1111/j.1530-9134.2012.00339.x.

Benson, Susan Porter. *Counter Cultures: Saleswomen, Managers, and Customers in American Department Stores, 1890–1940*. Urbana: University of Illinois Press, 1986.

Bonacich, Edna, and Khaleelah Hardie. "Wal-Mart and the Logistics Revolution." In *Wal-Mart: The Face of Twenty-First-Century Capitalism*, edited by Nelson Lichtenstein, 163–187. New York: New Press, 2006.

Bonacich, Edna, and Jake Wilson. *Getting the Goods: Ports, Labor, and the Logistics Revolution*. Ithaca, NY: Cornell University Press, 2008.

Cochoy, Franck, Johan Hagberg, and Hans Kjellberg. "The Technologies of Price Display: Mundane Retail Price Governance in the Early Twentieth Century." *Economy and Society* 47, no. 4 (2018): 572–606.

Cohen, Lizabeth. *Making a New Deal: Industrial Workers in Chicago, 1919–1939*. Cambridge, UK: Cambridge University Press, 1990.

Deloitte. "Global Powers of Retailing." 2022. https://www2.deloitte.com/content/dam/Deloitte/global/Documents/Consumer-Business/gx-global-powers-of-retailing-2022.pdf.

Deutsch, Tracey A. *Building a Housewife's Paradise: Gender, Politics, and American Grocery Stores in the Twentieth Century*. Chapel Hill: University of North Carolina Press, 2010.

Dreiser, Theodore. *Sister Carrie*. New York: Signet Classics, 2000 [1900].

Enstad, Nan. *Cigarettes, Inc.: An Intimate History of Corporate Imperialism*. Chicago: University of Chicago Press, 2018.

Fawcett, Stanley E., and Gregory M. Magnan. "The Rhetoric and Reality of Supply Chain Integration." *International Journal of Physical Distribution and Logistics Management* 32, no. 5 (2002): 339–361.

Geissler, Heike. *Seasonal Associate*. Translated by Katy Derbyshire. Cambridge, MA: MIT Press, 2018.

Gent, Ed. "The Battle for India's Street Corner." *MIT Tech Review*, June 21, 2022, 58–65.

Gereffi, Gary, John Humphrey, and Timothy Sturgeon. "The Governance of Global Value Chains." *Review of International Political Economy* 12, no. 1 (2005): 78–104.

Ginsberg, Allen. "A Supermarket in California." In Ginsberg, *Collected Poems, 1947–1997*, 144. New York: HarperCollins, 2006.

Gomory, Ralph, and Richard Sylla. "The American Corporation." *Daedalus* 142, no. 2 (2013): 102–118. https://doi.org/10.1162/DAED_a_00207.

Hamilton, Shane. *Supermarket USA: Food and Power in the Cold War Farms Race*. New Haven, CT: Yale University Press, 2018.

Harland, C. M. "Supply Chain Management: Relationships, Chains and Networks." *British Journal of Management* 7, no. 1 (1996): 63–80. https://doi.org/10.1111/j.1467-8551.1996.tb00148.x.

Herod, Andrew, Graham Pickren, Al Rainnie, and Susan McGrath Champ. "Global Destruction Networks, Labour and Waste." *Journal of Economic Geography* 14, no. 2 (2014): 421–441. https://doi.org/10.1093/jeg/lbt015.

Howard, Vicki. *From Main Street to Mall: The Rise and Fall of the American Department Store*. Philadelphia: University of Pennsylvania Press, 2015.

Ikeler, Peter. *Hard Sell: Work and Resistance in Retail Chains*. Ithaca, NY: Cornell University Press, 2016.

Kline, Ronald R. *Consumers in the Country: Technology and Social Change in Rural America*. Baltimore: Johns Hopkins University Press, 2000.

Lamoreaux, Naomi, and William J. Novak, eds. *Corporations and American Democracy*. Cambridge, MA: Harvard University Press, 2017.

LeCavalier, Jesse. *The Rule of Logistics: Walmart and the Architecture of Fulfillment*. Minneapolis: University of Minnesota Press, 2016.

Levinson, Marc. *The Great A&P and the Struggle for Small Business in America*. New York: Hill and Wang, 2011.

Lichtenstein, Nelson. "Supply Chains, Workers' Chains, and the New World of Retail Supremacy." *Labor: Studies in Working-Class History of the Americas* 4 (Spring 2007): 17–31.

Lichtenstein, Nelson. "Two Cheers for Vertical Integration: Corporate Governance in a World of Global Supply Chains." In *Corporations and American Democracy*, edited by Naomi Lamoreaux and William J. Novak, 329–358. Cambridge, MA: Harvard University Press, 2017.

Lucic, Karen. *Charles Sheeler and the Cult of the Machine*. Cambridge, MA: Harvard University Press, 1991.

Manaugh, Geoff, and Nicola Twilley. "The Philosophy of SimCity: An Interview with the Game's Lead Designer." *The Atlantic*, May 9, 2013. https://www.theatlantic.com/technology/archive/2013/05/the-philosophy-of-simcity-an-interview-with-the-games-lead-designer/275724/.

McCraw, Thomas K. *Prophet of Innovation: Joseph Schumpeter and Creative Destruction*. Cambridge, MA: Belknap, 2007.

Moreton, Bethany. *To Serve God and Wal-Mart: The Making of Christian Free Enterprise*. Cambridge, MA: Harvard University Press, 2009.

National Retail Federation. "Top 100 Retailers." 2022. https://nrf.com/resources/top-retailers/top-100-retailers/top-100-retailers-2022-list.

Oliver, R. Keith, and Michael D. Webber. "Supply-Chain Management: Logistics Catches Up with Strategy." *Outlook* 5, no. 1 (1982): 42–47.

Orenstein, Dara. *Out of Stock: The Warehouse in the History of Capitalism*. Chicago: University of Chicago Press, 2019.

Peterson, Hayley. "The Retail Apocalypse Is Still in Its 'Early Innings'—and Thousands More Stores Will Close Before It Ends." *Business Insider*, October 3,

2018. https://www.businessinsider.com/retail-apocalypse-is-still-in-early-innings-cowen-says-2018-10.

Rahmandad, Hazhir, and Zeynep Ton. "If Higher Pay Is Profitable, Why Is It So Rare? Modeling Competing Strategies in Mass Market Services." *Organization Science* 31, no. 5 (2020): 1053–1071. https://doi.org/10.1287/orsc.2019.1347.

Rome, Adam. *The Bulldozer in the Countryside: Suburban Sprawl and the Rise of American Environmentalism*. Cambridge, UK: Cambridge University Press, 2001.

Sanchez-Vidal, Maria. *Retail Shocks and City Structure*. Centre for Economic Performance Discussion Paper no. 1636. London: London School of Economics and Political Science, 2019.

Schlereth, Thomas J. "Country Stores, County Fairs, and Mail-Order Catalogues: Consumption in Rural America." In *Consuming Visions: Accumulation and Display of Goods in America, 1880–1920*, edited by Simon J. Bronner, 339–375. New York: W. W. Norton, 1989.

Scranton, Philip. *Endless Novelty: Specialty Production and American Industrialization, 1865–1925*. Princeton, NJ: Princeton University Press, 1997.

Scroop, Daniel. "The Anti-Chain Store Movement and the Politics of Consumption." *American Quarterly* 60 (December 2008): 925–949.

Sheffi, Yossi. *The Resilient Enterprise: Overcoming Vulnerability for Competitive Advantage*. Cambridge, MA: MIT Press, 2005.

Spellman, Susan V. *Cornering the Market: Independent Grocers and Innovation in American Small Business*. Oxford: Oxford University Press, 2016.

Statista. "Big-Box Real Estate in North America." 2022. https://www-statista-com/study/48279/big-box-real-estate-in-north-america/.

Tangires, Helen. *Movable Markets: Food Wholesaling in the Twentieth-Century City*. Baltimore: Johns Hopkins University Press, 2019.

Tolbert, Lisa C. "The Aristocracy of the Market Basket." In *Food Chains: From Farmyard to Shopping Cart*, edited by Warren J. Belasco and Roger Horowitz, 179–195. Philadelphia: University of Pennsylvania Press, 2009.

Tsing, Anna Löwenhaupt. *Friction: An Ethnography of Global Connection*. Princeton, NJ: Princeton University Press, 2004.

Tuan, Yi-Fu. *Space and Place: The Perspective of Experience*. Minneapolis: University of Minnesota Press, 1977.

INDEX

Abbey, Edward, 28
Abercrombie and Fitch (A&F), 140–41, 147, 148, 195
absentee leasing, 93
access privileges. See catch shares
access, consumer goods, 192
Aceto, Joe, 61
acreage, wetland mitigation banks, 124f
Adams, Noah, 53–54
adventure expeditions, 140, 145–46, 195
affordability of consumer goods, 4, 140, 195
African Americans. See people of color
Agriculture, US Department of, 193–94
agriculture/agribusiness, 21–22, 115, 116f
Air Management, Bureau of, 59
air quality: distribution centers, 55; government regulations, 66; ground level ozone, 64, 67–68; monitoring, 29, 71; New York State, 30, 31; non-point sources, 65–66; Oconomowoc distribution center, 59, 63; traffic congestion, 29; Walmart, 37; Williston, Vermont, 29; Wisconsin, 65–66
Alaska, Pebble Mine campaign, 160, 174–77
Aldi, 86
Alex C. Walker Foundation, 92
Alibaba (China-based conglomerate), 187
Allen, Wes, 138
alligators, wetlands, 118
Amazon: e-commerce, 6; Fortune 500 rankings; logistics formula, 40; sales, 188
Ambassador Town Center, 112f, 113f, 124–25
American Camper, 144–45
American retailing, 3, 4, 58
American Society of Planning Officials, 114–15
Andel, Tom, 69
Anderson, Lars, 63–64
Anderson, Lloyd and Mary, 142

anti-chain legislation, 5
Archery Hall of Fame and Museum, 169, 170
architecture of big box stores, 195–96
Argentina, Walmart retail outlet in, 35
Arkansas: Bentonville, 32f, 191; federal funding, 21; Ozarks, 10; right-to-work legislation, 22
Army Corps of Engineers. See United States Army Corps of Engineers
Asian population. See people of color
assessments, fisheries certification, 88
athlete-oriented merchandise, 140
Audubon, John James, 164
Australia, big box stores in, 187, 188

banking policy. See mitigation banking
bankruptcy, Gander Mountain, 152
barcode. See UPC barcode
bargaining practices, fixed prices, 5
Barquist, David, 68
bass fishing, natural history, 161
Bass Pro Shops: business model, 139; Cabela's, 152, 163; catalogs, 162, 166–69; conservation, 160, 169, 171, 178–79; consumer goods, 167; cultural identity, 160, 162, 171, 178–79; destination travel, 162, 163, 164; diversity and inclusion, 173; environmental impact, 160, 174–78; flagship store, 163, 169; growth and expansion, 163; indoor nature experience, 150; job discrimination, 171–73; Memphis Pyramid, 158f, 159–60, 163–64; messaging, 162, 163, 164; NASCAR sponsorship, 173; National Rifle Association's (NRA) National Sporting Arms Museum, 169, 170; nostalgia, 167, 169; Pebble Mine campaign, 160, 176–78; people of color, 164–65, 167, 168, 175, 178; retail outlets, 162–66; sales, 147; shopping experience, 160, 162, 164, 165f, 170, 171, 178, 197, 198; square footage of stores, 151, 169; Trump presidential rally, 175f, 176; white male consumer base, 173–75
Ben and Jerry's, 24, 25
Ben Franklin five-and-dime store, 19

BenDor, Todd, 124
Bentonville, Arkansas, 6, 17, 20f, 21, 32f, 33f, 34–36, 40, 79, 191
Best Buy, Williston, Vermont, 29
Bezos, Jeff, 6, 40
Big Bazaar, India, 187
big box capitalism, 198
big box stores: architecture, 195–96; brand appeal, 11, 144–46, 150; business model, 138, 140, 147, 150, 192–93; closeouts, 144; consolidation, 189; corporate responsibility, 194; creative destruction, 191; cultural education, 8; development, 29–30; distribution networks, 5; e-commerce, 6; economic power, 194; entrepreneurship, 200–1; environmental impact, 7, 10, 39, 201; expedition sponsorships, 145–46; governance, 191; history, 3–8, 10, 191, 195; international, 34, 35, 37, 188; locations, 9, 111, 200; logistics, 57–58; mail-order, 5; mass production, 56; monopolies, 192; opposition, 54, 190; organizational structures, 190; outdoor industry, 140, 142, 143, 152; outlets, 6, 34, 35, 162–66; regulations, 188, 193; scholarship, 6–7; space, 141, 188; specialty shops, 139; square footage, 9, 57, 114–15, 150, 151f; "squeeze," 35, 39; tourist attractions, 151; transnational, 78; unionization, 192
Big Three, 57
biodiversity, wetlands, 122
biomass, fisheries, 79, 92, 94
Black Diamond Equipment, 137
Black population. See people of color
Black Rifle Coffee Company, 165, 166f
bluefin tuna fisheries, 90
Borders, 150
bottom trawling, 89
Bradley Foundation (Sand County Foundation), 92
brand identity, 138, 140–41, 150, 178
Branson (Missouri), Table Rock Dam, 161
Brazil, Walmart retail outlet in, 34
Bristol Bay (Alaska), 176–78
Browner, Carol, 123

brownfields, ecological footprint, 8
Bruntland Commission (United Nations/1987), 78
building displays, in-store environment, 8
bureaucracy, Environmental Impact Statement (EIS), 63, 64
Bush, George H.W., 121
Bush, George W., 122
business history of big box retail, 7, 10
business model: investors, 192; outdoor retailers, 139, 143; specialty stores, 152; supply-chain management, 192–93; value architecture, 192; Walmart, 97, 98, 143, 152
business-environment research, 7, 10
Butler brothers' franchise, 19
Buy American campaign, 34

Cabela, Dick, 148
Cabela, Jim, 148
Cabela's: Bass Pro Shops, 152, 163; business model, 139, 147; cultural identity, 147, 148f; customer experience, 11, 148–50; growth and expansion, 138–39, 149; heritage, 149; house-brand products, 139; indoor nature experience, 147–49, 150; museums, 148–49; political identity, 148f, 149; sales, 147; square footage, 151
California wetlands, 115, 117f, 118
camping equipment: big box stores, 143; Costco, 143; mass merchandising, 143; outdoor industry, 139; popularity, 142; Walmart, 143
Canada, 34
Canning-Hofmann, Bonnie, 30, 31
capital accumulation, transnational retailers, 78
carbon monoxide, 63
carbon offsetting, 11, 114, 125–26
Carlson, Tucker, 176–77
Carr, Archie, 118
Carrefour, 9, 12, 86, 96, 187
Carter, Jimmy, 119
catalogs from big box stores, 147, 148, 162, 166–69

Catch Share Design Manual, 93
catch shares, 10, 77, 91-95, 97
Cavelle, Peter, 25
census data, wetlands drainage, 116f
Central Valley wetlands, 115, 117–18
certification: choice editing, 86; ecosystems, 89–90; fisheries, 83, 85, 88; FishWise, 85–86; Marine Stewardship Council (MSC) environmental impact, 83, 85, 88–90; seafood supply chain, 83, 85, 88–89; third party, 90; sustainability, 82, 83, 84f, 85, 97
chain stores: cleanliness, 196; hardware, 190; independent retailers, 114; lighting, 196; non-discrimination, 196; opposition, 190; shopping experience, 195–96
Champs Sports, 147
Charles C. Koch Foundation, 92
Chicago market, 56, 57, 71, 122, 124
child labor, 36, 82
Chile, fisheries sustainability, 89–90, 94
China, supply chains, 34, 35, 187
choice editing, 86, 96, 96
choice, consumers, 188, 189, 191
Circuit City, 150
citizen-consumers, 114
city centers, 63, 200
class, mass consumption, 114
Clean Air and Water Acts: Federal Water Pollution Control Act, 118–19; Pebble Mine, 177; reforms, 56, 66, 69–70; Section 301, 119; Section 404, 113–14, 119; wetlands mitigation, 122
cleanliness, chain stores, 196
climate change, 171
Clinton, Bill, 122
closeouts, outdoor sportswear, 144–46
clothing. *See* sportswear retailers
Co-op. *See* REI
coastal wetlands, 117–18
Cohen, Ben, 24
Cohen, Lizabeth, 114
Coleman, 143, 144
Coler Mountain Bike Preserve, 33f
commercial ecology, Arkansas Ozarks, 10
commercial leverage, Bass Pro Shops, 178

community fit, small-town locations, 69
community quotas, 91
company brands, big box retailers, 144–46
compensatory mitigation. *See* mitigation banking
competition, American retailing, 21, 58
Competitive Enterprise Institute, 92
conditional use permits, 60–64
Confederate flags, 173
Congress, Environmental Protection Agency (EPA), 70
Connecticut, 118
conservation: conservatism, 177–78; fish population, 79; messaging, 164, 165f, 166f, 169; Pebble Mine campaign, 176; political identity, 178–79; promotion, 160; stewardship, 169
Conservation International, 83
conservationist, 149
conservatism, conservation, 177–78
consolidation: seafood supply chains, 92, 93; United State retail sector, 189; wetlands, 115, 121, 126
consumer goods: affordability, 195; Bass Pro Shops, 167; low prices, 81; pricing, 35, 39, 57–58, 192; supply-chain management, 19
consumer experience. *See* shopping experience
consumption, nature of, 195
control of supply chains, 96, 97
convenience of big box retail stores, 57
corporate culture, 4, 23
corporate governance: catch shares, 97; greening initiatives, 38, 46, 77, 81; partnerships, 86–87; responsibility, 78, 194; sustainability practices, 79, 85, 86, 97–98
corporate greenwashing, 89, 91, 98
corporate tax breaks. *See* tax subsidies
Corps. *See* United States Army Corps of Engineers (USACE)
cost of living, 28, 67
Costco, 3, 112, 143, 144, 147, 188, 192
Covid-19, 12, 71, 96, 152, 197
creative destruction, 191
credit accounts, department stores, 5

credits, carbon offsetting, 121–22, 124–26
Cruse, Valencia, 172
Cullen, Michael, 5
cultural identity, shopping experience, 8, 147, 148f, 160, 162, 171, 178
cultural norms, 3, 191
customers. *See* shopping experience
Cypremort-Teche Mitigation Bank, 125

Dalzell, Rick, 40
Dance, Bill, 159–60
Daniels, Mark, Jr., 167
Dateline, 34, 36
David and Lucile Packard Foundation, 87
Davis, Jeffrey, 25, 26, 27
Dayton-Hudson Corporation, 5, 57, 145
Dayton, George Draper, 56
decline of local businesses, 30, 127
decoration, in-store environment, 8
definition of sustainability, 97–98
delivery schedules, supply chains, 193
demographics of big box customers, 174
Denver (Colorado), REI store in, 150–52
department stores, 4–5, 6, 9, 190, 195
dependency models, supply chains, 95
depletion, seafood supply chain, 82, 89
destination travel experiences, 162, 163, 164
Deuter, 137
development: challenges, 56; conditional use permits, 60–64; environmental governance, 25, 126–27; greenfields, 54; large-impact, 62; Section 404 compliance, 122; wetlands, 111, 112, 113f, 117–18, 120, 121
Dick's Sporting Goods, 3, 112, 144
direct policy interventions, 78
discount pricing, 57–58
discount stores, 139, 140, 144–45
discrimination, 36, 171–73
Disney Wilderness Preserve mitigation site, 122–23
displacement of independent retailers, 114
disruption of cultural norms, 191
distance, shopping experience, 198
distinctiveness, specialty stores, 140
distribution centers: business model,

192–93; conditional use permits, 60–62; environmental impact, 41, 55, 58–59, 124, 200; geography, 58; government intervention, 67; greenhouse gas emissions, 39; grocery stores, 5; growth and expansion, 71; legal challenges, 67–70; locations, 55, 71; logistics, 32, 57–58, 199; long-haul trucking, 24f, 55, 56; mass production, 56; opposition, 10, 54, 55, 58–60, 65–66, 67–67; product lines, 192; retail stores, 5; road transportation, 55; scaling operations, 57; square footage, 61f, 188; Summit, Town of, 60–62; Target Stores, 53–54, 55, 56, 57–58, 61f, 63–64, 68; Wisconsin, 58, 59–60; zoning classifications, 61
diversity, lack of, 167, 168–69, 173, 197
domestic earnings, Walmart, 35
draining wetlands, 115, 116f, 117–18
Dreiser, Theodore, 195, 197
Duane, Daniel, 138, 139
Ducks Unlimited National Waterfowl Heritage Center, 169
dynamite, 89

e-commerce, 6
Eastern Mountain Sports, 139, 150
eco-crusaders, 27–28
ecological footprint of big box stores, 4, 8, 10, 35, 37–40, 116
ecological outcome, regenerative initiatives, 98
economic growth, 3, 58, 59–60
economic power of big box retailers, 194
economic value, retail governance, 191
ecosystems: conservation ecology, 79; endangered species, 31, 90, 118; fisheries, 81, 89–90; geographic distributions, 114; government regulation, 62; greenwashing, 89, 91, 98; international, 34; legislation, 25; marine mammal populations, 90; shifts, 78–79; sustainability, 79; Walmart impact, 126; wetlands, 118
Eddie Bauer, 147, 148
Edina (Minnesota), 56–57
Einck, Virg, 67

Einstein, Albert, 164, 165f
electrification, hydroelectric dams, 161
elitism, outdoor industry, 143, 144, 145, 146, 147, 152
Elmore, Bart, 10, 160, 197
Emerald Square Mall, 127–28
emotional shopping experience, 194–95
employees: big box capitalism, 198; productivity, 192; skills set, 192; undocumented immigrant workers, 36; wages, 21, 22, 192; working conditions, 81, 192, 193
employment statistics, 60, 171
enclosed shopping centers. *See* malls
endangered species, 31, 90, 118
enthusiasts, shopping experience, 162
entrepreneurship, outdoor industry, 142, 200–1
Environmental Decade, 67–68
Environmental Defense Fund (EDF), 92–93
Environmental Impact Statement (EIS), 62, 63, 64, 66
environmental impact: activism, 37; air quality, 59, 63, 64; awareness, 174; Bass Pro Shops, 160, 174–78; big box stores, 30, 31, 201; catch shares, 94; concerns, 28, 36, 37; corporate governance, 78, 126–27; damage, 119; developers, 25, 62; distribution centers, 41, 55, 58–59, 66–67, 200; education, 8; environmental footprint, 37, 80; groundwater runoff, 58–60; history, 7, 10–12, 197; justice, 171; long-haul trucking network, 30, 31; Marine Stewardship Council (MSC) certified fisheries, 89–90; non-government organizations (NGOs), 122–23; outdoor industry, 141; overfishing, 89; parking lots, 66; regulations, 10–11, 56, 62, 66, 69–70, 193–94; supply chains, 39, 41; transformation, 3; transportation of goods, 35; violations, 28–29, 40, 80; wetlands, 7–8, 121
Environmental Protection Agency (EPA), 28–29, 36–37, 70, 119, 120, 127
Environment Program (United Nations), 85

Equal Employment Opportunity Commission (EEOC), 171–73
Etienne, Jean-Louis, 145
Europe, 35, 188
Everglades, 116, 122–23
expeditions, sponsorships, 145–46
experience of retail workers, 198
expert-oriented merchandise, 140
externalities, environmental history, 197
extraction, marine ecosystems, 80
exurbs, 199
Exxon Corporation, 125

factories, overseas, 7, 34, 36, 38, 190, 198
family-oriented merchandise, 140
farming. *See* agriculture/agribusiness
federal regulations. *See* regulations
Federal Water Pollution Control Act, 118–19
female customer base / employees, 36, 138
fill material, 113–14
fishing industry / fisheries: African Americans, 167; Bristol Bay, 176–78; catch shares, 92–94, 174; conservation ecology, 79; depletion, 89; economic impact, 177; extraction, 80; federal management plans, 93–95; fishery improvement plans (FIPs), 97; harvesting, 81; healthy oceans, 79, 82; large-scale, 77; market-driven production, 82, 85; neoliberal market-based strategies, 91; overfishing, 78–79, 88–89, 92; privatization, 91; regulatory efforts, 97; techniques, 89; transnational, 82; tuna, 90; wetlands, 118; *See also* seafood supply chains; supply chains
fishing and hunting industry, 32*f*, 138, 147, 162, 163, 171, 164, 168, 174
Fishman, Charles, 81
FishWise, 85–86
five-and-dime stores, 4, 5, 19, 32*f*
fixed pricing, 5
flagship stores, 150, 151*f*, 152, 163, 169
fleece, 144
fleet efficiency of long-haul trucking network, 37
flood control, hydroelectric dams, 161

Florida, 116, 118, 122–23
flow of goods. *See* transportation of goods
Fortune 500 rankings, 40
France, 90, 187, 191
free markets, sustainability initiatives, 9, 96, 193–94
free will, shopping experience, 197
freight handling, 57–58

Gander Mountain, 151, 152
GDP (gross domestic product), 139
Geissler, Heike, 198
gender, mass consumption, 23, 114
general discount stores. *See* discount stores
geographic distributions, 114
geography, big box stores, 4, 20, 21, 58
Geomar, 94
Georgia, 61, 118
Germany, 35, 126
Geronimo, 170
ghost acres, 80, 200
ghost stores, 191
Gifford, Kathie Lee, 36
Ginsberg, Allen, 196
Glass, David, 36
global environments, 3
global supply chains. *See* seafood supply chains; supply chains
global value chains (GVC) theory, 189
goods. *See* manufactured goods
Gore-Tex, 145
governance structure, 78, 87–89, 189, 191, 193–94
government regulations. *See* regulations
grassroots efforts. *See* opposition to big box stores
Great Atlantic & Pacific (A&P) Tea Company, 5
Great Depression, 6
Greatland, 144–46
green buffers, 127
Greenfield, Jerry, 24, 25
greenfields, development, 54
greenhouse gas emissions, 35, 38, 39, 125–26

Greenpeace, 87
greenwashing, 89, 91, 98
grocery stores. *See* supermarkets
gross domestic product (GDP), 139
Gross, Rachel S., 11, 160, 162, 196
ground level ozone: air quality assessments, 64, 67–68; regulations, 65–66
groundwater runoff. *See* storm water runoff
growth and expansion: agribusiness, 21–22; discount stores, 140; distribution centers, 71; outdoor retailers, 138–40, 142–43, 149, 163; supermarkets, 142–43; political obstacles, 69; Walmart, 20–21, 79
Grunt Style (apparel company), 165–66
Guidelines, Environmental Protection Agency, 119

Hamilton, Shane, 11
harvesting fisheries, 81, 92
headquarters of Walmart, 79
health insurance, 36
Heavey, Bill, 163
heritage, shopping experience, 149, 171
hierarchy of supply-chain management, 189, 193
hiking, growth in popularity, 142
Hilary brand, 144–45
Hill, Rich, 138
Hispanic population. *See* people of color
historic building renovations, 8
history of American retailing, 4, 191
Holubar, 141
home delivery systems, 5
Home Depot, 29, 35, 188
HomeGoods, 112
Honduras, 36
Hudson Corporation, 57
Hugelmeyer, Frank, 144–45
Humble Oil and Refining Company, 125
Humes, Edward, 36
hunting and fishing, 32*f*, 138, 147, 162, 163, 171, 164, 168, 174
hydroelectric dams, 161
hypermarché, 187

IFQs4Fisheries, 92–93
Ikea, 9, 86
Illinois wetlands, 117*f*
immigrant customers, 196
impact of development on wetlands. *See* environmental impact
impartiality of fisheries certification, 88
implementation of Section 404, 120
imports, seafood, 80
in-store environment, 8
incentives. *See* tax subsidies
inclusiveness, shopping experience, 178–79
increasing catch shares, 93
independent retailers: chain store wars, 5; decline, 30, 191; discrimination, 196; displacement, 114; kiranas, 188; outdoor industry, 138, 143; regulations, 188; replacement by big box stores, 191; shopping experience, 188, 195–96
India, 187, 188
Indiana wetlands, 115, 117*f*
indirect greenhouse gas emissions, 39
individual consumer choice, 188, 189
individual tradable quotas (ITQs), 91, 93
Indonesia, 35, 94
indoor nature experience, 147, 148–49, 150
industrial space, 54, 65, 188
influence of Walmart on supply chains, 77, 78
infrastructure improvements, 21, 24–27, 29
Intermodal Transportation and Efficiency Act of 1991, 55
international big-box retail stores, 9, 12, 187, 188, 192
international earnings, Walmart, 33–35
International Union for the Conservation of Nature, 90
internet shopping, 12, 193
intersections, stroads, 195, 196, 198, 200
interstate transportation. *See* long-haul trucking network
investors, business models, 192
Iowa, 30–32, 117*f*
Ish, Teresa, 78, 85–86, 96
Ithaca (New York), 31–32

J.C. Penney, 4–5
J.M. Burguières Co. Ltd., 125
Jackson Hole (Wyoming), 31–32
James, Jesse, 170
Japan, 90, 188
job discrimination, 171–73
job growth, 58, 59–60, 71
Johnny Morris Wonders of Wildlife National Museum and Aquarium, 169–70; Native American Hall, 170
Johnson, John, 115
Jon, Linda, 67
jurisdictional wetlands, 113–14

Kelty, 141, 144, 147
Kernaghan, Charles, 36
Kids R Us, 127
King Kullen, 5, 6
kiranas in India, 188
Kmart, 6, 57, 114–15, 127, 139, 143, 144, 150, 187
Kresge, S.S., 4
Kroger, 5, 188
Kurtz, Fred, 68

labor unions, 22
Lafayette wetlands, 111, 112*f*, 113*f*
Lager, Fred "Chico," 25
landfills, 200
land use retail expansion, 54
large-format store layouts, 5
large-impact developments, 62
large-scale fishing industry, 77
largemouth bass, 161
LeCavalier, Jesse, 198, 199
legal challenges to developments, 56, 67–69, 70
legislation. *See* regulations
LEKI, 137
Leopold, Aldo, 164
Les Halles, 191
Lewis and Clark, 169–70
lifestyle-centered identity, 150. *See* cultural identity; political identity
light pollution, 53
lighting in chain stores, 196
limited regulation, 96

Linens 'n Things, 150
Little Village (Chicago), 71
L.L. Bean, 147, 148
local governments, zoning laws, 69, 188, 193
local stores. *See* independent retailers
location of stores, 55, 111, 198–99
logistics network, 20, 57–58, 192–93, 199
long-haul trucking network: environmental pollution, 30, 31, 56; fleet efficiency, 37; legislation, 55, 56; transportation of goods, 199; Walmart, 23, 24*f*
long-lining, 89, 90
Lormax Stern, 127
Louisiana, 111, 112*f*, 113*f*, 115, 117, 121, 124*f*, 125
low wages, 81
low-margin goods, 57–58
loyalty to products, 146
lures, fishing, 161
luxury goods, 57, 190

Macy, Rowland H., 4–5
mail-order catalogs. *See* catalogs from big box stores
Main Street establishments, 30
Maine wetlands, 118
Malden Mills, 144
male customer base, 140, 162, 171, 173–74
malls: citizen-consumers, 114; community life, 114; decline, 128–30; independent retailers, 114; shopping center, 56–57; suburbs, 114
management of catch shares, 93–94
managerial positions, 23, 192
Manion, Daniel (Judge), 70
manufactured goods, 4, 5, 6, 138, 188
marginalized consumers, 178
marine ecosystems, 77, 80, 81, 90
Marine Stewardship Council (MSC): corporate partnerships, 86–87; financial interests, 88; governance structure, 87–89; overfishing, 88–89; promotional materials, 89; sustainability certification, 11, 82, 83, 84*f*, 85, 89–90; Walmart Family Foundation, 77, 86, 87, 91
market-based incentives, 78, 121, 122, 126

market-driven fish production, 85, 87
Markin, Gene, 149–50
Marshalls, 112
Martin, Laura J., 11, 160, 198–99
Massachusetts, 127
mass consumerism, 114, 143
mass production, 56
McDonald's, 87
McMillan, Doug, 98
mega-format, 187
Memphis Pyramid Bass Pro Shops. *See* Bass Pro Shops
men in managerial positions, 23
Mercadona, 192
merchandising, 139–41, 143, 144, 145, 146, 149–50
messaging, conservation, 162, 163, 164, 165f, 166f, 169
Mexico, 34, 37, 94
middlemen, organizational structures, 190
Midwest Regional Distribution Center, 62
military surplus stores, 142
mineral leases, 125
minimum wage, 22
Minneapolis (Minnesota), 56
Missouri wetlands, 117f
Mitchell, Stacy, 38
mitigation banking: Ambassador Town Center, 124–25; banking policy, 121–22, 199; credits, 114, 121–22; developers, 120; environmental damage, 119; Environmental Protection Agency (EPA), 120; federal guidelines, 127; growth and expansion, 123; impact, 114; National Environmental Policy Act of 1969 (NEPA), 119; offsite preservation projects, 122–23, 126; onsite preservation projects, 121; permits, 120, 121; rural areas, 123–24; sequence, 119; urban areas, 123–24; wetlands, 11, 111–12, 124f
modern retailing, 189–90
monitoring seafood supply chain, 81
Monkey Wrench Gang, The, 28
monopolies, big box retailers, 192
monopsony, 81, 95
Montgomery Ward, 5, 143

Moosejaw, 137
Moreton, Bethany, 18, 22
Morris, Johnny, 159–62, 166, 173, 176–77
Motor Carrier Act of 1980, 55
mountain biking, 33f
Mountain Miser, 152
mountain shops, 138
multi-channel advertising, 145
museums, big box retailers and, 8, 148–49, 162, 169–71
mythology in outdoor industry, 149

NASCAR, 173, 178
National Environmental Policy Act of 1969 (NEPA), 119
National Fish and Wildlife Foundation, 126
National Marine Fisheries Service, 119
National Public Radio (NPR), 53–54
national regulations. *See* regulations
National Rifle Association's (NRA) National Sporting Arms Museum. *See* Bass Pro Shop
Native American Hall. *See* Johnny Morris Wonders of Wildlife National Museum and Aquarium
Natural Resources Conservation Service, 119
naturalist, 149
Nature Conservancy (TNC), 122–23, 126
nature indoor shopping experience, 141, 147, 148–50
nature messaging, 164, 165f, 166f
nature of consumption, 195
navigable waters, 119
neoliberal market-based strategies, 91
neoliberal trade policies, 34, 91, 193–94
Nestlé sustainability commitments, 96
New England Groundfish Fishery, 93
New York State, 30, 31
Niering, William, 118
Nixon, Richard, 62
No Net Loss of Wetlands agenda, 121
noise pollution, 30, 53
non-discrimination in chain stores, 196
non-government organizations (NGOs), 86

non-point-source pollutants, 65–66
non-white customers, 138
North Face (TNF), 141, 144
nostalgia, shopping experience, 167, 169

Oakley, Annie, 170
objection process, fisheries, 88
ocean ecosystem, 10–11, 77–79
Oceans of Abundance Project, 93
Oconomocow Target distribution center: air quality impact, 59, 63, 66–67; cost of living, 67; distribution center, 53–54, 55f, 58–60; government intervention, 67; legal challenges, 67–70; opposition, 55, 63–64, 66–67; proponents, 68; zoning, 62–64, 65
offsetting. *See* carbon offsetting
offsite compensatory mitigation preservation projects, 121–23, 126
Ohio wetlands, 117f
Old Navy, 144
Olive Garden, 87
onsite compensatory mitigation preservation projects, 121
open corridors, 196
opposition to big box stores: anti-development legislation, 25, 26; chain stores, 190; distribution centers, 10, 54, 55, 60–62, 63–66, 67–68; eco-crusaders, 27–28; Grassroots Outdoor Alliance, 138; individual stores, 54; Iowa City, Iowa, 31–32; Ithaca, New York, 31–32; Jackson Hole, Wyoming, 31–32; mail-order catalogs, 190; Pebble Mine, 176; retailing, 190; small towns, 30, 32; Steamboat Springs, Colorado, 31–32; Vermont, 23; Westford, Massachusetts, 31
organizational structure, 189, 190
origin of *big box* term, 195
Otsego County Conservation Association, 30
"out of stock," 58
outdoor industry: affordability, 140; big box chain stores, 140, 152; brand identity, 11, 138, 150; business model, 138–41, 143, 147; camping equipment, 139, 142, 143; clothing, 144–46; elitism, 143, 144, 145, 146, 147, 152; entrepreneurship, 142; environmental impact, 8, 141, 174; gross domestic product (GDP), 139; growth and expansion, 138–40; hiking, 142; independent retailers, 138, 143; merchandising, 145, 146, 149–50; Moosejaw, 137; pandemic, 152; people of color, 164–65, 158–59; popularity, 147; sales, 141, 142; shopping experience, 140, 141, 148–50, 162, 163, 196; specialty shops, 138, 140; travel expeditions, 145–46; Walmart, 137
Outdoor Recreation Coalition of America, 144–45
outlets, Walmart, 32
Outside, 138
overfishing, 78–79, 83, 85, 88–90, 92, 94
overseas suppliers, 34, 35
overtime compensation, 22
Ozark Mountains, 18–19
Ozark Trail, 144–45

pandemic, impact on big box stores, 12, 71, 96, 152, 197
Paris Accord, 38
parking lots, 28–29, 59, 66, 199–200
partnerships, supply-chain management, 193
Patagonia, 141, 173–74, 178
patriarchal organization of work, 9
Patterson, Ralph, 64
payroll. *See* wages
Pebble Mine campaign, 160, 174–77
Pellegrene, John, 146
people of color: impact of wetlands mitigation on communities, 124; outdoor industry, 164–65; job applicants, 171–73, 175; representation in catalogs, 167–69; shopping experience, 114, 164–65, 168, 175, 196, 197
permits: conditional use, 60–62; local governments, 69; pollutant discharge, 119; Section 404, 120, 123; United States Army Corp of Engineers, 113–114, 117–19, 120, 121, 123, 127
Peru, 94

Pescador Holdings, 94
PetSmart, 112
Pew Environmental Group, 87
philanthropy, 77
physical environment. *See* shopping experience
Piggly Wiggly, 5, 6
pipeline easements, 125
Plambeck, Erica L., 95
point of consumption, 200
point-of-sale, 19, 193, 197
poison fishing, 89
Polartec, 144
policy initiatives by Walmart, 77
political economy of supply chains, 198
political identity, shopping experience, 11, 148f, 149, 160, 162, 164, 165f, 171, 178–79
political leverage of Bass Pro Shops, 175, 178
pollution: discharge permits, 119; water systems, 66; wetlands, 118
popularity, outdoor activities, 140, 142, 147
power structures, modern retailing, 189
premium-oriented merchandise, 140
preservation of public lands, 121, 175
price fixing, 97
pricing consumer goods, 35, 39, 57–58, 81, 192, 193
Pritchett, Lou, 18–19
private corporate environmental governance, 78
private-sector-driven, choice editing, 86
privatization of the fishing industry, 91
Procter and Gamble, 18–19, 37
productivity of workers, 192
products: adding, 192; arrangement, 8; ecological footprint, 37–39; loyalty, 146; tie-ins, 145
profit-sharing program, Walmart, 22–23
profitability, big box stores, 92, 192, 198–99
Project Gigaton, 38
promotion, conservation, 93, 169
Property and Environment Research Council, 92–93
proponents, Target Stores, 68
protests. *See* opposition to big box stores
public lands, 175
public-private collaborations, 193–94
Publix, 96
PVC pipes, wetlands, 115
Pyramid Companies, 127

quotas. *See* catch shares

race to fish, 92
rail transportation, 4, 5, 55, 190
rainwater-runoff provisions, 69
Raman, Kal, 40
re-valuation of wetlands, 199
Reason Foundation, 92–93
reassessments, fishery certification, 83, 85
Recreational Equipment, Incorporated. *See* REI
Red Lobster, 87
redistribution of wetlands, 123
Redmond, Peter, 82, 83, 86, 95
reducing ecological footprint, 37
Reeves, Bass, 170
regenerative initiatives, 98
regional markets, 57
regulations, 21, 115, 116, 127; anti-development, 25, 26; catch shares, 92–93; choice editing, 86; Clean Air and Water Acts, 56, 69–70, 119; compensatory mitigation, 111–12; distribution centers, 67; ecosystems, 62; Environmental Impact Statement, 62, 63, 64; environmental laws, 40–41, 69–70, 193–94; fishery improvement plans (FIPs), 97; government, 62; ground level ozone, 65–66; independent shop owners, 188; international, 188; limited, 96; long-haul trucking network, 55, 56; pollution, 66, 119; public-private collaborations, 193–94; right-to-work, 22; supply chains, 96; sustainability certifications, 96; Walmart, 78; wetlands, 111, 118; zoning, 64, 65
REI (Recreational Equipment, Incorporated): business model, 139;

catalogs, 168–69; Co-op, 141–43; flagship store, 150, 151f; growth and expansion, 138–39, 142–43; house-brand products, 139; sales, 147; shopping experience, 11, 150, 151f, 173–74, 196; tax subsidies, 150, 151f
reliance on the global supply chain, 187–188
relocation, industry, 54
representation, people of color, 167–69
Republican National Committee, 177
research methodologies, big box environmental history, 10–12
reservoirs, 161
resistance. *See* opposition to big box stores
Retail Link, 19
retail stores. *See* big box stores
retail workers. *See* employees
revenue sales, big box stores, 79–80, 188
Rhode Island, 118
right-to-work legislation, 22
rights-based access privileges. *See* catch shares
Rittenhouse, Kyle, 166
road transportation, 55, 56, 116–17
Robertson, Morgan M., 122
Rohloff, Ed, 53, 64, 68
Roosevelt, Theodore, 169–170, 177
Ross Sea Chilean seabass fishery, 89–90
Roush, Darrell, 149–50
Rowland, Mike, 173
Ruben, Andy, 95
rugged frontiersman, 149
Rugiel, Ted, 120
runoff, water, 58–60
rural locations: aesthetic, 30, 32; distribution centers, 6, 10, 21, 199; long-haul trucking, 24f; mail-order catalogs, 190; wetlands mitigation, 123–24

sales positions, 23
sales tax, 115
sales revenue, 35, 147, 188
salmon, 176–78
sameness, American landscape, 3
San Francisco Bay, 117–18
Saravana, 187
SC Johnson, 37
scaling operations, 57
Schell, Orville, 38
scholarship, big box stores, 6–7
Schumpeter, Joseph, 191
Scott, H. Lee, 30, 31, 36, 37, 83
scouting Walmart locations, 20
seafood supply chains: certification, 82, 83, 85, 88, 90; choice editing, 86; consolidation, 92; FishWise, 85–86; imports, 80; sustainability, 10–11, 77–79, 86, 90, 94; vertical integration, 81, 92, 94; *See also* fishing industry / fisheries; supply chains
sea-lords, 93
Sears, Roebuck, 5, 139, 143, 144–45, 150
Seattle REI flagship store, 151–52
Section 301 (Clean Water Act), 119
Section 404 (Clean Water Act), 113–14, 119, 120, 121, 123, 128
self-service, grocery store business model, 5, 9, 190
Seligmann, Peter, 83
Seligmann's Conservation International, 93
selling, 9
sensory shopping experience, 194–95
service positions, 3, 23
Seventh Generation, 37
sharecroppers, 93
shareholders, 17–18
shark finning, 89
Sheeler, Charles, 188
Shell Oil, 125
Sheu, Sherri, 11, 196, 197
shipping containers, 23, 35, 39
shipping costs, 23
shopping centers. *See* malls
shopping experience: Abercrombie and Fitch (A&F), 140–41; Bass Pro Shops, 163, 164, 170, 197, 198; big box stores, 4, 11; brand appeal, 150; Cabela's, 148–50; chain stores, 195–96; choice, 86, 87, 188–89, 191; convenience, 57; cultural identity, 3–4, 147, 148f, 160, 162, 171, 178, 189–90; customer satisfaction, 192;

demographics, 138, 173–74; distance, 198; elitism, 143, 144, 145, 146, 147, 152; heritage, 149, 171; inclusiveness, 178–79; independent retailers, 188, 195–196; luxury items, 57; male customer base, 140, 162; nostalgia, 167; open corridors, 196; Patagonia, 173–74; people of color, 114, 164–65, 175, 196, 197; physical environment, 194–95; point of consumption, 200; political identity, 148f, 149, 160, 162, 164, 165f, 171, 178; REI, 150, 151f, 196; satisfaction, 192; shopping patterns, 12, 194–195; sovereignty, 189; standardization, 197; Walmart, 80, 196
shore-to-shelf seafood companies, 94
Sierra Club, 178
Sierra Designs, 141
Silver Lake (Wisconsin), 54, 55f, 67–68
SimCity, 199–200
simplifying supply chains, 77, 95
Singh, Ashok K., 63
Sister Carrie, 195, 197
small businesses. *See* independent retailers; specialty retailers
smallmouth bass, 161
small-town store locations, 30, 32, 69
social practices, disruption, 191
social value, retail governance, 191
Southdale (Edina, Minnesota), 56–57
sovereignty of the consumer, 189
Spain, 188, 192
spatial distortion, 198–99
specialty retailers: business models, 152; camping equipment, 143; distinctiveness, 140; general discount retailers, 139; hard goods, 145, 146; product loyalty, 146. *See also* outdoor industry sponsorships for travel expeditions, 145–46
sporting goods. *See* outdoor industry
Sportmart, 147
Sports Authority, 147
sports fishing, 177
sportsmen for sportsmen, 162
sportswear retailers: closeouts, 144–46; elitism, 144, 145, 146, 147; square footage, 169

square footage: big box stores, 9, 57, 114–15, 150, 151f; distribution centers, 53–54, 61f, 188; parking lots, 66, 199–200; supercenters, 57, 80; warehouses, 188
"squeeze," 35, 39, 81
St. Petersburg Times, 120
stagnation, wages, 28
standardization, freight handling, 57–58
state governments, 4, 58, 62, 77, 115, 116, 193
steam power, 115
Steamboat Springs (Colorado), 31–32
Steger, Will, 146, 150
stewardship, conservation, 92, 94, 169
Stirling Properties, LLC, 113–14, 125
Stone, Kenneth, 30
STOP TARGET Coalition, 65–66, 67–68
store locations, 111, 198–99
storm water runoff, 28–29, 36–37, 55, 58–60, 66, 70, 121, 127
stroads, 195, 196, 198, 200
structural organization, 189
subsidies. *See* tax subsidies
suburban locations, big box stores, 6, 9, 54, 56–57, 63, 114–15, 199
Summit (Wisconsin), 53–54, 60, 61f, 62, 63, 70
Sun Art, 187
Sunbelt, 9
supercenters, 8, 79, 80, 128, 187, 200
supermarkets: Agriculture, US Department of, 193–94; Great Depression, 6; growth and expansion, 142–43; kiranas in Indiana, 188; large-format layouts, 5; market share, 80; supply-chain management, 190
superstores, 187
supply chains: business models, 192–93; child labor, 36; consumer goods, 19; Covid-19 pandemic, 12, 71, 96, 152, 197; delivery schedules, 193; dependency models, 95; disruptions, 197; ecological footprint, 38–39, 80; environmental impact, 39, 41; governance, 189; greenhouse gas emissions, 35, 39; hierarchy, 193; long-haul trucking, 199; marine sustainability, 11; modernization, 189–90; monopsony, 95; partnerships,

193; point of consumption, 200; political economy, 198; pricing, 81, 193; regulatory efforts, 96; reliance, 187–88; Retail Link, 19; shipping containers, 35; simplifying, 77, 95; supermarkets, 190; transnational retailers, 78; transportation of goods, 199; UPC barcode, 193; Walmart, 77, 82–83, 84f, 96, 97; Woolworth's, 190. *See also* fishing industry / fisheries; seafood supply chains
surface water. *See* storm water runoff
sustainability: catch shares, 91–93; certification, 10–11, 82, 84f, 96; choice editing, 86; corporate governance, 85, 86, 97–98; definition, 78, 97–98; fisheries, 77–79, 89–90; FishWise, 85–86; goals, 90; index, 37–39; initiatives, 96; marine mammal populations, 90; Marine Stewardship Council (MSC), 83, 85; market-driven, 78; metrics, 79; overfishing, 88–89; supply chains, 77, 82–83, 85, 94; transnational retailers, 78
Sutton, Michael, 85
Swamp Land Acts, 115
swampland. *See* wetlands
sweatshop factories, 34, 36
Sweedens Swamp (Massachusetts), 127, 128
Switzerland, 126

Table Rock Dam, 161
Taft Corner Associates, 23, 25, 26, 29
Target Stores: American Camper, 144–45; Australia, 187; camping equipment, 139, 143; Chicago market, 56, 57; distribution centers, 10, 53–55, 57–60, 61f, 63, 66, 67–69, 70; Georgia, 61; Greatland label, 144–46; growth and expansion, 57, 69, 69, 127; opposition, 60–62, 63–63; pollution, 53; revenue, 188; scaling operations, 57; square footage, 57; STOP TARGET Coalition, 65–66, 67–68; suburban locations, 6, 114–15; traveling truck exhibit, 145, 146; urban markets, 6; water pollution, 53
tax subsidies, 58, 116, 150, 151f, 159–160, 164, 193

Teal, John and Mildred, 118
telegraph communication networks, 190
Temple Kirby, Jack, 30
Tennessee, 158f
Teotihuacán, 37
territorial use rights, 91
Tesco, 9, 86, 96
Therm-a-Rest, 137
Thompson, Tommy, 58, 59–60, 53
total allowable catch (TAC), 92, 94
tourist attractions, 151
Toys 'R' Us, 29, 127
trade industries, job growth, 71
Trader Joe's, 192
traffic congestion, 20, 29, 30, 31, 59
Trans-Antarctica Expedition, 145
transformation of consumer culture, 3–4, 198
transnational businesses, 78, 82
Transportation and Distribution, 69
transportation of goods, 35, 55, 56, 58–60, 71, 199
travel expeditions. *See* adventure expeditions
traveling truck exhibit, 145, 146
trends, shopping, 9–10
Trump, Donald, 176–77
Trump, Donald, Jr., 175f, 176
Trunzo, Robert, 53, 64
Tucker Carlson Tonight, 176–77
tuna industry, 90, 97

undocumented immigrant workers, 36
Unilever, 83
unionization, 192
United Kingdom, 35, 126, 187
United States: carbon credit buying, 126; history of retailing, 191; organization structure, 190; outlets, total, 21; pipeline easements, 125; retail sector, 188, 189; seafood imports, 80
United States Army Corps of Engineers (USACE): permits, 113–14, 116–18, 119, 123, 127; Section 404, 120; wetlands, 121, 124
unregulated pollutants, 66
UPC barcode, 57–58, 193, 197

urban locations, 6, 9–10, 63, 71, 123–24, 198–200
utilities industries, 71

value architecture, 192
value chain, 189
Van Neste, Aaron, 10, 193, 200
variety stores, 4
Vermont, opposition to Walmart, 23, 25, 26, 27
vertical coordination, 81, 92, 94
vetos, permits, 120

W.L. Gore and Associates, 145
wages: Costco, 192; discrimination, 36; labor market, 21; Mercadona, 192; minimum, 22; overtime, 22; payroll, 80; poverty-level, 81; stagnation, 28; workers, 192
Walmart (formerly Wal-Mart): business model, 81, 97, 98, 143, 152; Buy American campaign, 34; child labor, 82; competition, 21; corporate culture, 23; customers, 80; direct policy interventions, 78; domestic earnings, 35; ecological footprint, 10, 35, 37, 38–39, 80, 126; effect on local businesses, 30; environmental violations, 28–29, 36–37; Fortune 500 rankings, 40; gendered workspace, 23; ghost stores, 191; government partnerships, 78; greening initiatives, 38–39, 77, 78, 90; grocery market share, 80; growth and expansion, 20–21, 79; headquarters, 20f, 79; health insurance, 36; image, 83; international earnings, 33–35, 37; labor unions, 22; launch, 6; locations, 6, 10, 20, 21, 114–15, 199; long-haul trucking network, 23, 24f; Marine Stewardship Council (MSC), 86, 91; Moosejaw, 137; 1981 shareholders meeting, 17–18; opposition to, 26–28, 30–32, 37; outdoor industry, 137, 139, 143, 144; outlets, 32; Ozark Trail, 10, 144–45; Paris Accord, 38; philanthropy, 77; pricing practices, 35, 38, 81; procurement offices, 34; profit-sharing program, 22–23; Project Gigaton, 38; quality of goods, 138; regional markets, 57; Retail Link, 19; revenue, 79–80; seafood products, 82–83, 84f, 96, 97; shipping containers, 23, 35; shopping experience, 28, 196; supercenters, 80; supply chains, 34, 35, 36, 77, 80, 96, 97; sweatshop factories, 34, 36; undocumented workers, 36; UPC barcode, 197; wages, 22, 36, 80; website, 138
Walmart Global Responsibility Report, 44n73, 45n78, 45n81, 45n82, 45n84
Walmart Sustainability Hub, 37
Walmartization, 139, 143, 151
Walt Disney World Company, 122–23
Walton Family Foundation, 32f, 77, 78, 87, 93, 94
Walton, Alice, 17–18
Walton, Ben, 94
Walton, Helen, 17, 19, 32f
Walton, Lucy Ann, 94
Walton, Rob, 82–83
Walton, Sam: anti-union stance, 22; camping, 18; canoeing, 17; first five-and-dime store, 32f; hunting, 19, 32f; international ventures, 34; love of the Ozark Mountains, 10, 18; pickup truck, 20f; pilot's license, 20; Pritchett, Lou, 18–19
warehouses, 55, 58–60, 69, 71, 188, 190–91
wasted space, spatial distortion, 198–99
water pollution, regulations, 53, 66, 174–75
waterway transportation, 55
Waukesha County (Wisconsin), 53
WCRG. See Williston Citizens for Responsible Growth (WCRG)
Wenger, Dean, 60, 69
Westford (Massachusetts), 31
wetlands: biodiversity, 122; compensatory mitigation, 11, 114, 121–26, 199; consolidation, 115, 121, 126; development, 111, 112, 113f, 114, 121; ecosystem, 118; Georgia, 118; history, 115; jurisdictional, 113–14; loss of, 115, 116f, 117f, 118; Louisiana, 124f, 125; Massachusetts, 127; pollution, 118; PVC pipes, 115;

redistribution, 123; re-valuation, 199; Rhode Island, 118; road and highway construction, 116–17; soil-draining science, 115; store locations, 111, 199; storm water infrastructure, 127; Swamp Land Acts, 115
white male consumer base, 171, 173–75
Whittaker, Jim, 142–43
Whole Foods Market, 86
Williams, Johnathan, 10, 160, 192–93
Williams, city centers, 200
Williston Citizens for Responsible Growth (WCRG): opposition to Walmart, 25, 26, 27f
Williston: big box development, 29–30; eco-crusaders, 27–28; infrastructure, 24–27, 29; Walmart, 23, 28
Wisconsin: air quality, 65–66; Department of Development, 53; distribution centers, 58, 59–60; Natural Resources (DNR), Department of, 58–59; Silver Lake, 54, 55f; Target distribution centers, 53–54
women employees, sales and service positions, 23
Woolworth, Frank W., 4
Woolworth's, 190, 198
workers. *See* employees
working class customers, 28
World Trade Organization, 34
World Wildlife Fund (WWF), 83, 87, 88, 90
Wright, Jimmy, 40

younger customers, 83, 138

Zoma Capital, 94
zoning regulations, 61f, 62–65, 69

ABOUT THE AUTHORS

BART ELMORE is professor of environmental history and a core faculty member of the Sustainability Institute at Ohio State University. His work focuses on the ecological footprint of large multinational firms. He is the author of *Citizen Coke: The Making of Coca-Cola Capitalism* (W. W. Norton, 2015); *Seed Money: Monsanto's Past and the Future of Food* (W. W. Norton, 2021); and *Country Capitalism: How Corporations from the American South Remade Our Economy and the Planet* (Ferris and Ferris, 2023).

RACHEL S. GROSS is assistant professor of history at the University of Colorado Denver where she teaches U.S. environmental, business, and public history. She is the author of *Shopping All the Way to the Woods: How the Outdoor Industry Sold Nature to America* (forthcoming from Yale University Press).

SHANE HAMILTON is reader in Strategy, Management, and Society at the University of York. He is the author of *Supermarket USA: Food and Power in the*

Cold War Farms Race (Yale, 2018) and the award-winning *Trucking Country: The Road to America's Wal-Mart Economy* (Princeton, 2008). Shane has published articles on food and agribusiness in *Technology and Culture, Strategic Entrepreneurship Journal, History of Retailing and Consumption, Enterprise and Society, Business History Review, Business History,* and *Agricultural History.*

LAURA J. MARTIN is a historian and ecologist who studies the ways people shape the habitats of other species. She is the author of *Wild by Design: The Rise of Ecological Restoration,* and her writing can be found in the *Washington Post, Sierra Magazine, Scientific American,* and elsewhere. She is an environmental studies professor at Williams College.

SHERRI SHEU is a historian and the Haas Curatorial Fellow at the Science History Institute in Philadelphia. Sheu's research examines how environmental relationships shape cultures and institutions. Their work appears in *Environmental History,* the *Washington Post,* and other venues.

AARON VAN NESTE is an environmental historian and historian of science interested in how humans understand and manage complex multispecies environments, particularly food systems. He has a PhD in the history of science from Harvard University.

JOHNATHAN WILLIAMS is a historian who studies US retail, business, and modern environmental politics. He earned his PhD in history from Boston University and is the United States History Teaching Fellow at the University of Northern Iowa.

www.ingramcontent.com/pod-product-compliance
Lightning Source LLC
Chambersburg PA
CBHW052137070526
44585CB00017B/1858